EVERYMAN, I will go with thee,

and be thy guide,

In thy most need to go by thy side

GOTTFRIED WILHELM LEIBNIZ

Born in 1646 at Leipzig. Entered the University of Leipzig at the age of fifteen. Obtained a professorship at the University of Altdorf before he was twenty-one. Elected F.R.S. in 1670. In 1676 went to live at the Court of Hanover and died in 1716.

Leibniz:
Philosophical Writings

TRANSLATED BY
MARY MORRIS

INTRODUCTION BY
C. R. MORRIS, M.A.

DENT: LONDON
EVERYMAN'S LIBRARY
DUTTON: NEW YORK

All rights reserved
Made in Great Britain
at the
Aldine Press · Letchworth · Herts
for
J. M. DENT & SONS LTD
Aldine House · Bedford Street · London
First included in Everyman's Library 1934
Last reprinted 1965

193
L525p

NO. *905*

INTRODUCTION

GOTTFRIED WILHELM LEIBNIZ has been described as a man of universal attainments and of almost universal genius. A courtier, diplomat, scholar, mathematician and philosopher, he is perhaps the most brilliant figure among modern philosophers. The history of philosophy has always recognized him as one of the greatest of system-builders. Now in the twentieth century he receives in addition an even higher esteem for the brilliance of some of his particular ideas and for the close thinking of some of his detailed arguments. With Descartes he shares the merit of having a more authoritative insight into the method and value of mathematics and physics than any other philosopher of the first rank. And with Hume he shares the honour of setting the stage for the rejuvenation of modern philosophy in the critical philosophy of Kant.

Life and Character. Leibniz was born at Leipzig in July 1646, thirteen years after the birth of Spinoza, and four years before the death of Descartes. His father, who died in 1652, had been for some years Professor of Moral Philosophy at Leipzig. At the age of fifteen Leibniz entered the university of that city; and in 1666 he became a Doctor of Laws, but at Altdorf, the university town of Nuremburg, where he declined the offer of a professorship. In the following year he entered the political service of the powerful Elector-Archbishop of Mainz. Sent to Paris in 1672 on a diplomatic mission to Louis XIV, he was enabled to have some intercourse with learned men of his day, notably with Arnauld and Malebranche. Early in the next year he paid a short visit to London, where he met Oldenburg, the first secretary of the Royal Society, and Boyle. On his return to Paris he devoted himself to the study of geometry under the guidance of Huygens.

Previously he had mainly concerned himself with problems of logic and metaphysic. In 1676 he completed his discovery of the Differential Calculus. There is no doubt that Newton had been using a similar method for some years previously. But it seems probable that Leibniz discovered it independently; and the form in which he presented it has been universally adopted in preference to that of Newton.

After the death of the Elector of Mainz, he accepted in 1676, after some hesitation, the position of librarian to the learned John Frederick, Duke of Brunswick, and Hanover became his headquarters for the remaining forty years of his life. He thus lived in the atmosphere of the local politics of a German principality. But his writings make it clear that he was primarily interested in the wider development of European civilization. For a time he was connected with the learned life of Berlin through his friendship with the Electress Sophia and her daughter Sophia-Charlotte, afterwards Queen of Prussia. With the help of the latter he was largely responsible for the institution in 1700 of an Academy in Berlin, of which he was made life President. He made some attempts to secure the foundation of similar academies in Dresden, St. Petersburg, and Vienna; but Europe was too much interested in wars, and he met with no ultimate success. In 1712, on his last visit to Vienna, he received the honour of a Privy Councillorship and Barony of the Empire.

When he returned to Hanover, the Elector George had already gone to England. Leibniz wished to go to London for the coronation, but was ordered to remain at Hanover and to continue his work on his history of Brunswick. He seems never to have found favour with George I, whose displeasure increased after his accession to the throne of England; this was possibly due to the influence of friends of Newton. In the last years of his life Leibniz was almost entirely neglected, and his death in 1716 aroused no interest in London or Berlin. No one from the Court attended his funeral, his coffin being followed to the grave by his secretary alone. In Paris, however, a fitting memorial oration was pronounced by Fontenelle.

Throughout his life Leibniz was indefatigably industrious,

and was impatient of the ill-health that his long hours sometimes caused. He enjoyed social intercourse of all kinds, thinking that there must always be something that he could learn from everybody. This did not prevent him from being extremely proud of his own ideas, and extremely confident of the correctness of his own opinions. But he never lost his enthusiasm to learn, nor relaxed his determination to examine every problem which occupied him with complete thoroughness. In controversy he showed himself to be exceptionally patient and good-tempered; and in general, his secretary tells us, he spoke well of everybody and made the best of everything.

Philosophical System : the Monadology, etc. It has already been said that to-day the main philosophic interest of Leibniz lies less in his system, considered as a system, than in the particular arguments by which the development of that system was influenced. We shall therefore give here only a brief summary of his systematic doctrines, and then turn to consider at greater length his treatment of some special problems in his less formal writings.

Everything which has any reality, according to Leibniz, must itself either be a real unity or be made up of real unities. It is evident at once that bodies are not themselves real unities; they must therefore be aggregates of real unities. A real unity must be simple, indivisible, imperishable in the ordinary course of nature, and capable of variety without having parts. There is one thing in experience which we know to have all these characteristics, namely, a soul. Now the unities of which bodies are composed cannot actually be souls because they have no consciousness; they must therefore be, as it were, souls-without-consciousness, entities which have all the characteristics of souls except consciousness. We may say then that these souls-without-consciousness and souls, properly so called, are the only real unities conceivable to us. The name which Leibniz uses to cover all real unities is *monads*.

Since the monad has no parts it can only come into being all at once and end all at once; that is, it can come into being only by being created by God, and can come to an end only by being annihilated by God. For the same reason, Leibniz says, it cannot be changed internally by the action upon it of things outside it, as a compound could. Yet every monad has some character to distinguish it from every other monad, and is subject to change. Its character and its changes must therefore be determined by some internal principle, which is essential to it. So from the moment of its creation every monad is pregnant with its own future. No other monad can affect it in any way; what happens to it is determined by its own nature alone. The action by which it passes from one state to another Leibniz calls *appetition*.

Though the monads cannot act upon one another, they are nevertheless adapted to one another, so that taken all together they form a universe; in a word, they are connected together and adapted to one another *as if* they acted upon one another. This connection and adaptation is governed by two laws: the *principle of contradiction*, which determines what is possible and what is impossible, and the *principle of sufficient reason*, in accordance with which the Author of the universe, by free decisions of His will, selects out of the infinite possibilities that which is best and most fitted for existence. Each monad, in producing its own changes by its own internal principle,— since its changes fit in with the changes which are produced in themselves by all the other monads—may be said to express or represent the universe from its own point of view. The passing state of the monad, representing as it does the whole universe, is called *perception*.

Not every perception is *apperceived*. There are monads which never have any consciousness at all; and even minds have an infinite number of unconscious perceptions. Monads without consciousness, of which bodies are composed, act according to the laws of efficient causes; souls act according to the laws of final causes. Since the changes of every monad of whatever kind are adapted to the changes of every other, it is clear that the kingdom of efficient causes and the kingdom of final causes are in harmony with one another.

Among souls a distinction must be made between minds

and ordinary souls. In ordinary souls, for instance the souls of brutes, there is some connection between conscious perceptions in accordance with the laws of memory and imagination; but minds, which have clear and distinct apperceptions, are further gifted with reason. Ordinary souls are the living mirrors of the universe of created things, whereas minds are also images of the Divinity himself, the Author of nature, and are capable of knowing the system of the universe. This makes minds capable of entering into a kind of society with God, so that they are members of the City of Minds, the most perfect state under the most perfect of monarchs. Just as within the world of nature there is harmony, as we saw above, between the two kingdoms of efficient and of final causes, so there is a harmony between the physical kingdom of nature and the moral kingdom of grace; that is, there is accord between God as Architect of the machine of the universe and God as Monarch of the divine City of Minds.

By reason of this harmony, there is no good action without reward, and no evil action without punishment. All things work together for the good of the righteous in a universe which is the image of the infinite perfections of God.

Correspondence with Arnauld. Let us now attempt to discover what considerations led Leibniz to the main conclusions which are basic to the structure of his system; in other words, let us examine his more detailed discussion of some particular points, and try to find out what special problems he was primarily considering when he made up his mind on the most essential matters.

It is clear that one of the most fundamental of Leibniz's doctrines—it is certainly one of the most curious—is that every substance is a real unity, simple in the sense of having no parts, incapable of being acted upon by anything outside itself, and therefore productive of its own changes by an internal principle. It is generally recognized to-day that the best light on the development of this thesis is to be found in the letters to Arnauld, where Leibniz seems to be arguing that his whole view of the nature of substance follows from a basic principle of logic, which he takes to be axiomatic; namely, *verae propositionis semper praedicatum inest subjecto*—in a true proposition the predicate is always included in the subject. The implications of this in regard to general propositions have no doubt been recognized previously, says Leibniz; but its implications in regard to singular propositions are more startling. Certainly they startled Arnauld, part-author of the Port-Royal Logic. It has always been recognized, Leibniz argues, that the predicates which can truly be asserted of a sphere must be contained within the essential notion of a sphere; but it has not been seen that the same must hold of the *actual individual sphere* which Archimedes had placed upon his tomb. It must have been included within the original notion of that sphere that it would on a particular day be set upon that grave. To take a more striking instance, everything which can truly be predicated of Adam must be contained within the essential notion of Adam; that is, the original notion of Adam included once for all the notion of everything that was going to happen to him, and thereby to the rest of mankind, his descendants.

This doctrine at once stirred the theologian in Arnauld, by raising in his mind difficulties about the *freedom* of God; and Leibniz had to attempt to show that he was not a determinist in any theologically objectionable sense. But with this dispute we are not for the moment concerned. What concerns us is that Leibniz is arguing that the principle *praedicatum inest subjecto* involves the denial of any interaction between substances; and that in making his point he is emphasizing a distinction between predicates asserted of general concepts (*sub specie generalitatis*) and predicates asserted of individuals (*singulariter*). It is important to notice that he refuses to identify or confuse the individual with a highly differentiated general concept (i.e. with an *infima species*). Adam is not just the first man, the husband of Eve, or an inhabitant of the garden of Eden. He is the one unique Adam. And everything which happened to him happened to him because it followed from the essential motion of that one unique Adam by an absolute necessity.

Thus it seems to follow that *if* in a true proposition the

predicate is included in the notion of the subject, and *if* there can be any true propositions asserted of Adam *singulariter*, then Adam cannot have been ever acted upon by anything external to himself; and, more generally, individual substances are incapable of interaction. But, even if we pass without comment Leibniz's acceptance of the first of these hypotheses, we naturally ask ourselves why he did not regard his argument as amounting to a *reductio ad absurdum* of the notion of *individual* substances. Why did he not conclude that individuals are not substances, and that we have no knowledge of any true singular propositions?

It seems that Leibniz was convinced by reading Spinoza that any view which denied the substantiality of individuals was inadmissible. Beyond this it is very difficult to say anything clear and definite. Up to a point he is very cautious about the imputation of substantiality; and he thinks that philosophers generally are too ready to allow that things are substances. A body, he says, is evidently not a substance; a crowd is not a substance. But he seems to take it for granted that individual selves are substances. He further takes it for granted that, though bodies are not substances, they are real existences of some kind, and therefore they must be aggregates of substances. He also holds that all general notions are *incomplete* notions. No notion is complete except the notion of an individual. Thus the notion of the First Man is not the notion of a substance; but the notion of Adam *is* the notion of a substance. All this, however, seems hardly to amount to any proof. Leibniz seems to be doing no more than simply affirming again and again his thesis that a substance is essentially an individual or real unity, and that there is in the universe a plurality of such substances. There is, however, a basic *conviction* involved in the argument, namely, the conviction that individual selves are real unities and must be represented as substances. For this conviction Leibniz offers no defence, though perhaps he sometimes holds that we are directly conscious of being real unities.

Dynamics and Physics. There is no doubt that Leibniz

thought that his discoveries in regard to dynamics supported his general theory of substance. In view of the Cartesian doctrine that the essence of material substance was extension, he always regarded his refutation of Descartes's mechanics as a vital part of the defence of his own system.

Descartes taught that the total quantity of motion in nature is always the same. Leibniz argues that the quantity of motion in nature is not constant, but (what Descartes did not know) that the quantity of motion in any given direction is constant. This principle he formulated by saying that the total cause is *equivalent* to the total effect. It had always been recognized that effects were proportional to causes: but Leibniz now asserted that the total effect was not simply proportional, but equivalent to the total cause. In other words, to every action there is an equal reaction.

Leibniz also regarded himself as having proved that the total quantity of *force* in nature remains constant, force being proportional not, as Descartes thought, to the product of the mass and the velocity (mv), but to the product of the mass and the square of the velocity (mv^2, i.e. double what is now called kinetic energy). The two formulae (mv and mv^2) give the same result only in cases of equilibrium. In a system of moving bodies mv is demonstrably not constant; whereas mv^2 can be shown to be always the same. Since God has not made a faulty machine, it is evident that in nature the total quantity of force is conserved.

Thus if we wish to understand the principle of change in the physical universe, Leibniz argues, what we have to consider is not motion but force. Now force is calculated by looking at its effects. But it cannot be maintained, of course, that the force *is* its effect. The effects are in the future, whereas the force is in the body *now*. But what exactly is meant by saying that the force is *in* the body? We do not mean, according to Leibniz, that the body is actually being active. To say that a body is endowed with a certain force is different from saying that it is actually doing work. On the other hand we do not mean by force the mere *potency* of the Schoolmen; for that which has mere

potency requires the realization of some external condition
(that is, it requires the action of something outside upon it)
to turn its potency into actuality. Force is thus neither
actual activity nor mere potency, but something between
the two.

Leibniz thus concludes that his dynamics forces him to
maintain that physical objects are made up of units whose
essence it is to be endowed with force (*vis viva*), and
which, therefore, do not need the action of one unit upon
another in order to produce change. Actually, of course,
it is difficult to see how Leibniz can have thought that
his dynamics supported the doctrine that each unit is a
substance or real unity, quite incapable of being affected
by any other unit. As he sometimes admits, dynamics
must think in terms of interaction. But of this we shall
have more to say presently, when we come to consider the
Correspondence with Clarke.

The New System, and the Controversy with Bayle. Here
Leibniz is primarily concerned to explain and defend his
doctrine of pre-established harmony, with special reference
to the union of body and soul. In doing so he shows that
his general view of substance partly depends on a careful
investigation of the nature of the mind.

The doctrine of pre-established harmony, he says, really
follows from the conclusions already drawn about the
nature of substance. Since no substance can act on any
other substance, and yet the changes of the various substances are adapted to one another as if they did interact,
we must conclude that everything that happens to any
individual substance 'springs from within itself by a
perfect spontaneity with regard to itself, and yet in a
perfect conformity with things outside'. Committed to this
conclusion by his analysis of propositions, Leibniz here
seeks to show that he can give a satisfactory account of
the union of soul and body. He does this especially by
examining the nature of the mind, and trying to show that
the doctrine that the mind produces of itself its own experience by virtue of its own inner nature agrees with the
facts of experience. It accords well with the fact of free-

will, as maintaining that all the soul's actions are produced by itself alone, and with the fact of immortality, since if nothing can affect the soul nothing can bring it to an end, except a miracle; and on careful investigation we see he alleges that it also accords with the facts of perception.

There are two main objections to his doctrine which Leibniz here faces: first, that such automatism is inconceivable; secondly, that even if such automatism is possible, the facts of experience show that the mind is not in reality such an automaton.

To the first objection Leibniz urges that automata can actually be constructed which are capable of a great variety of behaviour. No doubt it is beyond the power of a human artificer to make an automaton which would behave as my body is behaving. But it certainly cannot be shown that such an automaton is in principle impossible. And we must remember that on any view there is a great difference between Nature's machines and ours, perhaps amounting to a difference in kind. In short, we must take it that there is no behaviour, however complicated, which is in principle beyond the power of automatism.

In the course of answering the second objection, namely, that the mind is not *in fact* such an automaton, Leibniz conducts some important psychological investigations. He reminds us first that it is inconceivable to us how body can act on mind or mind on body. Though it may appear, therefore, that when I am stung by a wasp, the pain felt by my mind is immediately caused by what happens to my body, we cannot accept that explanation. It is evident that the cause of what happens in the mind, since it cannot be sought in the body, must be sought in the mind. Nor need we be disturbed by the fact that previous philosophers have rejected the view that minds are automata. What they were rejecting was the contention that minds are mechanical, that is, that they are *corporeal* automata. This we shall not maintain, says Leibniz. We hold that bodies are automata and minds are automata, but that between the two kinds there is a great difference. Every mind changes as determined by its own essence in accordance with the laws of its own nature; and every body does the same. But the laws of the nature of mind are different from those of the nature of body.

We must look then for an explanation of the present state of a mind in previous states of the same mind, and nowhere else whatever. If this were not so, there could be no responsibility and no identity. Furthermore, we shall find that on this principle we can give some explanation of a number of obvious facts of experience which have hitherto been unexplained. But this Leibniz works out in more detail when he comes to consider the philosophy of Locke.

New Essays. Here, in considering the *Essay on the Human Understanding*, Leibniz perforce gives his main attention to problems connected with the nature of knowledge. His thought in this connection tends automatically to fall into two parts, the one part psychological and the other logical. In the first he argues rather in the manner of Locke, and seeks to propound an account of the nature of mind which will explain what he takes to be the observed facts of experience, e.g. memory, habit, etc. But, holding as he does that the conclusions of this part of his inquiry are not incompatible with the teaching of the established logic, he has, secondly, to expound what he takes to be the essential teaching of that logic. For though he does not think that the established logic needs any fundamental modification, it is obvious that he must needs give it a new and careful re-statement after studying Locke. This is an absolutely vital part of Leibniz's philosophy, because, as we have seen, his whole view of the nature of substance depends largely on pressing the implications of the logical principle *praedicatum inest subjecto*.

Let us first briefly consider Leibniz's psychological teaching in the *New Essays*. Here the most striking thing is perhaps his application of his law of continuity to mental phenomena. *Natura non facit saltum:* there are no big sudden changes in nature. When there appear to be big sudden changes, the appearances must be deceiving us. When a tennis ball, for instance, strikes a wall, it may *appear* that at one moment the ball is moving forward with a velocity of say 70 f.s., at the next moment it is at rest, and at the next it is moving back again with a velocity of 50 f.s. But this cannot really be the case. In order to pass from a velocity of 70 f.s. to a state of rest, the ball must have slowed up gradually and have passed through all the intermediate velocities between 70 f.s. and zero; and similarly when it acquires a velocity of 50 f.s. in the other direction. The same must be true, Leibniz says, of the mind's experience. If we appear to pass immediately from a feeling of pleasure to a feeling of acute pain, the appearance must be deceiving us. The mind must actually have passed through all the intermediate states. Since we are often not conscious of this gradual transition, we must admit that a great deal goes on in the mind of which we are not conscious. There are a great many perceptions which we do not apperceive, and all these perceptions go to make up the state of our minds at any given moment. The existence of such perceptions can often be inferred from the character of our conscious states, even though the perceptions cannot be themselves brought into consciousness.

All this brings Leibniz into conflict with Locke. To the latter it seems absurd to speak of something happening in the mind of which the mind is not conscious; though, as Leibniz points out, he modifies this later by saying that there can be nothing in the mind of which the mind *has never been* conscious—without ever acknowledging, however, the importance of this modification of his doctrine. But surely, Leibniz urges, it is Locke's view that is absurd. What are we to say of memory, and of habits and dispositions? It is impossible to explain memory or habits without supposing that there may be *in* the mind, in some sense, things of which the mind is not conscious. And if this be granted in principle, it is purely a matter for detailed investigation to discover whether or not there must be in the mind some perceptions of which, as far as we can discover, we have never been conscious at all. Leibniz thinks that there certainly are such perceptions. Suppose that it has been established that a wasp-sting normally causes pain *at the time*; and suppose that on a particular occasion my attention is so much engaged with what I am doing that I do not notice any pain until the tension of my excitement relaxes, although I must actually have been stung some time before. Are we to say that in this case the mind had no pain at all during the intervening time, though it would have had pain if I had not been otherwise excited? Are we to say, in fact, that a happening in my body is correlated with a happening in my mind at some times and not at others? Surely not, Leibniz urges. When something happens in my body, there is always a corresponding happening in my mind. We must not conclude, just because I am not conscious of any previous event in my mind relevant to the explanation of my present state, that there was no such event. Rather we must examine my present state and seek to determine what *must* previously have occurred in my mind, even though it cannot be found in my conscious experience.

It is evident that, though Leibniz is applying his principle of continuity over-crudely, he has here a very strong case. But what use does he make of it? His point is that since it cannot be maintained that there is nothing in the mind of which we are not conscious, Locke's attack on 'innate ideas' fails. Just as the veins, which are laid bare when a block of marble is cut, were there in the marble before they were discovered, so there are some ideas which are in the mind from the beginning whether or not they have yet been found there. Locke's argument fails to show that they cannot be there; and there are good, logical reasons for concluding that they must be there. For what account can be given otherwise of universal and necessary truths, such as are to be found in geometry and arithmetic? Knowledge of these cannot be derived from experience; for the observation of particular instances can never entitle us to assert a universal proposition.

Thus according to Leibniz Locke's attack on the basis of the established logic fails; and it is therefore open to Leibniz to fall back on a doctrine which accords with that logic to explain those necessary truths of which Locke cannot consistently give an account. Necessary truths are arrived at by the analysis of clear and distinct notions; and these notions in turn are, by a special technique, simply *found in the mind*. From the analysis of the original clear and distinct notions we come, by way of identical propositions, to non-identical propositions, and then by analysis of these to further propositions, and so on to the whole body of knowledge. The most powerful engine for producing this happy result, he says, is the syllogism, though it is a mistake to regard it as the only one.

Herein Leibniz shows himself to be a rationalist indeed. He even includes within this doctrine our knowledge of contingent fact. He distinguishes indeed between truths of reason and truths of fact. The first are in the sphere of necessity and are known *a priori*: the latter are in the sphere of contingency and are known *a posteriori*. But in the end these too, according to Leibniz, are arrived at by the analysis of clear and distinct notions which are found in the mind, and not by mere sense-observation. Because these truths are in the sphere of contingency, we must not make the mistake of thinking that they are any the less certain. True propositions about Adam follow as much from the original notion of Adam as true propositions about triangles follow from the original notion of triangularity. The latter follow in accordance with the law of contradiction, whereas the former follow by the law of sufficient reason. But both are equally certain.

Thus in the end, according to Leibniz, none of our knowledge is really derived from observation by the senses; all of it springs from the analysis of original notions which are in some sense found in the mind.

Correspondence with Clarke: Leibniz and Newton. In this controversy with an authoritative exponent of the views of Newton, Leibniz, in the closing years of his life, seeks finally to set in order and to defend his views with special reference to their bearing on mathematics and physics. In view of the intrinsic interest of this subject and of the at least superficial resemblance between Leibniz's teaching and modern physical theory, it is perhaps worth while to examine this issue at some length.

Leibniz agreed with the Cartesians in rejecting atoms. The reasons which make it impossible to believe that perceptible bodily masses are perfectly inelastic and indivisible hold in the end with equal weight against atoms. In this modern physicists would agree with Descartes and Leibniz. But the latter goes on to reject the former's primary elements, which, he says, are nothing but *mathematical points*; they have position, but no magnitude and no other characteristics whatever. But how can such elements be put together in such a way as to aggregate into a bodily mass? No number of nothings, when put together, can make a something. Yet this is what, according to Leibniz, the doctrine of Descartes requires.

Now the truth is, Leibniz continues, that it is not to extension, but to that which is extended, that we must turn our attention. If we do so we shall see that the essence of that which is extended is not extension, but something else. Let us for the sake of argument suppose that matter is passive, as Descartes thought, and let us consider a piece of matter at rest. This is as a matter of fact, says Leibniz, to speak abstractly, since real matter is not passive and is never at rest. But let that pass for the moment. Let us suppose that matter is passive, and let us consider a body at rest. Now the essence of the matter of the body is not its extension, but its solidity. This solidity shows itself in two ways: the body resists penetration and resists movement. Without impenetrability and inertia it would not be a body; unless it had these characteristics it could not be extended. Solidity cannot be explained in terms of extension. Therefore even Descartes, who held that matter was inert and passive, should have seen that that which makes a body solid is an essential character of body.

We have already seen how this criticism of the Cartesians is gathered up into Leibniz's constructive view that the essence of matter is *vis viva*, in terms of which both impenetrability and inertia can be explained.

At this point we should perhaps expect Leibniz to ask himself the question which he has just asked of Descartes with such destructive results. How can these elements, or *metaphysical points*, as he calls them, be compounded into a bodily mass? After all, they share with the Cartesian elements the characteristic of having no extended magnitude. It is true that, while Descartes's elements have no characteristic but position, those of Leibniz have the positive characteristic of *vis viva*. But does this help to explain mass? Can a number of parts, whose sole characteristic is active force, aggregate into a body?

To this problem modern readers, I think, will expect Leibniz to offer some such solution as the following:—Each unit has a certain quantity of force, and, though it has no extension, it always has position; that is to say, at any given moment the force always operates at a point. The units act upon one another, acting of course not by impact, but at a distance, as Newton held gravitation to act; and the result of this interaction is that the elements, which must be thought of as centres of force, move in such a way as to present to the human observer the *appearance* of a number of continuous bodily masses of finite size behaving in certain ways. Perceptible bodies, together with their changes and motions, are only appearances; the realities are the interacting centres of force.

It is true that this view gives rise to very great difficulties. Suppose we allow that movements of invisible particles can give rise to the appearance of a continuous surface; how can there be motion without a body to move? Can a centre of force move? But to the modern reader these are, for better or worse, accustomed difficulties; and he will probably expect Leibniz to inaugurate some such view. To do so would be to accept as ultimate realities the centres of force, space and time (as implied by their position and movement), and presumably a mind or minds (implied by the existence of appearances). And it would be allowed that the centres of force in moving could affect one another's motion by action at a distance.

But it is evident that this was *not* Leibniz's view. He held that the only ultimate realities are individual substances; that is, the metaphysical points, endowed with *vis viva*, and minds. Nothing else has ultimate reality; and it is clear to Leibniz that space and time are not individual substances. What then are space and time? In the first place Leibniz will have nothing to do with the notion of action at a distance, or with that of empty space. All motion takes place in a plenum, and all action of body on body is by impact. We have no experience, he says, of a vacuum in nature; and if there were such a thing as empty space, position or motion in it would be purposeless, since, as every point would be absolutely homogeneous with every other, there could be no reason for occupying one point rather than another, nor for moving from one point to another. Since there would be no reason for it, it would be contrary to reason.

Moreover, in nature, Leibniz argues, position and motion are never purposeless. A body cannot be moved from one position to another and remain the same body in every respect other than its position. To change the situation of bodies is, contrary to the opinion of those who believe in empty space, to change the bodies. If you move a block of marble from Genoa to Paris, it may appear to make no difference to anything but the mere position in space of the marble. But this is not so. It really makes a difference to the marble and to everything else in the universe. What makes the difference is, of course, not change of position in empty space, but the change in the interrelations of bodies —that is, in the end, a change in the order of active forces in the universe.

Thus space and time are nothing but the order of real existences, according to Leibniz. Perhaps his view can be more clearly stated in this way:—Bodies and movements of bodies are not real existences, but ideal existences created by the imagination. There is nothing real in the physical universe behind the curtain of sense except individual units of *vis viva*, which are not in space and time. Space and time themselves are even further removed from real existence than are bodies and movements of bodies. For the notions of bodies *in* space and of change *in* time can only be significant if there is empty space and empty time. If the physical world is a plenum, space is nothing but an arrangement of bodies, and time is nothing but an order of changes. Now the whole notion of empty space and empty time is a vulgar error. So space and time are not only not ultimately real like the monads; they are less real than bodies, being due to a confused perception of bodies.

In a word, if we wish to understand the true nature of reality we must banish from our minds all notions of space and time. Instead we must conceive of an order of relations between entities whose essence is active force. In conceiving of these entities as exercising their force in an ordered system we must not think of them as operating at points in space, or of the system as a mechanical system, excellently as such a fancy may seem to satisfy the imagination. We must think of real entities as acting intensively, rather in the manner that a soul acts, though without the consciousness which attends upon some of the activities of souls. If we think of the universe as a system, or ordered unity, of the activities of monads, we shall be in no danger of thinking of space and time as real existences. Such a mistaken notion would be entirely due to the action of the imagination.

Summary of Leibniz's Philosophy. We may now make a tentative attempt to gather together the various strands of thought which go to make the finished product of Leibniz's system; though it will now be clear to the reader that any such attempt at a final judgment must rest on a very precarious basis.

First, Leibniz was profoundly affected by his discovery of the implications of the fundamental principles of the Scholastic logic when applied to singular propositions. This convinced him that substances must be real unities, and cannot be affected by anything outside themselves. Secondly, he found that if the constituent elements of things are real unities, they must be the only real unities; since, if they are to keep their character as real unities, they can only be compounded by aggregation. Thirdly, he argued that we are given in experience an instance of such a real unity, namely, the self; this unity is thought of as indivisible into parts, but yet as capable of great variety. Fourthly, he considered that an examination of the nature of the mind bears out the view that it is unaffected in its experience by anything outside itself; this, so far as it goes, confirms the view that real unities are pregnant with their own future. Fifthly, a sound dynamics reveals that the essence of material substance is not extension, nor even

motion, but force, a character *in* things which is presupposed by solidity and motion; real unities must be conceived
to be endowed with force in the same manner as the soul
is endowed with activity. Sixthly, since there cannot be
any interaction between real unities, it follows that there
must be pre-established harmony, in order to give unity
to the universe; without this there would be a chaotic
plurality and everything would be purposeless, which is
absurd. Lastly, reality as such is governed not by mechanical laws, but by the law of sufficient reason; the real
world is not the only possible world, but the best of possible
worlds; everything is ordered not by a mechanistic necessity,
but by the moral necessity to work for the highest good of
minds; this is achieved by making the kingdom of nature
subservient to the kingdom of minds, God being at once the
Architect of the one and the Monarch of the other.

Remarks and Criticisms. It is now time to suggest a few
brief criticisms at each point of the argument as we have
here represented it. First, if Leibniz's view of substance
follows from the doctrine *praedicatum inest subjecto*, he
seems to offer no reason for subscribing to that doctrine
itself; he simply takes it as common ground between himself and the established logic. Secondly, when he maintains
that if parts are real unities wholes of those parts can only
be aggregates, he is arguing too much *a priori*, and is
reflecting too little on the implications of his own view that
all individual minds taken together form a unity in the
City of Minds under the monarchy of God. Moreover, his
contention that a simple being which has no parts is yet
capable of variety is insufficiently worked out; it is not
sufficient to refer to an instance in experience, namely, the
soul; he ought at least to indicate, for example, just how an
infinity of little perceptions go to make up the present state
of the soul. Thirdly, it is doubtful, as Hume emphasized,
whether it *is* clear in experience that the soul is entirely
simple and without parts. Fourthly, while Leibniz makes
good ground against Locke when he maintains that the
present experience of a particular mind is always partly
determined by the intrinsic nature of mind as such and

partly by the previous experience of the particular mind, and is never wholly determined (as it would be if the mind were a *tabula rasa*) by the present action of things outside it; yet his arguments stop short of proving that its experience is entirely determined by the mind's own original nature. Fifthly, though Leibniz was no doubt right in principle in urging that physics must explain everything in terms of force or activity of some kind, he seems to have been wrong in thinking that dynamical theory could conform to his doctrine of real unities; indeed he himself sometimes allows that as far as dynamics is concerned its objects behave as if there was interaction between them. Sixthly, since Leibniz allows that everything in the universe, even including minds, behaves in every way, because of the pre-established harmony, *as if* there was interaction, he seems to be left with no argument against the real interaction of body on body and of mind on mind except the logical argument from the principle *praedicatum inest subjecto*; and this principle seems to be open to objection. Lastly, Leibniz can show that many who argue that this is *not* the best of all possible worlds take insufficient account of the all-inclusive, all-pervading unity of the universe; but he has no argument to prove that this *is* the best possible world; the most that he can do is to show that his optimism cannot be finally refuted.

A brief note must be added here about Leibniz's teaching in regard to *freedom*. His stress on the principle of sufficient reason inevitably makes his ethical views central to his system. Yet his ethics, for whatever reason, is certainly the weakest part of his thought. It is really quite clear that he must believe in some kind of predestination; that is, he is, in ordinary non-Leibnizian language, some kind of a determinist. Yet he will never say so. He can pour scorn, of course, on the suggestion that God might leave the future of the universe to chance. He can show, more-over, that the principles underlying the determination of my actions are different from the principles of geometry or of mechanics. But though he may multiply distinctions between the various kinds of determination, the important fact remains that on his view my actions are determined, and are in principle predictable. It is difficult to see how such a doctrine can leave room for any real freedom of the will. It is true that, according to Leibniz, my actions are determined by nothing but my own nature. But so are the actions of the brutes, and of those monads which have no consciousness. He sometimes tries to mark the difference between the determination of minds and physical determination by saying that motives 'incline without necessitating'. But, as far as its bearing on freedom is concerned, this is nothing but words. The fact that I shall do this action freely, he says, does not mean that it is uncertain whether I shall do it. Nothing in the universe is uncertain, because nothing can occur without a sufficient reason. And this is Leibniz's last word. He points out some important distinctions, but they do not enable him to make out a case for free-will.

Influence of Leibniz. It may safely be said that until the twentieth century Leibniz's influence on the development of philosophy was exercised chiefly through Kant. Kant was brought up on the systematized Leibnizianism of Wolff. But the latter made no important original contribution, and it was on the basis of the ideas of Leibniz himself that Kant sought to revivify philosophy after the sceptical influence of Hume.

There is no doubt that, especially in the *New Essays*, Leibniz goes far towards leading up to Kant's Copernican revolution in logic. He carefully examines Locke's empiricism, and lays down the principle that the *tabula rasa* theory of mind cannot account for the existence of knowledge of universal and necessary truths, such as are found in geometry and arithmetic. This point is accepted without more ado as a starting-point by Kant and Hegel. So also is the method, here used by Leibniz, of attempting to refute a psychological theory of knowledge by arguing from the possibility of the existence of universal and necessary truths. Kant, who presses the method much further, calls it the 'transcendental method'.

Leibniz agrees with Kant in conceding to Locke that all knowledge must start with sense-experience, and also in denying that it can be wholly *derived from* sense-experience. He goes further and makes the pregnant suggestion, *nihil est in intellectu quod non fuerit in sensu*, excipe, *nisi ipse intellectus*—there is nothing in the understanding which was not previously in the senses, *except* the understanding itself. But it must be admitted that his happy phrase does not suggest to him, though it may well have suggested to Kant, the Kantian view that what is necessary to the possibility of universal truths is the existence of categories, that is, forms of spontaneous activity.

Leibniz further shows the way to Kant by emphasizing the distinction between *truths of reason* on the one hand, which are *a priori*, in the sphere of necessity, and concerned with general notions of possibilities, and on the other *truths of fact*, which are *a posteriori*, in the sphere of contingency, and concerned with individuals or real existences. He did not, however, see the necessity for abandoning what Kant called the 'dogmatic' position in regard to truths of fact. He recognized, with Kant, that particular facts cannot be deduced from original notions in accordance with the laws of contradiction; only general truths can be arrived at in this way, and these suffer under the disadvantage that their objects are not real existences. But he thought that he could save 'dogmatic' rationalism by introducing the new refinement of the principle of sufficient reason to bridge the gap between knowledge of general truths and knowledge of individuals. He did not see, what Kant learned from Hume, that in the sphere of real existences we cannot progress without a knowledge of causal relations, which is clearly not arrived at by any analysis of original notions. We have as a matter of fact no insight into the sufficient reason for the happening of any event to any individual. Because he did not see this, he did not recognize that our knowledge of truths of fact is synthetic. Instead, he stood by the established logic, and performed the service of showing Kant how that logic must be stated if it is to meet the difficulties, which he himself exhibited, in regard to our knowledge of the physical world.

In a word, Leibniz showed, as against Locke, that we cannot explain scientific knowledge if we suppose the mind to be a *tabula rasa*; nor can we do so if we suppose that nothing goes on in the mind except what meets the eye of introspection. So far he indicated to Kant what line · he should take in meeting Locke's psychological approach. But he allowed himself to be too much encouraged by his discovery that the doctrine of innate ideas cannot be certainly refuted by an empirical inventory of the contents of the mind; and so he thought that this doctrine could be defended absolutely, and that, with the added refinement of the principle of sufficient reason, 'dogmatic' rationalism could be made to stand in despite of Locke. It is quite true that the mind *might* be born with some kind of innate knowledge of certain universal notions; but, as Hume shows, even if this were so, it could not help to explain our knowledge of real existences, since it could not explain our knowledge of causal relations. It is on this rock that Leibniz's rationalism breaks.

C. R. MORRIS.

SELECT BIBLIOGRAPHY

In the lifetime of Leibniz only one complete work of his on philosophy was published: *Essais de Théodicée sur la bonté de Dieu, la liberté de l'homme, et l'origine du mal*, 1710. Other important philosophical works are: the correspondence with Samuel Clarke on the principles of natural philosophy and religion (published by Clarke, 1717); *La Monadologie*, a sketch of his philosophic system (German trans. 1720, original French not until 1840 in Erdmann's edition); *Nouveaux Essais sur l'Entendement Humain* (Raspe edition, 1765), being an answer to John Locke's *Essay on the Human Understanding*; the *Systema Theologicum* (1819), which is an exposition of the doctrines of the Roman Catholic Church, written in the cause of reunion between Protestantism and Catholicism (the title was probably given to the work by an over-zealous Catholic).

Translations of the above (other than the Clarke correspondence, which contained a translation by Clarke of Leibniz's words in the original 1717 edition) are: *A System of Theology*, trans. by C. W. Russell, 1850; *The Philosophical Works of Leibniz*, trans. by G. M. Duncan (containing *The Monadology*, the Clarke correspondence, many of the shorter philosophical papers, an abridgment of the *Theodicy*, and selections from the *New Essays*), 1890; *The New Essays*, trans. by A. G. Langley (1896). Other translations: *The Monadology*, etc., trans. by R. Latta, 1898 and 1925; *The Monadology* by H. W. Carr,

1930; *A summary Account of Leibnitz's Memoir, addressed to Louis XIV*, recommending the Conquest of Egypt, 1803; *Discourse on Metaphysics, Correspondence with Arnauld*, and *The Monadology*, trans. by G. R. Montgomery, 1902; *Early Mathematical Manuscripts of Leibniz*, trans. by J. M. Child, 1920.

There exists at present no complete edition of the works of Leibniz, and it may be said that all editions are supplementary in some way or other. The best edition is that of C. J. Gerhardt (philosophical writings, 1875–90; mathematical writings, 1855–63). Next comes Onno Klopp's edition of the historical and political writings (1864–77); and then that of Foucher de Careil (1859–75), which contains the theological works besides the political works, and the writings bearing on the foundation of academies. To these should be added the first 'collected' edition of L. Dutens (1768), and that of G. H. Pertz (1843–63); the editions of the philosophical works by Raspe (1765), Erdmann (1840), Jacques (1846), and Janet (1866). There is, however, in course of preparation, a complete edition of the works of Leibniz, including all the papers in the Library of Hanover, under the direction of the *Akademie der Wissenschaften* of Berlin. It is intended to consist of forty quarto volumes, arranged in seven series: (1) General, Political, and Historical Correspondence (11 vols.); (2) Philosophical Correspondence (6 vols.); (3) Mathematical, Scientific, and Technical Correspondence (5 vols.); (4) Political Writings (4 vols.); (5) Historical Writings (4 vols.); (6) Philosophical Writings (6 vols.); (7) Mathematical, Scientific, and Technical (4 vols.).

The standard biography is that by G. E. Guhrauer (1842). Works in English are: J. T. Merz: *Leibniz,* 1884 (new edition, 1948); Bertrand Russell: *A Critical Exposition of the Philosophy of Leibniz,* 1900 (reprint with new preface, 1937); H. W. Carr: *Leibniz,* 1929; G. J. Jordan: *The Reunion of the Churches,* 1927 (a study of Leibniz's attempt at reunion); P. Schrecker: *Leibniz,* 1937; R. Klibansky: *Leibniz's Unknown Correspondence with English Scholars and Men of Letters,* 1941; H. W. Joseph: *Lectures on the Philosophy of Leibniz,* 1949. Mention should also be made of E. Bodemann's catalogue, *Die Leibnizschriften in der Königlichen Bibliothek zu Hannover* (1895), from which are translated one or two extracts in this volume.

TRANSLATOR'S PREFACE

THE passages from Leibniz's philosophical writings given in this book are almost all taken from the seven volumes of Gerhardt's edition. A few extracts in Part III are not taken from Gerhardt, but their sources are indicated in footnotes.

Part I contains the three best known works among Leibniz's more formal expositions of his system—*The Monadology* (1714), *Principles of Nature and of Grace* (1714), and *On the Ultimate Origination of Things* (1697). These are given complete. The *Monadology* is printed first in spite of its date, because in addition to being the most famous of Leibniz's writings, it is also, so to speak, his title-piece.

Part II represents an attempt to give evidence for a balanced judgment about the scope and development of the thought of Leibniz, and is arranged chronologically. Except in the case of the *Letter to Foucher* (1676), the *Letter to Bayle* (1687), and the *New System of the Nature and Communication of Substances* (1695), substantial abridgment has been necessary. Where the omissions are not made clear by the numbering of the chapters or paragraphs, they have been indicated by dots (. . . .) or by footnotes. I have tried, in abridging, only to cut out arguments which are better or more appropriately dealt with elsewhere, so as to concentrate attention on what seemed the central points in the various works. In the *Correspondence with Arnauld* (1686–7) I have regarded Leibniz as chiefly concerned with deriving his doctrine of substance from the analysis of propositions; in the controversy with Bayle (1695–1702) I have represented his mathematician's interest in machines and automata; in the *New Essays* (1702–3) passages are given showing the development of his psychology and indicating his statement of his logical doctrines, with special reference to his attitude to the syllogism; and in the *Correspondence with Clarke* (1715) I have concentrated attention on his defence of his physical and dynamical ideas, and of his doctrines about space and time, since these writings represent Leibniz's last and greatest attempt to state his case against the theories of Newton.

Part III consists of short extracts which are intended to illustrate the breadth and variety of Leibniz's interests, and also his attitude to other men of learning of his time. A few passages are included as specimens of his more fanciful writing. The last (taken from the concluding pages of the *Theodicy*) also gives as clear an idea as any other passage of his standpoint with regard to freedom and predestination.

In translating I have thought it better to come to a definite decision on all occasions, rather than to cumber the text with footnotes about difficulties of interpretation. The disadvantages of this method are perhaps seen at their greatest in §§ 12, 13 of the *Monadology*. Here, as elsewhere, I have tried to give an exact rendering of the text rather than to tighten it up, as it were, into accuracy or consistency. Where Leibniz uses a vague word or phrase, I have tried to give a correspondingly vague word or phrase in English. Even so, however, I am aware that my translation is throughout affected by my own interpretation of the author's meaning; but I have tried to make it as philosophically exact as possible.

To avoid multiplying footnotes I have given short notes on the persons mentioned in the text in the Index of Proper Names, and have added a full Philosophical Index to take the place of cross references at the bottom of the page.

Of the existing English versions I have found Latta's to be the best; though I have sometimes differed from him. I have also consulted the translations of Wildon-Carr, Montgomery, Duncan, and Langley.

M. M.

CONTENTS

CONTENTS

PART I

THE PHILOSOPHICAL SYSTEM OF LEIBNIZ

1. The *monad*, of which we shall speak here, is nothing but a simple substance which enters into compounds; *simple*, that is to say, without parts.

2. And there must be simple substances, because there are compounds; for the compound is nothing but a collection or *aggregatum* of simples.

3. Now where there are no parts, there neither extension, nor shape, nor divisibility is possible. And these monads are the true atoms of nature and, in a word, the elements of things.

4. Moreover, there is no fear of dissolution, and there is no conceivable way in which a simple substance could perish in the course of nature.

5. For the same reason there is no way in which a simple substance could begin in the course of nature, since it cannot be formed by means of compounding.

6. Thus it may be said that monads can only begin and end all at once, that is to say they can only begin by creation and end by annihilation, whereas what is compound begins or ends by parts.

7. There is also no means of explaining how a monad can be altered or changed within itself by any other created thing, since it is impossible to displace anything in it or to conceive of the possibility of any internal motion being started, directed, increased, or diminished within it, as can occur in compounds, where change among the parts takes place. Monads have no windows, by which anything could come in or go out. Accidents cannot become detached, or wander about outside substances, as the 'sensible species' of the

Scholastics used to do. Thus neither substance nor accident can enter a monad from without.

8. Monads, however, must have some qualities, otherwise they would not be beings at all. And if simple substances did not differ by their qualities, there would be no way of perceiving any change in things, since what is in the compound can only come from its simple ingredients; and if monads were without qualities, they would be indistinguishable from one another, since they do not differ in quantity either. And consequently, supposing space to be a plenum, each place would always only receive, when motion occurred, the equivalent of what it had before; and one state of things would be indistinguishable from another.

9. Indeed, every monad must be different from every other. For there are never in nature two beings, which are precisely alike, and in which it is not possible to find some difference which is internal, or based on some intrinsic quality.

10. I also take it as granted that every created thing, and consequently the created monad also, is subject to change, and indeed that this change is continual in each one.

11. It follows from what we have just said, that the natural changes of monads come from an *internal principle*, since an external cause would be unable to influence their inner being.

12. But besides the principle of change, there must be *differentiation within that which changes*, to constitute as it were the specification and variety of simple substances.

13. This differentiation must involve a plurality within the unity or the simple. For since every natural change takes place by degrees, something changes, and something remains; and consequently the simple must contain a large number of impressions and relations, although it has no parts.

14. The passing state, which involves and represents a plurality within the unity or simple substance, is nothing other than what is called *perception*, which must be carefully

distinguished from apperception, as will appear presently. And herein lies the great mistake of the Cartesians, that they took no account of perceptions which are not apperceived. It is this also which made them believe that minds alone are monads, and that neither brutes nor other entelechies have souls. For the same reason also they fell into the common error of confusing death, properly so called, with a prolonged unconsciousness; and this made them favour the Scholastic conviction that souls are entirely separate from bodies, and even confirmed some ill-balanced minds in the opinion that souls are mortal.

15. The action of the internal principle which produces the change or passage from one perception to another may be called *appetition*; it is true that the appetite cannot always attain completely the whole of the perception at which it aims, but it always attains something of it, and arrives at new perceptions.

16. We ourselves experience plurality within a simple substance, when we find that the least thought of which we are conscious involves a variety in its object. So everyone who acknowledges that the soul is a simple substance must acknowledge this plurality within the monad; and M. Bayle should not have found any difficulty in this, as he does in his *Dictionary*, in the article 'Rorarius'.

17. We are moreover obliged to confess that *perception* and that which depends on it *cannot be explained mechanically*, that is to say by figures and motions. Suppose that there were a machine so constructed as to produce thought, feeling, and perception, we could imagine it increased in size while retaining the same proportions, so that one could enter as one might a mill. On going inside we should only see the parts impinging upon one another; we should not see anything which would explain a perception. The explanation of perception must therefore be sought in a simple substance, and not in a compound or in a machine. Moreover, there is

nothing else whatever to be found in the simple substance except just this, viz. perceptions and their changes. It is in this alone that all the *internal actions* of simple substances must consist.

18. We may give the name *entelechies* to all created simple substances or monads. For they have in themselves a certain perfection (ἔχουσι τὸ ἐντελές); there is a self-sufficiency (αὐτάρκεια) in them which makes them the sources of their internal actions — incorporeal automata, if I may so put it.

19. If we wish to give the name 'soul' to everything which has *perceptions* and *appetites* in the general sense I have just explained, all created simple substances or monads might be called souls; but as feeling is something more than a simple perception, I agree that the general name—monad or entelechy—should be enough for simple substances which have no more than that, and that those only should be called souls, whose perception is more distinct and is accompanied by memory.

20. For there is to be found in our ordinary experience a state, in which we remember nothing and have no distinguishable perception; as when we fall into a swoon, or when we are overcome by a deep dreamless sleep. In this state the soul does not sensibly differ from a simple monad; but as this state is not permanent, and as the soul emerges from it, the soul is something more.

21. And it does not follow that when in that state the simple substance has no perception at all. Indeed, that is not possible for the above reasons; for it cannot perish, nor can it subsist without being affected in some way, and this affection is nothing but its perception. But when there are a very great number of small perceptions with nothing to distinguish them, we are stupefied, just as it happens that if we go on turning round in the same direction several times running, we become giddy and go into a swoon, so that we

can no longer distinguish anything at all. And death can throw animals [1] into this state for a time.

22. And as every state of a simple substance is a natural consequence of its preceding state, so that the present state of it is big with the future,

23. and since, on awakening from our stupor, we *are conscious* of our perceptions, it must be the case that we received the perceptions the moment before, though we were not conscious of them; for a perception cannot arise in the course of nature except from another perception, as one motion can only arise in the course of nature from another motion.

24. From this we see that if we had nothing in our perceptions to distinguish them, nothing so to speak heightened and of a keener savour, we should always be in this stupor. And this is the state of bare monads.

25. We see also that Nature has given heightened perceptions to animals from the care she has taken to provide them with organs which collect several rays of light, or several undulations of the air, so as to make these effective by being united. There is something of the kind in smell, taste, and touch, and perhaps in many other senses which are unknown to us. I will explain later how what occurs in the soul represents what takes place in the organs.

26. Memory provides souls with a kind of *consecutiveness,* which copies reason but must be distinguished from it. What I mean is this: we often see that animals, when they have a perception of something which strikes them, and of which they had a similar perception previously, are led, by the representation of their memory, to expect what was united with this perception before, and are carried away by feelings similar to those they had before. For example, when dogs

---

[1] By 'animals' Leibniz means all living creatures up to and including man. The lower animals, as distinguished from man, he refers to as 'brutes'.

are shown a stick, they remember the pain which it has caused them in the past, and howl or run away.

27. The powerful imagination, which strikes and moves them, arises either from the magnitude or from the number of the preceding perceptions. For often a vivid impression has in a moment the effect of long *habit*, or of many ordinary perceptions oft repeated.

28. Men act like brutes in so far as the sequences of their perceptions arise through the principle of memory only, like those empirical physicians who have mere practice without theory. We are all merely empiricists as regards three-fourths of our actions. For example, when we expect it to be day tomorrow, we are behaving as empiricists, because until now it has always happened thus. The astronomer alone knows this by reason.

29. But it is the knowledge of necessary and eternal truths which distinguishes us from mere animals, and gives us *reason* and the sciences, raising us to knowledge of ourselves and God. It is this in us which we call the rational soul or *mind*.

30. Further it is by the knowledge of necessary truths and by their abstractions that we are raised to *acts of reflection*, which make us think of what is called the *self*, and consider that this or that is within *us*. And it is thus that in thinking of ourselves, we think of being, of substance, of the simple and the compound, of the immaterial and of God Himself, conceiving that what is limited in us, in Him is limitless. And these acts of reflection provide the chief objects of our reasonings.

31. Our reasonings are based on two great principles: the *principle of contradiction*, by virtue of which we judge to be false that which involves a contradiction, and true that which is opposed or contradictory to the false;

32. and the *principle of sufficient reason*, by virtue of which we consider that no fact can be real or existing and no pro-

position can be true unless there is a sufficient reason, why it should be thus and not otherwise, even though in most cases these reasons cannot be known to us.

33. There are also two kinds of *truths*: truths of *reasoning* and truths of *fact*. Truths of reasoning are necessary and their opposite is impossible; those of fact are contingent and their opposite is possible. When a truth is necessary, the reason for it can be found by analysis, that is, by resolving it into simpler ideas and truths until the primary ones are reached.

34. It is in this way that in mathematics speculative *theorems* and practical *canons* are reduced by analysis to *definitions*, *axioms*, and *postulates*.

35. Finally there are simple ideas of which no definition can be given; there are also axioms or postulates, or in a word *primary principles*, which cannot be proved and have no need of proof. These are *identical propositions*, whose opposite contains an express contradiction.

36. But a *sufficient reason* also must be found in the case of *contingent truths* or *truths of fact*; that is to say, in the case of the series of things spread over the universe of created things; otherwise resolution into particular reasons might go on into endless detail on account of the immense variety of things in nature and the division of bodies *ad infinitum*. There are an infinite number of shapes and motions, both present and past, which enter into the efficient cause of my present writing; and there are an infinite number of minute inclinations and dispositions of my soul, both present and past, which enter into its final cause.

37. And as all this differentiation involves only other prior or more differentiated contingent things, all of which need a similar analysis to explain them, we are no further advanced: and the sufficient or ultimate reason must be outside the *series* of this differentiation of contingent things, however infinite it may be.

38. This is why the ultimate reason of things must lie in a necessary substance, in which the differentiation of the changes only exists eminently as in their source; and this is what we call *God*.

39. Now since this substance is a sufficient reason of all this differentiation, which is itself likewise all connected, *there is only one God, and this God is enough*.

40. We may also judge that since this Supreme Substance, who is unique, universal, and necessary, has nothing outside Himself independent of Himself, and is a simple series of possible being, He must be incapable of being limited, and must contain just as much reality as is possible.

41. Whence it follows that God is absolutely perfect, since *perfection* is nothing but magnitude of positive reality, in the strict sense, setting aside the limits or bounds in things which are limited. And there, where there are no bounds, that is to say in God, perfection is absolutely infinite.

42. It follows also that created things owe their perfections to the influence of God, but that they owe their imperfections to their own nature, which is incapable of being without limits. For it is in this that they are distinguished from God.

43. It is true likewise, that in God is the source not only of existences but also of essences, in so far as they are real, that is of all the reality there is in possibility. This is because the Understanding of God is the region of eternal truths and of the ideas on which they depend, and because without Him there would be nothing real in the possibilities—not only nothing existent, but also nothing possible.

44. For if there is a reality in essences or possibilities, or indeed in eternal truths, this reality must be founded on something existent and actual; and consequently on the existence of the Necessary Being in whom essence involves existence, or in whom to be possible is itself to be actual.

45. Thus God alone (or the Necessary Being) has the

privilege that He must exist if He is possible. And as nothing can prevent the possibility of that which has no limits, no negation, and consequently no contradiction, this alone is necessary to make us know the existence of God *a priori*. We have proved it also by the reality of eternal truths. And we have now just proved it *a posteriori* also, since there exist contingent beings, which can only have their ultimate or sufficient reason in the Necessary Being, who has the reason for His being in Himself.

46. We must not, however, imagine, as some do, that because the eternal truths are dependent on God, they are therefore arbitrary and depend on His will, as Descartes, and after him M. Poiret, seem to have thought. This is true only of contingent truths, whose principle is *fitness* or the choice of *the best*; whereas necessary truths depend solely on His understanding, of which they are the internal object.

47. Thus God alone is the primary Unity, or original simple substance, from which all monads, created and derived, are produced, and are born, so to speak, by continual fulgurations of the Divinity from moment to moment, limited by the receptivity of the created being, which is of its essence limited.

48. There is in God *power*, which is the source of everything, *knowledge*, which contains the differentiation of the ideas, and finally *will*, which causes change and production according to the principle of what is best. And these correspond to what provides the ground or basis in created monads, the perceptive faculty and the appetitive faculty. But in God these attributes are absolutely infinite or perfect, while in created monads or in *entelechies* (or *perfectihabiae*, as Hermolaus Barbarus translated this word) there are only limitations of them, in proportion to the perfection there is in the monad.

49. The created thing is said to *act* outwardly in so far as it has perfection, and to be *passively affected* by another in so

far as it is imperfect. Thus *activity* is attributed to the monad in so far as it has distinct perceptions, and *passivity* in so far as it has confused perceptions.

50. And one created thing is more perfect than another when there is found in it that which explains *a priori* what happens in the other; and it is because of this that we say that it acts upon the other.

51. But in simple substances the influence of one monad over another is *ideal* only; it can have its effect only through the intervention of God, inasmuch as in the ideas of God a monad rightly demands that God, in regulating the rest from the beginning of things, should have regard to itself. For since it is impossible for a created monad to have a physical influence on the inner nature of another, this is the only way in which one can be dependent on another.

52. And this is why actions and passions are mutual between created things. For when God compares two simple substances he finds in each reasons which oblige Him to adapt the other to it, and consequently what is active in certain aspects is passive from another point of view: *active* in so far as what is distinctly known in it explains what occurs in another, and *passive* in so far as what occurs in it is distinctly known in another.

53. Now as there is an infinite number of possible universes in the ideas of God, and as only one can exist, there must be a sufficient reason for God's choice, determining Him to one rather than to another.

54. And this reason can only be found in the *fitness*, or in the degrees of perfection, which these worlds contain, each possible world having the right to claim existence in proportion to the perfection which it involves.

55. And it is this which causes the existence of the best, which God knows through His wisdom, chooses through His goodness, and produces through His power.

56. Now this *connection* or adaptation of all created

things with each, and of each with all the rest, means that each simple substance has relations which express all the others, and that consequently it is a perpetual living mirror of the universe.

57. And just as the same town, when looked at from different sides, appears quite different and is, as it were, multiplied *in perspective,* so also it happens that because of the infinite number of simple substances, it is as if there were as many different universes, which are however but different perspective representations of a single universe from the different points of view of each monad.

58. And this is the means of obtaining as much variety as possible, but with the greatest order possible; that is to say, it is the means of obtaining as much perfection as possible.

59. Further it is this hypothesis alone (which I venture to regard as proved) which properly exalts the greatness of God. This M. Bayle recognized, when in his *Dictionary* (in the article 'Rorarius') he made objections, in which he was even inclined to believe that I attributed too much to God, and more than is possible. But he could not advance any reason why this universal harmony, which causes each substance exactly to express all the others through the relations which it has with them, should be impossible.

60. Moreover, it is evident from what I have just said that there are *a priori* reasons why things could not be otherwise than they are: namely, because God in regulating the whole had regard to each part, and particularly to each monad. The nature of the monad is representative, and consequently nothing can limit it to representing a part of things only, although it is true that its representation is confused as regards the detail of the whole universe and can only be distinct as regards a small part of things; that is to say as regards those which are either the nearest or the largest in relation to each of the monads; otherwise each monad would be a divinity. It is not in the object, but in the modification

of the knowledge of the object, that monads are limited. In a confused way they all go towards the infinite, or towards the whole; but they are limited and distinguished from one another by the degrees of their distinct perceptions.

61. And in this the compounds symbolize the simples. For as the whole is a plenum, which means that the whole of matter is connected, and as in a plenum every movement has some effect on distant bodies in proportion to their distance, so that each body not only is affected by those which touch it, and is in some way sensitive to whatever happens to them, but also by means of them is sensitive to those which touch the first bodies by which it is itself directly touched; it follows that this communication stretches out indefinitely. Consequently every body is sensitive to everything which is happening in the universe, so much so that one who saw everything could read in each body what is happening everywhere, and even what has happened or what will happen, by observing in the present the things that are distant in time as well as in space; σύμπνοια πάντα, as Hippocrates said. But a soul can only read in itself what is distinctly represented there; it is unable to develop all at once all the things that are folded within it, for they stretch to infinity.

62. Thus although each created monad represents the whole universe, it represents more distinctly the body which is particularly affected by it, and whose entelechy it is: and as this body expresses the whole universe by the connection of all matter in the plenum, the soul represents the whole universe also in representing the body which belongs to it in a particular way.

63. The body belonging to a monad, which is that body's entelechy or soul, constitutes together with the entelechy what may be called a *living thing*, and with the soul what is called an *animal*. Now this body of a living thing or animal is always organic; for since every monad is in its way a mirror of the universe, and since the universe is regulated in a

perfect order, there must also be an order in that which represents it, that is to say in the perceptions of the soul, and consequently in the body, according to which order the universe is represented therein.

64. Thus each organic body of a living thing is a kind of divine machine, or natural automaton, which infinitely surpasses all artificial automata. Because a machine, which is made by the art of man, is not a machine in each of its parts; for example, the tooth of a metal wheel has parts which as far as we are concerned are not artificial and which have about them nothing of the character of a machine, in relation to the use for which the wheel was intended. But the machines of nature, that is to say living bodies, are still machines in the least of their parts *ad infinitum*. This it is which makes the difference between nature and art, that is to say between Divine art and ours.

65. And the Author of nature was enabled to practise this divine and infinitely marvellous artifice, because each portion of matter is not only infinitely divisible, as the ancients recognized, but is also actually subdivided without limit, each part into further parts, of which each one has some motion of its own: otherwise it would be impossible for each portion of matter to express the whole universe.

66. Whence it is evident that there is a world of created beings—living things, animals, entelechies, and souls—in the least part of matter.

67. Each portion of matter may be conceived as a garden full of plants, and as a pond full of fish. But every branch of each plant, every member of each animal, and every drop of their liquid parts is itself likewise a similar garden or pond.

68. And although the earth and the air interspersed between the plants in the garden, or the water interspersed between the fish in the pond, are neither plant nor fish, yet they still contain them, though most usually of a subtlety which renders them imperceptible to us.

69. Thus there is nothing waste, nothing sterile, nothing dead in the universe; no chaos, no confusions, save in appearance. We might compare this to the appearance of a pond in the distance, where we can see the confused movement and swarming of the fish, without distinguishing the fish themselves.

70. Thus we see that each living body has a dominant entelechy, which in the case of an animal is the soul, but the members of this living body are full of other living things, plants and animals, of which each has in turn its dominant entelechy or soul.

71. But we must not imagine, as some have done who have misunderstood my view, that each soul has a mass or portion of matter appropriate or attached to itself for ever, and that it consequently possesses other inferior living things, for ever destined to its service. For all bodies are in a perpetual flux like rivers, and parts are passing in and out of them continually.

72. Thus the soul only changes its body bit by bit and by degrees, so that it is never despoiled of all its organs all together; in animals there is often metamorphosis, but never metempsychosis, nor transmigration of souls: neither are there any entirely *separate souls*, nor *superhuman spirits* without bodies. God alone is entirely detached from body.

73. It is because of this also that there is never, strictly speaking, absolute generation nor perfect death, consisting in the separation of the soul. And what we call *generation* is a development and a growth, while what we call *death* is an envelopment and a diminution.

74. Philosophers have been much embarrassed over the origin of forms, entelechies or souls. But to-day when exact researches on plants, insects, and animals have revealed the fact that the organic bodies of nature are never produced from a chaos or from putrefaction, but always from seeds, wherein there was certainly some *preformation*, we conclude

not only that the organic body was already present before conception, but also that there was a soul in this body; that, in a word, the animal itself was present, and that by means of conception it was merely prepared for a great transformation, so as to become an animal of another kind. We even see something of this kind apart from birth, as when worms become flies, and caterpillars become butterflies.

75. The *animals*, of which some are raised by means of conception to the rank of the larger animals, may be called *spermatic*; but those among them which remain in their own kind (and they are the greater number) are born, multiply, and are destroyed like the large animals; and there is only a small number of elect ones who pass to a wider sphere.

76. But this is only half the truth. And so I judged that if the animal never begins naturally, neither does it end naturally; and that not only will there be no birth, but also no complete destruction, no death, strictly speaking. And these reasonings, which are *a posteriori* and derived from experience, agree perfectly with the principles I previously deduced *a priori*.

77. Thus one may say that not only is the soul (the mirror of an indestructible universe) itself indestructible, but so also is the animal itself, although its machine may often perish in part, and cast off or put on particular organic integuments.

78. These principles provide me with a way of explaining naturally the union, or rather the conformity, of the soul and the organic body. The soul follows its own laws, and the body its own likewise, and they accord by virtue of the *harmony pre-established* among all substances, since they are all representations of one and the same universe.

79. Souls act according to the laws of final causes by appetitions, ends, and means. Bodies act according to the laws of efficient causes by motions. And the two kingdoms, of efficient and of final causes, are in harmony with one another.

80. Descartes recognized that souls cannot give force to bodies because there is always the same quantity of force in matter. He believed, however, that the soul could change the direction of bodies. But this is because in his day the law of nature was not known which affirms the conservation of the same total direction in matter. Had he noticed this, he would have stumbled upon my system of Pre-established Harmony.

81. Under this system, bodies act as though, *per impossibile*, there were no souls: and souls act as if there were no bodies, and both act as if each influenced the other.

82. As for minds or rational souls, although I find that what I have just been saying is at bottom true of all living beings and animals (that is to say that the animal and the soul only begin with the world and do not come to an end any more than the world comes to an end), yet rational animals are peculiar in this, that their little spermatic animals, so long as they are that merely, have only ordinary or sensitive souls; but as soon as those which are, so to speak, elect arrive by an actual conception at human nature, then their sensitive souls are raised to the rank of reason and to the prerogative of minds.

83. Among other differences which exist between ordinary souls and minds, some of which I have already pointed out, there is also this, that souls in general are the living mirrors or images of the universe of created things, whereas minds are also images of the Divinity Himself, or the Author of nature, capable of knowing the system of the universe, and of imitating something of it by architectonic patterns, each mind being as it were a little divinity in its own department.

84. This it is which renders minds capable of entering into a kind of society with God, and makes His relation to them not only that of an inventor to his machine (which is God's relation to the rest of created things) but also that of a prince to his subjects, and even of a father to his children.

85. From this it is easy to conclude that the assemblage of all minds must make up the City of God, that is to say the most perfect possible state under the most perfect of monarchs.

86. This City of God, this truly universal monarchy, is a moral world in the natural world, and is the most exalted and the most divine of God's works, and in it truly consists His glory, since He could not be glorified if His greatness and goodness were not known and wondered at by minds: it is also in relation to this divine City that He may properly be said to have goodness, whereas His wisdom and power are manifested everywhere.

87. As we have established above a perfect harmony between two natural kingdoms, the one of efficient and the other of final causes, we ought here also to point out another harmony between the physical kingdom of nature and the moral kingdom of grace; that is to say between God as Architect of the machine of the universe, and God as Monarch of the divine City of Minds.

88. This harmony means that things conduce to grace by the very ways of nature, and that this globe, for example, must be destroyed and repaired by natural ways at the times demanded by the government of minds for the chastisement of some and the reward of others.

89. It can further be said that God as Architect satisfies God as Lawgiver in everything, and that thus sins carry their punishment with them by the order of nature, and by virtue of the mechanical structure of things itself; and that in the same way noble actions will attract their rewards by ways which are mechanical as far as bodies are concerned, although this cannot and should not always happen immediately.

90. Finally, under this perfect government there will be no good action without reward, no evil action without punishment, and everything must turn out for the good of the righteous, of those, that is, who are not dissatisfied in this

great State, who trust in Providence when they have done their duty, and who love and imitate fittingly the Author of all good, delighting in the consideration of His perfections after the manner of true *pure love*, which makes us take pleasure in the happiness of the beloved. This it is which makes the wise and virtuous work for whatever seems to conform with the presumptive or antecedent will of God, and yet leaves them satisfied with what God in fact causes to happen by His secret will, which is consequent and decisive, recognizing as they do that if we could sufficiently understand the order of the universe, we should find that it surpasses the desires of the most wise, and that it is impossible to make it better than it is, not only for the whole in general, but also for ourselves in particular, if we are attached as we should be to the Author of the whole, not merely as to the Architect and efficient Cause of our being, but also as to our Master and the final Cause which must constitute the whole end of our will, and which alone can constitute our happiness.

PRINCIPLES OF NATURE AND OF GRACE, FOUNDED ON REASON. 1714

1. *Substance* is a being capable of action. It is simple or compound. *Simple substance* is that which has no parts. *Compound substance* is the combination of simple substances or *monads*. *Monas* is a Greek work which signifies unity or that which is one. Compounds or bodies are pluralities, and simple substances—that is lives, souls, minds—are unities. There must necessarily be simple substances everywhere, because without simple substances there could be no compounds; consequently the whole of nature is full of life.

2. Monads, having no parts, cannot be made or unmade. They can neither begin nor end naturally, and consequently they last as long as the universe, which will be changed but not destroyed. They cannot have shapes, otherwise they would have parts. Thus one monad, in itself and at a particular moment, can only be distinguished from another by internal qualities and activities, which can be nothing else but its *perceptions* (that is to say, the representations in the simple of the compound or of that which is outside) and its *appetitions* (that is to say, its tendencies to pass from one perception to another), which are the principle of change. For the simplicity of substance does not preclude the possibility of a multiplicity of modifications, which indeed necessarily exist together in the same simple substance, and these modifications must consist in the variety of the relations of the simple substance to things which are outside. Just as in a *centre* or point, in itself perfectly simple, are found an infinite number of angles formed by the lines which meet there.

3. All nature is a plenum. Everywhere there are simple substances, effectively separated from one another by actions of their own which are continually altering their relations; and each simple substance or distinct monad, which forms the centre of a compound substance (e.g. of an animal) and the principle of its oneness, is surrounded by a *mass* composed of an infinite number of other monads which constitute the body belonging to this central monad; corresponding to the affections of its body it represents, as in a kind of *centre*, the things which are outside of it. And this *body* is *organic*, when it forms a kind of automaton or natural machine, which is a machine not only as a whole but also in its smallest observable parts. And since because the world is a plenum everything is connected together, and each body acts on every other body more or less according to the distance, and is affected by it by reaction, it follows that every monad is a mirror that is alive or endowed with inner activity, is representative of the universe from its own point of view, and is as much regulated as the universe itself. The perceptions in the monad spring from one another according to the laws of the appetites or the *final causes of good and evil*, which consist in the observable perceptions, regulated or unregulated—in the same way as the changes of the bodies and the phenomena outside spring from one another according to the laws of *efficient causes*, that is to say of motions. Thus there is a perfect *harmony* between the perceptions of the monad and the motions of the bodies, pre-established at the outset between the system of efficient causes and the system of final causes. Herein consists the concord and the physical union of the soul and the body, which exists without the one being able to change the laws of the other.

4. Each monad, together with a particular body, makes a living substance. Thus there is not only life everywhere, joined to members or organs, but there are also infinite degrees of it in the monads, some of them more or less

dominating over others. But when the monad has its organs adjusted in such a way that by means of them the impressions they receive, and consequently the perceptions which represent them, are distinguished and heightened (as, for example, when by means of the shape of the humours of the eye rays of light are concentrated and act with more force), this may amount to *sensation*, that is to say, to a perception accompanied by *memory*—a perception, to wit, of which a certain echo long remains to make itself heard on occasion. Such a living being is called an *animal*, as its monad is called a *soul*. And when this soul is raised to the level of *reason*, it is something more sublime, and is reckoned as a mind, as will be explained later. It is true that animals are sometimes in the condition of simple living beings and their souls in the condition of simple monads, to wit, when their perceptions are not sufficiently distinguished to be remembered, as occurs in a deep dreamless sleep or in a swoon. But perceptions which have become entirely confused must necessarily be developed again in animals, for reasons I shall give below (12). Thus it is well to distinguish between *perception* which is the inner state of the monad representing external things, and *apperception*, which is *consciousness*, or the reflective knowledge of this inner state, and which is not given to all souls, nor at all times to the same soul. It is for want of this distinction that the Cartesians made the mistake of taking no account of perceptions which are not apperceived, as common people take no account of insensible bodies. It is this also which made these same Cartesians believe that minds alone are monads, and that there are no souls in animals, and still less other *principles of life*. And while, in thus denying sensations to animals, they have gone against the common opinion of men too much, so they have, on the other hand, taken too much account of the prejudices of the vulgar, in confusing a *long stupor*, which arises from a great confusion of perceptions, with *actual death*, in which all perception would cease. This teaching of theirs has confirmed the ill-founded belief in the destruction of some souls, and the pernicious view of certain people, supposed to be free-thinkers, who have denied the immortality of ours.

5. There is a connection between the perceptions of animals, which bears some resemblance to reason: but it is based only on the memory of *facts* or effects, and not at all on the knowledge of *causes*. Thus a dog runs away from the stick with which he has been beaten, because memory represents to him the pain which was caused by that stick. And men, in so far as they are empiricists, that is to say in three-fourths of their actions, only act like brutes. For example, we expect that day will dawn tomorrow, because we have always experienced it to be so; it is only the astronomer who foresees it by reason, and even this prediction will ultimately fail when the cause of daylight, which is not eternal, ceases. But true reasoning depends on necessary or eternal truths (like the truths of logic, numbers, and geometry) which make the connection of ideas indubitable, and the sequences inevitable. Animals in which such sequences cannot be observed are called *brutes*; but those which know these necessary truths are called *rational animals*, and their souls are called *minds*. These souls are capable of performing acts of reflection, and of considering what is called self, substance, soul, mind—those things and truths, in short, which are immaterial. It is this which makes us capable of understanding science or demonstrative knowledge.

6. The researches of the moderns have taught us, and it is approved by reason, that the living things whose organs we know, that is to say plants and animals, do not come from putrefaction or chaos as the ancients believed, but from *pre-formed* seeds, and consequently from the transformation of pre-existing living things. There are little animals in the

seeds of the large ones, which by means of conception assume a new vesture, which they appropriate, and which enables them to be nourished and to grow, so as to pass on to a wider stage, and propagate the large animal. It is true that the souls of human spermatic animals are not rational and only become so when through conception these animals are destined for human nature. And as animals are usually not born completely in conception or *generation*, so neither do they perish completely in what we call *death*; for it is reasonable that what does not begin naturally should not come to an end in the order of nature either. Thus, casting off their masks or their rags, they merely return to a more subtle scene, on which, however, they can be as sensible and as well ordered as on the greater one. And what has just been said of large animals occurs also in the generation and death of these spermatic animals themselves; that is to say, they have grown from other smaller spermatic animals, in comparison with which they can be reckoned large; for everything in nature proceeds *ad infinitum*. Thus not only souls but animals also are ingenerable and imperishable: they are only developed, enveloped, reclad, stripped, transformed; souls never leave the whole of their body, and do not pass from one body to another which is entirely new to them. Thus there is no *metempsychosis*, but there is *metamorphosis*. Animals change, take on and put off parts only: in nutrition this takes place bit by bit, and by small insensible parts, but continually, while in conception and death when much is acquired or lost all at one time the change takes place rarely, but all at once and in a way that can be noticed.

7. Up till now we have spoken as *physicists* merely; now we must rise to *metaphysics*, making use of the *great principle*, commonly but little employed, which holds that *nothing takes place without sufficient reason*, that is to say that nothing happens without its being possible for one who has enough knowledge of things to give a reason sufficient to determine

why it is thus and not otherwise. This principle having been laid down, the first question we are entitled to ask will be: *Why is there something rather than nothing?* For 'nothing' is simpler and easier than 'something'. Further, supposing that things must exist, it must be possible to give a reason *why they must exist just as they do* and not otherwise.

8. Now this sufficient reason of the existence of the universe cannot be found in the series of contingent things, that is to say, of bodies and of their representations in souls. For since matter is in itself indifferent to motion or to rest, and to one motion rather than another, it cannot itself contain the reason of motion, still less of a particular motion. And although the present motion which is in matter arises from the one before it, and this in its turn from the one before that, we are no further on however far we go; for the same question always remains. Thus the sufficient reason, which needs no further reason, must be outside this series of contingent things, and must lie in a substance which is the cause of this series, or which is a being that bears the reason of its existence within itself; otherwise we should still not have a sufficient reason, with which we could stop. And this final reason of things is called *God*.

9. This simple primary substance must include eminently the perfections which are contained in the derivative substances which are its effects. Thus it will have perfect power, knowledge, and will; that is to say, it will have omnipotence, omniscience, and supreme goodness. And as *justice*, taken in a very general sense, is nothing other than goodness in conformity with wisdom, there must clearly also be supreme justice in God. Reason, which has made things exist through Him, makes them also depend on Him in their existence and operation; and they are continually receiving from Him that which endows them with some perfection; but any imperfection which they retain comes from the essential and original limitations of the created thing.

10. It follows from the supreme perfection of God that in producing the universe He chose the best possible plan, containing the greatest variety together with the greatest order; the best arranged situation, place, and time; the greatest effect produced by the simplest means; the most power, the most knowledge, the most happiness and goodness in created things of which the universe admitted. For as all possible things have a claim to existence in the understanding of God in proportion to their perfections, the result of all these claims must be the most perfect actual world which is possible. Otherwise it would not be possible to explain why things have happened as they have rather than otherwise.

11. The supreme wisdom of God has made Him choose especially the *laws of motion*, which are the best adjusted and the most fitted to abstract and metaphysical reasons. According to them there is always conserved the same quantity of total and absolute force or activity; the same quantity of relative force or reaction; the same quantity, finally, of force of direction. Moreover the activity is always equal to the reaction, aud the whole effect is always equivalent to its full cause. It is surprising that those laws of motion discovered in our day, some of which I have myself discovered, cannot be explained merely by the consideration of *efficient causes* or of matter. For I have found that it is necessary to have recourse to *final causes*, and that these laws do not depend on the *principle of necessity* as do the truths of logic, arithmetic, and geometry, but on the *principle of fitness*, that is to say on the choice of wisdom. Thus it is one of the most effective and sensible proofs of the existence of God for those who are able to go deeply into these matters.

12. It follows, further, from the perfection of the Supreme Author, that not only is the order of the whole universe the most perfect possible, but also that each living mirror which

represents the universe from its own point of view, that is to say each *monad*, each substantial centre, must have its perceptions and appetites regulated in the best way which is compatible with all the rest. From which it follows that *souls*, that is to say the most dominant monads, or rather animals themselves, cannot fail to wake up from the state of stupor in which they may be placed by death or by some other accident.

13. For everything is regulated in things once for all with as much order and agreement as possible, since supreme wisdom and goodness cannot act without perfect harmony: the present is big with the future, what is to come could be read in the past, what is distant expressed in what is near. The beauty of the universe could be learnt in each soul, could one unravel all its folds which develop perceptibly only with time. But as each distinct perception of the soul includes an infinite number of confused perceptions which embrace all the universe, the soul itself does not know the things which it perceives, except in so far as it has perceptions of them which are distinct and heightened: and it has perfection in proportion to its distinct perceptions. Each soul knows the infinite, knows everything, but confusedly. Just as when I am walking along the shore of the sea and hear the great noise it makes, though I hear the separate sounds of each wave of which the total sound is made up, I do not discriminate them one from another; so our confused perceptions are the result of the impressions which the whole universe makes on us. It is the same with each monad. God alone has a distinct knowledge of everything, for He is the source of everything. It has been very well said that as a centre He is everywhere; but His circumference is nowhere, since everything is present to Him immediately, without being removed from this centre.

14. As regards the rational soul or *mind*, there is in it something more than in monads, or even in simple souls.

It is not only a mirror of the universe of created things, but also an image of the Deity. The mind not only has a perception of the works of God, but is even capable of producing something like them, though on a small scale. For, not to mention the wonders of dreams, in which we invent without effort (but also without will) things we could only discover after much thinking when awake, our soul is architectonic in its voluntary activities also, and, discovering the sciences in accordance with which God had regulated things (*pondere, mensura, numero*,[1] etc.), it imitates in its own sphere, and in the little world in which it is allowed to act, what God performs in the great world.

15. For this reason all minds, whether of men or superhuman spirits, entering as they do by virtue of reason and the eternal verities into a kind of society with God, are members of the City of God, that is to say of the most perfect state, formed and governed by the greatest and best of monarchs: where there is no crime without punishment, no good action without proportionate reward, and finally as much virtue and happiness as is possible; and this, not by any derangement of nature, as if what God has in store for the soul might disturb the laws of the body, but by the actual order of natural things, by virtue of the harmony pre-established from all time between the realms of nature and of grace, between God as Architect and God as Monarch, in such a way that nature itself leads to grace, and grace perfects nature in making use of it.

16. Thus although reason cannot teach us the details of the great future, which are reserved for revelation, we can rest assured by this same reason that things are accomplished in a manner which exceeds our desires. Since, too, God is the most perfect and the most happy and consequently the most lovable of substances, and since *pure true love* consists in the state which causes pleasure to be felt in the perfections

[1] 'by weight, measure, number', etc.

and happiness of the beloved, this love ought to give us the greatest pleasure of which a man is capable, when God is the object of it.

17. It is easy to love Him as we ought if we know Him as I have described. For although God is not sensible to our external senses, He is none the less very lovable and gives great pleasure. We see how much pleasure men derive from honours, although they do not consist of qualities that appear to the external senses. Martyrs and fanatics (although the affection of the latter is ill regulated) show of what the pleasure of the mind is capable: and what is more, even the pleasures of the senses are in the last resort intellectual pleasures, confusedly known. Music charms us although its beauty only consists in the harmony of numbers, and in the account which we do not notice, but which the soul none the less takes, of the beating or vibration of sounding bodies, which meet one another at certain intervals. The pleasures which the eye finds in proportions are of the same kind, and those caused by the other senses amount to much the same thing, although we may not be able to explain it so distinctly.

18. It may even be affirmed that love of God gives us here and now a foretaste of future felicity. And although it is disinterested, it constitutes of itself our greatest good and interest, even though we may not seek them in it, and consider only the pleasure which it gives without regard to the utility it produces; for it gives us a perfect confidence in the goodness of our Author and Master, which produces a true tranquillity of mind, not as in the Stoics, who resolutely force themselves to patience, but by a present contentment, which further assures us a future happiness. And apart from the present pleasure, nothing could be more useful for the future, for the love of God also fulfils our hopes, and leads us in the way of supreme happiness, because in virtue of the perfect order established in the universe, everything

is done in the best possible way, as much for the general good as also for the greatest particular good of those who believe in it, and who are satisfied by the Divine government: which cannot fail to be the case with those who know how to love the Source of all good.   It is true that supreme happiness (with whatever *beatific vision,* or knowledge of God, it may be accompanied) can never be complete because God, being infinite, cannot be entirely known.   Thus our happiness will never consist, and ought not to consist, in a complete enjoyment, in which there would be nothing left to desire, and which would make our mind stupid, but in a perpetual progress to new pleasures and new perfections.

ON THE ULTIMATE ORIGINATION OF THINGS

23 NOVEMBER 1697

BESIDES the world or aggregate of finite things we find a certain Unity which is dominant, not only in the sense in which the soul is dominant in me, or rather in which the self or *I* is dominant in my body, but also in a much more exalted manner. For the dominant Unity of the universe not only rules the world, but also constructs or makes it; and it is higher than the world and, if I may so put it, extramundane; it is thus the ultimate reason of things. Now neither in any one single thing, nor in the whole aggregate and series of things, can there be found the sufficient reason of existence. Let us suppose the book of the elements of geometry to have been eternal, one copy always having been written down from an earlier one; it is evident that, even though a reason can be given for the present book out of a past one, nevertheless out of any number of books taken in order going backwards we shall never come upon a full reason; though we might well always wonder why there should have been such books from all time—why there were books at all, and why they were written in this manner. What is true of the books is true also of the different states of the world; for what follows is in some way copied from what precedes (even though there are certain laws of change). And so, however far you go back to earlier states, you will never find in those states a full reason why there should be any world rather than none, and why it should be such as it is.

Indeed, even if you suppose the world eternal, as you will still be supposing nothing but a succession of states and will not in any of them find a sufficient reason, nor however many states you assume will you advance one step towards giving a reason, it is evident that the reason must be sought elsewhere. For in things which are eternal, though there may be no cause, nevertheless there must be known a reason; which reason in things that are permanent is necessity itself or essence, but in the series of changeable things (if this be supposed to be an eternal succession from an earlier to a later) it will be, as will be presently understood, the prevailing of inclinations, in a sphere where reasons do not necessitate (by an absolute or metaphysical necessity, in which the contrary implies a contradiction), but incline. From this it is evident that even by supposing the world to be eternal we cannot escape the ultimate, extra-mundane reason of things, or God.

The reasons of the world then lie in something extra-mundane, different from the chain of states, or series of things, whose aggregate constitutes the world. And so we must pass from physical or hypothetical necessity, which determines the subsequent things of the world by the earlier, to something which is of absolute or metaphysical necessity, for which itself no reason can be given. For the present world is necessary physically or hypothetically, but not absolutely or metaphysically. In other words, when once it is determined that it shall be such and such, it follows that such and such things will come into being. Since then the ultimate root must be in something which is of metaphysical necessity, and since there is no reason of any existent thing except in an existent thing, it follows that there must exist some one Being of metaphysical necessity, that is, from whose essence existence springs; and so there must exist something different from the plurality of beings, that is the world, which, as we have allowed and have shown, is not of metaphysical necessity.

Let me explain a little more distinctly how out of truths that are eternal or essential or metaphysical there arise truths that are temporal, contingent, or physical. First we must notice, from the very fact that something exists rather than nothing, that there is in things that are possible, or in possibility of essence itself, a certain need for existence, or (if I may so put it) a claim to exist; and, to put it bluntly, that essence in itself tends towards existence. From this it further follows that all things which are possible, or express essence or possible reality, tend by equal right towards existence in proportion to the quantity of essence or reality which they include, or in proportion to the stage of perfection which belongs to them; for perfection is nothing else than quantity of essence.

Hence it is seen to be most evident that out of the infinite combination of possibles, and the infinite possible series, that one exists by whose means the greatest possible amount of essence or possibility is brought into existence. There is always, I take it, to be found in things a principle of determination which turns on considerations of greatest and least; namely, that the greatest effect should be produced with (if I may so put it) the least expenditure. And the time, the place, or (in a word) the receptivity or capacity of the world, may here be taken to be the expenditure or ground, on which a building is to be raised as fittingly as possible, while the variety of forms is in accordance with the fitness of the building and with the number and elegance of its rooms. It is very much like what happens in certain games, in which all the spaces on the board have to be filled in according to certain rules: unless you show some ingenuity you will find yourself at the end kept out of certain refractory spaces, and thereby compelled to leave empty more spaces than you need have done, and more than you wished. There is, however, a definite formula by which the greatest possible success in filling the spaces is easily obtained. For instance, if we suppose ourselves told to construct a triangle, there being no other principle of determination, the result is that we draw an equilateral triangle; and if we are required to go from one point to another, and nothing further is added to determine the way, we shall choose the path that is easiest or shortest. Similarly, once it has been granted that a being is better than a not-being, that is, that there is a reason why something should exist rather than nothing, or that transition from possibility to actuality is to take place, then, even if nothing further is determined, the consequence is that there exists as much as is possible in view of the capacity of time and place (or of the possible order of existing)—in very much the same way as tiles are fitted together so as to put in as many as possible within the given area.

From this it is now wonderfully clear how in the very origination of things a certain Divine mathematics or metaphysical mechanics is employed, and how the greatest quantity comes to be determined. It is on this principle that of all the angles the right angle is the determined angle in geometry, and that liquids when placed in heterogeneous media form themselves into the most capacious shape, that is, the spherical; but the best instance of all is that in common mechanics itself, when several heavy bodies are operating against one another, the result is that movement which secures the greatest descent on the whole. For just as all things that are possible with equal right tend towards existence in proportion to their reality, so in the same way all weights with equal right tend towards descent in proportion to their gravity; and just as in the latter case there results a motion involving the greatest possible descent of the heavy bodies, so in the former case there results a world involving the greatest production of things that are possible.

Thus we now have physical necessity based on metaphysical necessity. For although the world is not metaphysically necessary, so that its contrary would imply a contradiction or logical absurdity, nevertheless it is necessary physically, that is, determined in such a way that its contrary would imply imperfection or moral absurdity. And as possibility is the principle of essence, so perfection or degree of essence (which makes the largest number of things compossible) is the principle of existence. This makes it evident at the same time how there can be freedom in the Author of the world, although He does everything determinately, because He acts from the principle of wisdom or perfection. Indifference arises from ignorance, and the wiser a man is, the more is he determined to that action which is most perfect.

But (you will say) this comparison of a certain metaphysical determining mechanism with the physical mechanism of heavy bodies, elegant though it may appear, has nevertheless this fault: there really exist heavy bodies acting against one another, but possibilities or essences prior to or beyond existence are imaginary or fictitious, and therefore it is of no use to seek in them the reason of existence. I answer, that neither the essences nor the truths about them which are known as eternal truths, are fictitious; they exist (if I may so put it) in a certain region of ideas, that is, in God Himself, the fount of all essence and of the existence of everything. That this is no merely arbitrary assertion is shown by the very existence of the actual series of things.   For since in the series a reason cannot be found, as I have shown above, but must be sought in metaphysical necessities or eternal truths; since, too, existent things cannot come into being except from existent things, as I have explained previously; it follows that eternal truths must have their existence in some subject which is absolutely or metaphysically necessary, that is in God, through whom these truths, which would otherwise be imaginary, are (to use a barbarous but expressive word) *realized*.[1]

And indeed in actual fact we find that everything in the world takes place in accordance with the laws of the eternal truths, not only geometrical but also metaphysical laws;

[1] The word *realisentur* is a barbarism in Latin.

that is, not only according to material necessities, but also according to formal necessities. This is not only true in general, in regard to the reason (which I have just explained) why the world should exist rather than not, and why it should exist just as it is rather than otherwise (this reason is certainly to be found in the tendency of what is possible towards existence); but more than this, if we come down to details, we see the marvellous way in which metaphysical laws hold sway in the whole of nature—the laws of cause, of potency, of activity,—and how they prevail even over the purely geometrical laws of matter themselves, as I found to my great wonder when I was giving an account of the laws of motion; so much so, indeed, that though from my early youth, when I was more of a materialist, I had defended the law of the geometric composition of forces, I was finally forced to abandon it, as I have explained at greater length elsewhere.

Here then we have the ultimate reason of the reality both of essences and of existences in a Unity, which must certainly be greater, higher, and prior to the world itself, since through it alone not only the existent things, which the world contains, but also the things that are possible have their reality. It cannot be found except in one single source, because of the interconnection of all these things with one another. It is evident that from this source existent things are continually issuing and being produced, and have been produced, since it is not clear why one state of the world rather than another, yesterday's state rather than today's, should flow from the world itself. It is also evident how God acts not only physically but also freely; and how there lies in Him not only the efficient but also the final cause; and how from Him proceeds the reason not only of the greatness or potency that there is in the mechanism of the universe as now established, but also of the goodness or wisdom involved in the establishing of it.

In case someone may think that moral perfection or goodness is here being confused with metaphysical perfection or
greatness, and may admit the latter while denying the
former, it should be pointed out that it follows from what has
been said not only that the world is the most perfect physically, or, if you prefer it, metaphysically, or in other words
that that series of things will be forthcoming which in actual
fact affords the greatest quantity of reality, but also that
the world should be the most perfect morally, because true
moral perfection is physical perfection in minds themselves.
Hence the world is not only the most wonderful machine,
but also in regard to minds it is the best commonwealth, by
whose means there is bestowed on minds the greatest possible
amount of felicity or joyfulness; and it is in this that their
physical perfection consists.

But, you will say, we find in the world the very opposite
of this. Often the worst of sufferings fall upon the best men;
the innocent (I speak not only of the brutes, but of men also)
are afflicted, and are slain even with tortures; indeed the
world, especially if we look at the government of the human
race, seems rather a confused chaos than an affair ordained
by some supreme wisdom. So it appears at first sight, I
allow: but on deeper examination it must be agreed that the
opposite is the case. It is evident *a priori* from those very
principles which I have adduced that without doubt there is
secured in the world the highest perfection that there could
possibly be of all things, and therefore of minds.

And indeed it is unreasonable, as the lawyers say, to
give a judgment without inspecting the whole law. We have
knowledge of a tiny part of that eternity which stretches out
immeasurably. For how small a thing is the memory of the
few thousand years which history hands down to us! And
yet out of so little experience we rashly make judgments
about the immeasurable and the eternal; just as men who
had been born and bred in prison or in the subterranean

salt-mines of Sarmatia might think that there was no other
light in the world than the treacherous flicker of torches,
which was hardly sufficient to guide their footsteps. Look
at the most lovely picture, and then cover it up, leaving
uncovered only a tiny scrap of it. What else will you see
there, even if you look as closely as possible, and the more so
as you look from nearer and nearer at hand, but a kind of
confused medley of colours, without selection, without art!
And yet when you remove the covering, and look upon the
whole picture from the proper place, you will see that what
previously seemed to you to have been aimlessly smeared
on the canvas was in fact accomplished with the highest
art by the author of the work. What happens to the eyes in
painting is equally experienced by the ears in music. The
great composers frequently mingle discords with harmonious
chords so that the listener may be stimulated and pricked as
it were, and may become eager to know what is going to
happen; presently when all is restored to order he feels so
much the more content. In the same way we may take
pleasure in small dangers, or in the experience of ills, from
the very sense or proof they give us of our own power or
felicity. Or again at the spectacle of rope-walking or sword-
dancing we are delighted by the very element of fear that is
involved, and we ourselves in play with children hold them
as if we were going to throw them out of the window, and
half let them go—in very much the same way as the ape
carried Christian, King of Denmark, when he was still an
infant wrapped in long clothes, to the edge of the roof, and
then, when everybody was in terror, turned it into jest and
put him back into his cradle safe and sound. On the same
principle it has an insipid effect if we always eat sweet things;
sharp, acid, and even bitter things should be mixed in to
stimulate the taste. He who has not tasted what is bitter
has not earned what is sweet, nor will he appreciate it. This
is the very law of enjoyment, that positive pleasure does not

come from an even course; such things produce weariness, and make men dull, not joyful.

What I have said, however, about the possibility of a part being disturbed without upsetting the harmony of the whole must not be interpreted to mean that no account is taken of the parts; or that it is sufficient for the whole world to be completed at all points, even though it should turn out that the human race was wretched, and that there was in the universe no care for justice and no account was taken of us—as is maintained by some people whose judgment about the sum of things is ill-grounded.   For the truth is that, just as in a well regulated commonwealth care is taken that as far as possible things shall be to the interest of the individual, in the same way the universe would not be sufficiently perfect unless, as far as can be done without upsetting the universal harmony, the good of individual people is considered. Of this there could be established no better measure than the very law of justice itself, which dictates that each should have a part in the perfection of the universe and in his own happiness in proportion to his own virtue and to the extent to which his will is directed towards the common good; by which is fulfilled what we call the charity and love of God, in which alone, according to the judgment of wise theologians also, stands the whole force and power of the Christian religion.   Nor ought it to seem remarkable that all this deference should be paid to minds in the universe, since they bear the closest resemblance to the image of the supreme Author, and their relation to Him is not that of machines to their artificer (like the rest of the world) but rather that of citizens to their prince; moreover they will endure as long as the universe itself, and they, in some manner, express and concentrate the whole in themselves; so that it might be said that minds are whole parts.

As for the afflictions of men, and especially of good men, we must hold ourselves assured that they contribute to the greater good of those who suffer them; and this is true not only theologically, but physically also, just as a grain of wheat cast into the earth must suffer before it bears fruit. And in general it is true to say that afflictions are for the time being evil, but in effect good, since they are short cuts to a greater perfection. Similarly in physics the liquids which ferment slowly are also more slowly purified, whereas those in which there is a more violent disturbance throw off the foreign parts with greater force and so more quickly become pure. You might fairly say that this is a case of taking a step back in order to make a stronger leap forward (*reculer pour mieux sauter*). These things must be allowed to be not only pleasant and consoling, but also most true. Indeed in general I hold that there is nothing truer than happiness, and nothing happier and sweeter than truth.

Further, we realize that there is a perpetual and a most free progress of the whole universe in fulfilment of the universal beauty and perfection of the works of God, so that it is always advancing towards a greater development. Thus, even now a great part of our earth has received cultivation, and will receive it more and more. And though it is true that there are times when some parts of it go back again to virgin forest, or are destroyed again and oppressed, this must be understood in the same sense as I just now interpreted the meaning of affliction, namely, that this very destruction and oppression contributes to achieve something greater, so that in some way we receive profit from our very loss.

To the objection that may perhaps be offered that if this were so the world would long ago have become a paradise, the answer is at hand: although many substances have already come to great perfection, yet owing to the infinite divisibility of what is continuous, there always remain in the abyss of things parts that are asleep, and these need to be awakened and to be driven forward into something greater and better—in a word, to a better development. Hence this progress does not ever come to an end.

PART II

THE DEVELOPMENT OF LEIBNIZ'S PHILOSOPHY

LETTER TO FOUCHER.[1] 1676

I AGREE with you that it is important to examine our pre-suppositions, thoroughly and once for all, in order to establish something solid. For I hold that it is only when we can prove all that we bring forward that we perfectly understand the thing under consideration. I know that the common herd take little pleasure in these researches, but I know also that the common herd take little pains thoroughly to understand things. Your scheme, as I understand it, is to examine the truths which assert that there is something outside us. In this you appear to be very just, for thus you grant us all the truths which are hypothetical, and which assert not that there is something outside us, but only what would happen if there were. Thus at the outset we save arithmetic, geometry and a great number of metaphysical, physical, and moral propositions, whose convenient expression depends on definitions arbitrarily chosen, and whose truth depends on axioms which I am accustomed to call identical; as for instance, that two contradictories cannot both exist, that a thing at one and the same time is what it is—for instance, it is as big as it is, equal to itself, like itself, etc.

Now although you do not enter *ex professo*[2] into the examination of hypothetical propositions, I am nevertheless of opinion that it should be done, and that none should be admitted that have not been absolutely proved and resolved into identicals.

As regards those truths which deal with what is in fact

---

[1] Simon Foucher (1644–96), a Canon of Dijon, who professed philosophical scepticism. Cf. pp. 109–18.
[2] i.e. it is no part of your professed purpose to enter . . .

outside us, this is the subject with which your inquiries are primarily concerned. Now in the first place it cannot be denied that the very truth of hypothetical propositions themselves is something which is outside us and which does not depend on us. For all these hypothetical propositions assert what would or would not be, granting something or its contrary; and consequently they assure us that the supposition at the same time of two things that agree, or that a thing is possible or impossible, necessary or unnecessary, and also this possibility, impossibility, or necessity (for the necessity of one thing is the impossibility of its contrary), are none of them chimeras of our own making; since all we do is to recognize them in spite of ourselves and in a constant manner. Thus of all things which actually are, the possibility itself or impossibility of being is the first. Now this possibility or necessity forms or composes what are called essences or natures, and the truths which we are accustomed to call eternal; and we are right so to call them, for nothing is so eternal as what is necessary. Thus the nature of the circle with its properties is something which exists and is eternal: that is to say there is some constant cause outside us which makes all those who think about it carefully discover the same thing, and not merely that their thoughts agree with one another; this might be attributed simply to the nature of the human mind, but for the fact that phenomena or experiences confirm them whenever some appearance of a circle strikes our senses. And these phenomena necessarily have some cause outside us.

But though the existence of necessities comes first of all in itself and in the order of nature, I agree none the less that it is not the first in the order of our knowledge. For you see that in order to prove its existence I have taken for granted that we think and that we have sensations. Here then are two absolute general truths, truths that is to say which treat of the actual existence of things: the one that we think, the other that there is a great variety in our thoughts. From the first it follows that we are, from the other it follows that there is something other than us; something other, that is to say, than that which thinks, which is the cause of the variety of our appearances. Now the one of these two truths is as incontestable and as independent as the other; and through fastening on the first only in the order of his meditations, M. Descartes failed to reach the perfection which he had aimed at. If he had exactly followed what I call the *filum meditandi*,[1] I think that he would have brought to completion *first philosophy*.[2] But the greatest genius in the world is unable to force matters, and we must of necessity enter by the gates provided by nature if we are not to go astray. Moreover, one man alone cannot do everything at the outset; and for my part when I consider all the fine things M. Descartes has said, and said by himself, I marvel rather at what he has done than that there is something that he failed to do. I admit that I have not yet been able to read his writings with all the care I intend to devote to them, and my friends are aware that it has so happened that I read almost all the recent philosophers before him. Bacon and Gassendi were the first to fall into my hands; their familiar and easy style was more suited to a man desirous of reading everything. It is true that I often glanced at Galileo and Descartes, but as I have only recently become a geometrician, I was soon put off by their manner of writing, which necessitated serious thought. And personally, although I have always taken pleasure in meditations of my own, I have always found it difficult to read books which cannot be understood without much thought; for in following one's own meditations one follows a certain natural bent, and gains profit and pleasure at the same time, whereas one is terribly put out at having to follow the meditations of another. I always liked

---

[1] *lit.* 'the thread of thinking', i.e. his actual train of thought.
[2] i.e. metaphysics.

books which, while containing some fine thoughts, could be read straight through without stopping, for they gave rise in me to ideas which I followed at fancy, and pursued as the spirit moved me. This also prevented me from reading books on geometry, and I readily admit that I have not yet been able to make myself read Euclid in any different way from that in which one generally reads histories. I have learnt from experience that this method is in general a good one, but I have also learnt none the less that an exception must be made in the case of some authors, such as Plato and Aristotle among the ancient philosophers, and Galileo and M. Descartes among those of our day. Still, such knowledge as I have of M. Descartes's metaphysical and physical meditations has been almost entirely derived from reading a number of books written in a rather more familiar style which expound his opinions. And it may be that I have not yet properly understood him. None the less, in so far as I myself have glanced at his work, I seem to myself at least to get a glimpse of what he has not done, nor attempted to do; and this is among other things, to resolve all our presuppositions. For this reason I am accustomed to commend all those who examined the least truth thoroughly; for I know that it is a great thing to understand a thing perfectly, however small and easy it may seem. This is the way to go well ahead and to set up finally the art of discovery which depends on a knowledge (though it must be distinct and perfect) of the easiest things. And for this reason I do not condemn the design of M. de Roberval, who wished to prove everything in geometry, even including certain axioms. I admit that we must not try to force others to be so exact, but I think it is well to force ourselves.

I return to the truths which come first for our purpose among those which assure us that there is something outside us; that is to say, that we think, and that there is a great variety in our thoughts. Now this variety of thoughts cannot come from that which thinks, since one single thing cannot itself be the cause of the changes which are in it. For everything remains in the state in which it is if there is nothing to change it: and since it is not of itself determined to have certain changes rather than others, we could not begin to attribute to it any variety, without saying something for which we admit there is no reason, which is absurd. And even if we sought to maintain that there is no beginning to our thoughts, besides the fact that we should be obliged to assert that each of us has existed from all eternity, we should still not escape the difficulty; for we would still be obliged to admit that there is no reason for this variety which has existed in our thoughts from all eternity, since there is nothing in us which determines us to this thought rather than to another. Thus there must be some cause outside us for the variety of our thoughts. And as we agree that there are some subordinate causes of this variety, which nevertheless need a cause themselves, we have thereby established some particular beings or substances, whose actions we can recognize, that is to say, such that we conceive that from a change in them follows some change in us. And so we advance by great strides to the construction of what we call matter and body.

But at this point you are right to hold us up a little, and to renew the pleas of the Academy of old. For at bottom, all our experiences assure us of two things only, namely that there is a connection in our appearances which gives us a means of successfully predicting future appearances; and secondly that this connection must have a constant cause. But from all this it does not strictly follow that there is matter or that there are bodies, but only that there is something which presents us with appearances which follow properly on one another. For if an invisible power were to delight in giving us dreams properly connected with our preceding life, and in conformity with one another, could we

distinguish them from realities except after awakening? Now
what is it that prevents the course of our life being one long
well-arranged dream, about which we could be undeceived in
an instant? And I do not see that this power would therefore
be imperfect, as M. Descartes asserts, besides the fact that
its imperfection is not under discussion. For it might
be some subordinate power, or some superhuman spirit who
was able to take a hand, I know not why, in our affairs, and
who had at least as much power over someone, as that caliph
who had a drunken man carried into his place, and there made
him taste of the paradise of Mahomet when he was awakened,
until he was once more drunk and in a condition to be taken
back to the place from which he had been brought. When this
man returned to his senses, he naturally took for a vision
what seemed to him irreconcilable with the course of his life,
and retailed to the people maxims and revelations which he
believed he had learnt in this supposed paradise; and this
was what the caliph desired. Now since a reality has passed
for a vision, what prevents a vision from passing for a reality?
It is true that the more we see a connection in what happens
to us, the more we are confirmed in the opinion that there is
reality in our appearances; and it is true also that the more
nearly we examine appearances, the better connected we find
them to be, as microscopes and other ways of making experiments show us. This perpetual agreement gives us great
assurance; but after all it will be no more than a moral
assurance until somebody discovers *a priori* the origin of the
world which we see, and probes in the depths of its essence
to find the reason why things are as they seem. When that
is done, it will be proved that what appears to us is a reality,
and that it is impossible that we should ever be disabused
about it. But I think that this would be very like the
beatific vision, and that it is difficult to pretend to such
vision in the state in which we are. Still we learn from this
how confused the knowledge which we commonly have of

body and of matter must be, since we think that we are assured that they exist, and then find in the last analysis that we may be mistaken.

And this confirms M. Descartes's beautiful thought concerning the proof of the distinction between body and soul, since it is possible to cast doubt on the one, without questioning the other. For if there were nothing but appearances or dreams, we should be no less assured of the existence of that which thinks, as is very well said by M. Descartes; and I myself add that we could still prove just as well the existence of God, by methods different from those employed by M. Descartes, and which, in my view, take us further. For we have no need whatever to suppose a Being who will guarantee that we shall not be deceived, since it lies in our power to undeceive ourselves about many things, and at least about the most important. I hope, sir, that your meditations on this subject will have all the success you desire; but to that end it is a good thing to proceed in order and to establish propositions. This is the way to gain ground and to progress with certainty. I think that you would oblige the public further by publishing from time to time chosen passages from the Academy, and especially from Plato; for I know that there are to be found in them some things that are more beautiful and sounder than is ordinarily thought.

CORRESPONDENCE WITH ARNAULD

To Landgraf Ernst von Hessen-Reinfels. 1/11 Feb. 1686

BEING recently at a place where for several days I had
nothing to do, I composed a small *Discourse on Metaphysics*,
about which I should be very glad to have the opinion of
M. Arnauld.[1] For the questions of grace, of the relations of
God with His creatures, of the nature of miracles, the cause
of sin and the origin of evil, the immortality of the soul,
ideas, etc., are touched upon in a manner which seems to
provide new opportunities for throwing light on very great
difficulties. I enclose herewith a summary of the articles
contained in it, as I have not yet had time to make a fair
copy. I beg Your Serene Highness to have this summary
sent to him, and to ask him to consider it somewhat and
express his opinion; for as he excels equally in theology and
in philosophy, in learning and in the power of thought, I can
think of no one more fitted than he to judge of it. I should
very much appreciate having a critic as exact, as enlightened,
and as reasonable as M. Arnauld, being myself as ready as
any man in the world to yield to reason. Perhaps M.
Arnauld will find this little matter not altogether unworthy
of his consideration, especially as he has been much occupied
in examining these questions. If he finds any obscurity, I
will explain myself sincerely and frankly; and if he finds me
worthy of his instruction, I will see to it that he has reason
to be not ill satisfied with me. I beg Your Serene Highness

[1] Antoine Arnauld (1612–94), known as 'the great Arnauld';
a distinguished theologian, philosopher, and mathematician.
He defended the Jansenists against the Jesuits.

to attach this to the summary which I am sending for him, and to send both on to M. Arnauld.

SUMMARY OF THE 'DISCOURSE ON METAPHYSICS'

1. Of Divine perfection, and that God does everything in the most desirable manner.

2. Against those who maintain that there is no goodness in the works of God; or rather that the rules of goodness and of beauty are arbitrary.

3. Against those who think that God might have done better.

4. That love of God demands that we should be completely satisfied with and should acquiesce in all that He does.

5. Wherein the rules of perfection of the Divine conduct consist, and that the simplicity of the means is exactly balanced by the richness of the effects.

6. That God does nothing which is out of order, and that it is not even possible to imagine events which are not regular.

7. That miracles are in conformity with the general order, although they go against subordinate maxims. Concerning what God wills or permits, and concerning general and particular will.

8. In order to distinguish God's activities from those of created beings, an explanation is offered of wherein consists the notion of an individual substance.

9. That each single substance expresses the whole universe in its own way, and that in its notion are included all the events which will happen to it with all their circumstances, and the whole series of things outside it.

10. That the theory regarding substantial forms has something in it, but that these forms do not change anything in phenomena, and must not be used to explain particular effects.

11. That the meditations of the theologians and of the philosophers known as Schoolmen are not wholly to be despised.[1]

12. That the notions which depend upon extension include an imaginary element, and cannot constitute the substance of body.

13. As the individual notion of each person includes once and for all everything that will ever happen to him, in it can be seen the *a priori* proofs, or reasons of the truth of every event, or why one thing has happened rather than another. But these truths, although they are assured, are none the less contingent, since they are based on the free choice of God and of created beings. It is true that there are always reasons for their choice, but these reasons incline without necessitating.

14. God produces different substances, according to the different views which He has of the universe; and by the intervention of God the proper nature of each substance is such that what happens to one corresponds to what happens to all the others, without their acting immediately one upon another.

15. The action of one finite substance upon another consists only in an increase of the degree of its expression together with a decrease of that of the other, inasmuch as God has so formed them in advance that they shall agree together.

16. The extraordinary intervention of God is included in what is expressed by our essence; for this expression extends to everything. But it surpasses the forces of our nature or of our distinct expression, which is finite and follows certain subordinate maxims.

17. An example of a subordinate maxim of the law of

[1] This section of the *Discourse* itself is purely general. Leibniz does not mention any instances of truths to be found in the Schoolmen. He mentions St. Thomas with special honour.

nature, in which it is shown that God always regularly conserves the same force, but not the same quantity of motion, contrary to the teaching of the Cartesians and some others.

18. The distinction between force and quantity of motion is important, among other things as showing that it is necessary to have recourse to metaphysical considerations distinct from extension in order to explain the phenomena of bodies.

19. The value of final causes in physics.

20. A memorable passage from Socrates in Plato's *Phaedo* [1] against a too materialistic philosophy.

21. If the laws of mechanics depended on geometry alone without metaphysics, phenomena would be quite other than they are.

22. A reconciliation of two methods, one of which proceeds by final causes and the other by efficient causes; which will satisfy both those who explain nature mechanically and those who have recourse to incorporeal natures.

23. Returning to immaterial substances, an explanation is offered how God acts on the understanding of minds, and whether we always have an idea of what we are thinking about.

24. Of the nature of knowledge, clear or obscure, distinct or confused, adequate or inadequate, intuitive or supposititious; of nominal, real, causal, and essential definition.

25. In what cases our knowledge goes always with the contemplation of the idea.

26. We have within us all the ideas there are; and of Platonic reminiscence.

27. Of how our soul may be compared to a *tabula rasa*,[2] and of how our notions come from the senses.

[1] In this section of the *Discourse* itself a gap is left, into which Leibniz evidently intended to transcribe the passage from Plato.
[2] 'a blank tablet', i.e. a wax writing tablet with no impressions on it, or (to use the language of Locke) a piece of white paper. Cf. p. 143.

28. God is the sole immediate object of our perceptions, which exists outside of us, and He alone is our light.

29. Nevertheless we think immediately by our own ideas, and not by those of God.

30. How God inclines our soul without necessitating it; that we have no right to complain; that we must not ask why Judas sins, since that free action is included in his notion, but only why Judas the sinner is admitted into existence preferably to some other possible people. Of original imperfection or limitation before sin, and of the degrees of grace.

31. Of the motives of elective choice, of faith foreseen, of mean science,[1] of absolute decree; and that everything is reduced to the reason why God chose to admit into existence such and such a possible person, whose notion includes the particular succession of acts of grace and of free actions. This at once puts an end to all difficulties.

32. Value of these principles in matters of piety and religion.

33. Explanation of the intercourse between the soul and the body, which has been regarded as inexplicable or as miraculous, and of the origin of confused perceptions.

34. Of the difference between minds and other substances, souls or substantial forms. And that the immortality we desire requires memory.

35. Excellence of minds: that God considers them above other created things; that minds express God rather than the world, and that other simple substances express the world rather than God.

36. God is the Monarch of the most perfect commonwealth composed of all minds, and the happiness of the City of God is His chief design.

---

[1] *Science moyenne.* In the corresponding section of the *Discourse* itself there is no reference to it whatever. From the *Theodicy* it appears to refer to knowledge of 'conditional events', which Leibniz regards as intermediate between knowledge of possibilities and knowledge of actual facts.

37. Jesus Christ has revealed to mankind the mystery and the admirable laws of the Kingdom of Heaven and the greatness of the supreme happiness which God prepares for those who love Him.

To Landgraf Ernst von Hessen-Rheinfels. 12 April 1686

... I said in the thirteenth article of my Summary that the individual notion of each person includes once for all everything which will ever happen to him. He [1] draws from this the consequence that everything which happens to a person, and even to the whole human race, must happen by a more than fatalistic necessity—as if notions or previsions rendered things necessary, and as if a free action could not be contained in the notion or perfect vision which God has of the person to whom it will belong. He adds that perhaps I shall find nothing to trouble me in the conclusion he draws. And yet I had expressly protested in the very same article that I did not admit such a conclusion. So either he must doubt my sincerity, for which I have given him no reason, or else he has not sufficiently examined the view he is rejecting. Still I will not reproach him for this, as it seems I have a right to do, since I bear in mind that he was writing at a time when some indisposition did not allow him the free use of all his mind, as is witnessed by his letter itself.[2]

[1] Arnauld.

[2] Arnauld had complained of a bad cold in the previous letter; and he had added, 'All that I can now do is to say in two words to Your Highness that I find in these meditations so many things which frighten me, and which, unless I am much mistaken, all mankind will find so shocking, that I do not see that any purpose would be served by a piece of writing which will manifestly be rejected by the whole world. . . . Would it not be better for him to abandon these metaphysical speculations, which can be of no value either to him or to any one else, and to apply himself earnestly to the matter which is of the greatest importance of all to him, namely to assure his own salvation by returning to the Church . . . ?' Arnauld afterwards sincerely apologized for this rather off-hand treatment of Leibniz.

And I wish to have it known how much respect I feel for him.

If that is the case, he says (namely that the individual notion of each person includes once for all everything which will ever happen to him), *God was not free to create all that has happened to the human race and all that will ever happen by a more than fatalistic necessity* (there is some fault in the copy but I think I have succeeded in restoring it as above). *For the individual notion of Adam included his having so many children, and the individual notion of each of these children included everything that they would do and all the children they would have, and so on. God had, then, no more freedom in all this, supposing that He had once willed to create, than He had freedom not to create a being capable of thought.*[1] These last words should strictly contain the proof of the consequence; but it is very clear that they confuse *necessitatem ex hypothesi*[2] with absolute necessity. A distinction has always been drawn between what God is absolutely free to do and what He is obliged to do by virtue of certain resolutions already taken (and He does not take any without previous regard to all). It is not worthy of God to conceive of Him (under pretext of vindicating His liberty), in the manner of some Socinians, as being like a human being who takes his resolutions in consideration of circumstances, and as now being no longer free to create what He considers good, if His earliest resolutions in regard to Adam or others already include a relation to everything already connected with their posterity. On the contrary every one is agreed that God has ordered

---

[1] Arnauld's own letter reads as follows: *God had then no more freedom in all this, supposing He had once willed to create Adam than to argue that God was free, supposing He had once willed to create me, not to create a being capable of thought.* (This sentence is somewhat confused, but it sufficiently indicates the line of argument. It will be seen that the whole passage is loosely and confusedly written, as if Leibniz were in some difficulties to state his view.)

[2] i.e. that which necessarily follows from a given hypothesis.

from all eternity the whole succession of the universe, without its diminishing His freedom in any way.

It is evident also that this objection separates off from one another acts of will on the part of God, which are really connected together. We must not consider God's will to create a particular Adam as separated from all His other acts of will in regard to the children of Adam and all the human race; as if God first made the decision to create Adam without any relation to his posterity, and none the less by that decision, according to my view, deprived Himself of the freedom to create the posterity of Adam, as seemed to Him good. This would be a strange way of reasoning. Rather we should think of God as choosing, not just any Adam vaguely, but a particular Adam, of whom there exists among the possible beings in the ideas of God a perfect representation, accompanied by certain individual circumstances, and possessing among other predicates that of having in the course of time certain posterity; we must think of God, I say, as choosing him with an eye to his posterity, and so as equally at the same time choosing the one and the other. I cannot see what harm there is in that. If He acted otherwise, He would not be acting like God. Let me suggest a comparison. A wise prince, when he chooses a general whose connections he knows, in effect chooses at the same time a number of colonels and captains, whom he well knows the general will appoint, and whom he will not want to reject for reasons of prudence: yet they do not in any way destroy his absolute power, nor his freedom. The case is exactly the same with God for much stronger reasons. Therefore, to be exact, we must recognize in God a certain more general and comprehensive will, in which He has an eye to the whole order of the universe, since the universe is like a whole which God apprehends in a single view. This will virtually includes all the other acts of will about what is to come into this universe, and among the rest it includes that of creating a

particular Adam, who is connected with the whole succession
of his posterity, which God has also chosen as it is. We
might even say that these particular acts of willing the
details only differ from the willing of the whole general
purpose in a simple respect, very much as the situation of a
town considered from a particular point of view differs from
its ground-plan.[1] For these particular acts of will all of
them express the whole universe in the same way as each
situation expresses the town. In fact the wiser a man is,
the less does he have *detached acts of will*, and the more do
his views and his acts of will become comprehensive and
connected. And each particular act of will includes a relation
to all the others, so that they are as well harmonized as
possible. Far from finding in all this something shocking, I
should have thought that the contrary would destroy the
perfection of God. And in my opinion it must have been a
matter of great difficulty, or else of great prejudice, to find in
opinions so innocent, or rather so reasonable, an occasion for
such strange exaggerations as those which were sent to Your
Serene Highness.

Moreover, some slight consideration of what I have said
will show that it is evident *ex terminis*.[2] For by the individual
notion of Adam I undoubtedly mean a perfect representation
of a particular Adam, with given individual conditions and
distinguished thereby from an infinity of other possible
persons very much like him, but yet different from him
(just as every ellipse is different from the circle, however
closely it approaches to it). God preferred him to all these
others, because it pleased Him to choose just this particular
order of the universe; and all that follows from this decision
of His is necessary only by a hypothetical necessity, and in

[1] *Plan géométral:* a plan drawn to scale, showing the true
measurements in proportion, i.e. having no regard to perspective.
Cf. p. 84.
[2] 'from the terms themselves', i.e. from an analysis of the
meaning of the terms.

no way derogates from the freedom of God nor from that of created minds. There is one possible Adam whose posterity is such and such, and an infinity of others whose posterity would be different; is it not the case that these possible Adams (if I may so speak of them) are different from one another, and that God has chosen only one of them, who is exactly our Adam? There are so many reasons which prove the impossibility, not to say the absurdity and even impiety, of the contrary, that I think that at bottom all men are of the same opinion, when they give a little thought to what they say. Perhaps, too, if M. Arnauld had not held about me the prejudiced view with which he started, he would not have found my propositions so strange and would not have drawn from them the consequences which he did. . . .

To Landgraf Ernst von Hessen-Rheinfels. 12 April 1686

. . . Every man who acts wisely considers all the circumstances and connections of the decision he is taking, and the more so in proportion to his capacity. Will God, who sees everything perfectly and with a single glance, fail to have taken His decision in conformity with everything He sees? Can He have chosen a particular Adam without considering and deciding as well everything which has any connection with him? Consequently it is ridiculous to say that this free decision of God's takes away His liberty. Otherwise, to be free it would be necessary to be for ever undecided. . . .

Remarks on M. Arnauld's letter about my proposition that the individual notion of each person includes once for all everything that will ever happen to him. May 1686

. . . He admits in good faith that he understood my opinion to be that everything that happens to an individual can be deduced from his individual notion in the same way and with the same necessity as the properties of a sphere can be deduced from its specific notion or definition; and that he supposed I had been considering the notion of the individual in itself, without regarding the manner in which it exists in the understanding or will of God. *For* (he says) *it appears to me that we are not accustomed to consider the specific notion of a sphere in relation to what is represented in the Divine understanding, but in relation to what it is in itself, and I supposed it was the same with the individual notion of each person;* but he adds that, *now that he knows what my view is, that is enough to enable him to grant it sufficiently to try and find out whether it removes all the difficulties;* a matter of which he is still in doubt.

I see that M. Arnauld has not remembered, or at least has not concerned himself about, the opinion of the Cartesians, who hold that God establishes by His will the eternal truths, like those regarding the properties of the sphere. But as I am not of their opinion any more than M. Arnauld, I will simply explain why I hold that we must philosophize differently about the notion of an individual substance than we do about the specific notion of a sphere. This is because the notion of a *species* includes eternal or necessary truths only, whereas the notion of an individual includes *sub ratione possibilitatis* [1] what is fact, or what is related to the existence of things and to time; and consequently it depends on certain free decisions of God, considered as possible. For truths of fact or of existence depend upon God's decisions. Further, the notion of a sphere in general is incomplete or abstract; that is to say we only consider the essence of a sphere in general or in theory, without regard to individual circumstances. Consequently the notion does not include in any way what is required for the existence of a certain sphere. But the notion of the sphere which Archimedes

---

[1] 'considered under the head of possibility'; i.e. that which is, as a matter of fact, an actual fact is considered, not as actual fact, but as *possible*.

had placed upon his tomb is a fully worked out notion, and is bound to include everything which belongs to the object of that form. This is why in the case of individual considera-tions, or considerations of practice, *quae versantur circa singularia*,[1] besides the form of the sphere there enter in the matter of which it is made, the place, the time, and the other circumstances, which by a continual chain would in the end cover the whole series of the universe, if it were possible to follow out all that these notions include. For the notion of this piece of matter, of which the sphere is made, involves all the changes which have ever happened or will ever happen to it. According to my view, every individual substance always contains traces of all that has ever happened to it and marks of all that ever will ever happen to it for all time. What I have just said may suffice to explain my train of thought.

. . . As regards the objection that possibles are independent of the decisions of God, I grant that they are so of actual de-cisions (though the Cartesians do not agree with this); but I hold that possible individual notions include a number of possible free decisions. For example, if this world were possible only, the individual notion of any body in this world, which includes certain movements as possible, would include our laws of motion (which are free decisions of God), but it would include them as possible only. For as there is an infinity of possible worlds, there is also an infinity of laws, some proper to one world, others to another; and each possible individual of any world includes in its notion the laws of its world.

The same thing can be said of miracles or the extraordinary

---

[1] 'which are concerned with individuals', what is individual being opposed to what is general. The point of introducing these Latin phrases is, of course, that Leibniz wishes to indicate that he is following orthodox logical doctrine of the Schools.

operations of God, which none the less belong within the general order; they are in conformity with the principal designs of God, and consequently are included in the notion of this universe, which is a result of those designs. Just as the idea of a building results from the ends and designs of the builder, so the idea or notion of this world is a result of these designs of God, considered as possible. For everything must be explained by its cause; and the cause of the universe is the ends of God. Now each individual substance, according to my view, expresses the whole universe from a certain point of view, and consequently it also expresses the said miracles. All this must be understood of the general order, of the designs of God, of the series of the universe, of individual substance, and of miracles, whether they are taken in their actual state or are considered *sub ratione possibilitatis*.[1] For another possible world will have all those things too in their own manner, though the designs of our own world have been preferred.

It will be seen too, from what I have just said about the designs of God and about the primary laws, that this universe has a certain principal or primary notion, of which particular happenings are merely consequences—without, however, eliminating freedom and contingency, to which certainty is in no way inimical, since the certainty of events is partly based on free actions. . . . To speak exactly, it should be said that it is not so much because God decided to create this Adam that he decided on all the rest; the truth is rather that both His decision regarding Adam and His decision about other particular things are a consequence of His decision in regard to the whole universe and of the principal designs which determine its primary notion and establish in it this general inviolable order, with which everything is in conformity, without even excepting miracles, which are without doubt in conformity with the principal designs of

[1] i.e. not as facts, but as possibilities.

God, although they do not always observe the particular maxims which are called laws of nature.

I said before that the supposition from which all human events can be deduced is not simply that of the creation of a vague Adam, but that of the creation of a particular Adam determined in all his circumstances and chosen from among an infinity of possible Adams. This has given M. Arnauld occasion to object, not without reason, that it is as impossible to conceive of several Adams, taking Adam as a unique nature, as it would be to conceive of several *I*s. I agree; but I must add that in speaking of several Adams, I was not taking Adam as a determined individual. I must explain myself; this is what I meant. When in considering Adam we consider a part of his predicates, as for instance that he is the first man, set in a pleasure garden, from out of whose side God took a woman, and similar things conceived *sub ratione generalitatis*[1] (i.e. without naming Eve, Paradise, or other circumstances which fix individuality), and we give the name Adam to the person to whom these predicates are attributed, all this is not sufficient to determine the individual; for there might be an infinity of Adams, that is to say of possible persons, different from one another, to whom all that is appropriate. Far from disagreeing with what M. Arnauld says against such a plurality of one and the same individual, I used the same argument myself to make it clear that the nature of an individual must be complete and determined. I am indeed entirely persuaded of what St. Thomas had already taught in regard to intelligences, and which I hold to be of general application, namely that it is not possible that there should be two individuals entirely alike, or differing *solo numero*.[2] We must not then conceive of a vague Adam, that is to say a person to whom certain of Adam's attributes

---

[1] i.e. considered in general, as opposed to considered in respect of its unique, individual character.

[2] 'numerically only.'

belong, when it is a question of determining whether all human happenings follow from the supposition of him; we must attribute to him a notion so complete that everything that can be attributed to him can be deduced from it. Now there is no room for doubt but that God could form such a notion of him, or rather that He finds it ready made in the country of possibles, that is, in His understanding.

It follows also that he would not have been our Adam, but another, if he had had different events; for nothing prevents us from saying that he would be another. Therefore he is another. It appears evident to us that this square of marble brought from Genoa would have been in all respects the same, if it had been left there, because our senses only make us judge superficially; but at bottom, because of the inter-connection of things, the whole universe with all its parts would be quite different, and would have been a quite different universe from the beginning, if the least thing went differently from the way it does go. It is not for this reason that all that happens is necessary; it is because everything that happens is certain after God made choice of this possible universe, whose notion contains this series of things. I hope that what I am going to say will make even M. Arnauld agree with me.

Let there be a straight line ABC representing a certain time. And let a certain individual substance, for instance myself, remain or exist throughout the given time. Let us first take the I which exists during the time AB, and then the I which exists during the time BC. Since then the presumption is that it is the same individual substance enduring throughout, or rather that it is I who exist in the time AB, being then in Paris, and that it is still I who exist in the time BC, being then in Germany, it follows necessarily that there is a reason which makes us say truly that we endure, that is, that I who was in Paris am now in Germany. For if there is no reason, we should have as much right to say that it is another person. It is true that my internal experience convinces me *a posteriori* of this identicalness, but there must be a reason *a priori*. Now it is not possible to find any other except that both my attributes in the preceding time and state and my attributes in the later time and state are predicates of one and the same subject: *insunt eidem subjecto.*[1] Now what is meant by saying that a predicate is in a subject, except that the notion of the predicate is in some way included in the notion of the subject? And since from the time when I began to exist it was possible to say of me truly that this or that would happen to me, it must be acknowledged that these predicates were laws included in the subject, or in the complete notion of me which caused me to be called *I*, which is the foundation of the interconnection of all my different states, and which was perfectly known to God from all eternity.

After this I think that all doubts should disappear, for when I say that the individual notion of Adam includes everything that will ever happen to him, I do not mean anything other than what all the philosophers mean when they say *praedicatum inesse subjecto verae propositionis.*[2] It is true that the consequences of so evident a doctrine are paradoxical; but that is the fault of the philosophers, who do not follow up sufficiently the clearest notions.

I think that M. Arnauld, being as penetrating and fair-minded as he is, will now no longer find my proposition so strange, even if he is not yet able to approve of it entirely (though I almost persuade myself that he will approve). I agree with what he says so judiciously about the circumspection that is necessary in attempting to use the Divine knowledge[3] to find out what we ought to discover from the

---

[1] 'they are included in the same subject'.

[2] 'in a true proposition the predicate is included in the subject'.

[3] i.e. because God's knowledge is inaccessible to us as finite intelligences. We should not suppose that we can understand

notions of things. But, rightly understood, what I have just said must be allowed, since God would only be brought in as much as is necessary. For we should not need to assert that God, in considering the Adam whom He is deciding to create, sees in him everything that will happen to him; it is enough that we can always prove that there must be a complete notion of this Adam which contains them. For all the predicates of Adam either depend upon other predicates of the same Adam, or they do not so depend. Putting on one side, then, those which do depend on others, we have only to take together the primary predicates in order to form the complete notion of Adam, which is sufficient to make it possible to deduce from it everything which must happen to him, as far as is necessary to give an explanation of it. It is evident that God can invent, and even does in fact conceive, such a notion, which is sufficient to account for all the phenomena which belong to Adam; but it is no less evident that it is possible in itself. It is true that we must not, unless it is necessary, involve ourselves in the investigation of Divine knowledge and Divine will because of the great difficulties therein; still, we can explain all of this which we need for our question without entering into the difficulties mentioned by M. Arnauld — for example, whether the simplicity of God is reconcilable with the distinctions we are obliged to make with regard to Him. It is also extremely difficult to explain perfectly how God has a knowledge which He might not have had, namely the knowledge of *vision*[1]; for if contingencies in the future did not exist, God would have no vision of them. It is true that He would have simple knowledge, which is vision, none the less, for having joined to it His will; so that this difficulty perhaps reduces

God's knowledge, and infer from this the nature of particular things. We must start from the notions of things which we find in ourselves.

[1] *vision* in the sense in which the prophets had visions.

itself to such difficulty as there is about His will, that is, how God is free to will. This is without doubt beyond us, but it is not so necessary to understand it in order to solve our problem.

As for the manner in which we conceive that God acts in choosing the best among several possibles, M. Arnauld is right in finding some obscurity there. Yet he seems to recognize that we are led to conceive that there is an infinity of possible first men, each with a great following of persons and events, and that God chose the one who together with his following pleased Him. All that is not as strange as it had first appeared to him. It is true that M. Arnauld testifies that he is very much inclined to think that substances that are purely possible are nothing but chimeras. About this I do not want to enter into dispute: but I hope that in spite of that he will grant me what I need. I agree that there is no other reality in pure possibilities but that which they have in the Divine understanding; and from this it can be seen that M. Arnauld himself will be obliged to fall back on the Divine knowledge to explain them, whereas he seemed to mean just now that they ought to be looked for in themselves. Since I should admit also the proposition, of which M. Arnauld is convinced and which I do not deny, namely that we do not conceive of any possibility except through ideas which are to be found in the things which God has created, this objection does not affect my argument. For when I speak of possibilities, I am quite satisfied that it should be possible to form true propositions about them. For example, if there were no perfect square in the world, we should still see that it does not involve any contradiction. And if we absolutely reject pure possibilities, this means that there is no contingency; for if nothing is possible except what God has in fact created, what God has created would be necessary, supposing He had once decided to create anything.

Finally, I agree that in order to judge of the notion of

an individual substance it is a good thing to consider that
which I have of myself, just as it is necessary to consider
the specific notion of a sphere in order to judge of its properties. And yet there is a considerable difference; for the
notion of *me* and of every other individual substance is
infinitely more extended and more difficult to understand
than a specific notion like that of a sphere, which is incomplete only. It is not enough that I feel myself a
substance which thinks, it would be necessary to conceive
distinctly what distinguishes me from all other minds; but
of this I have only a confused experience. The result is
that, though it is easy to determine that the number of
feet in the diameter is not included in the notion of the
sphere in general, it is not so easy to determine whether the
journey which I intend to make is included in my notion;
otherwise it would be as easy for us to be prophets as to
be geometers. I am uncertain whether I shall go on the
journey; but I am not uncertain that, whether I go or not,
I shall still be the same *I*. It is an unreflective conviction,[1]
which must not be confused with a notion or distinct apprehension. These things only seem to us to be undetermined
because the foreshadowings or marks which are there in
our substance are not recognizable by us. In the same
way those who take no account of anything but the senses
will treat with ridicule any one who says that the least
movement communicates itself on and on as far as matter
extends, because this could not be learnt from experience
alone; but when we consider the nature of motion and of
matter, we are convinced. It is the same here: when I
consider the confused experience I have of the individual
notion of *me* in particular, I take no care to perceive this
connection of events; but when I consider the general,
distinct notions which enter into the notion of *me*, I come

---

[1] *Prévention.* There is not, I think, a sufficiently exact English
equivalent; and this cumbrous phrase seems to be unavoidable.

upon that connection. In fact, in considering the notion that I have of every true proposition, I find that every predicate, necessary or contingent, past, present, or future, is contained in the notion of the subject; and I ask no more.

Indeed, I think that this will open up to us a way of reconciliation; for I imagine that M. Arnauld felt a repugnance against assenting to my proposition only because he took the connection, which I am maintaining, to be intrinsic and necessary at the same time, whereas I hold it to be intrinsic, but in no way necessary; and I have now sufficiently explained that it is founded on free decisions and actions. I do not mean any other connection between subject and predicate than that which is to be found in the most contingent truths; that is to say, there is always something to be conceived in the subject which provides the explanation why this predicate or this event belongs to it, or why a particular event happened rather than not. But the reasons of these contingent truths incline without necessitating. It is true then that I am not able to go on this journey, but it is certain that I shall go. This predicate or event is not certainly connected with my other predicates conceived incompletely or *sub ratione generalitatis*,[1] but it is connected certainly with my complete individual notion, since I suppose that this notion was expressly so constructed that it might be possible to deduce from it everything which happens to me. This notion is without doubt *a parte rei*;[2] and it properly is the notion of *me*, who find myself in a number of different states, since it is this notion alone which is capable of including them all. . . .

[1] Cf. p. 65, note 1.
[2] 'from the side of the thing itself'; i.e. the notion is of something really existing, and not of an imaginary or merely possible object.

To Arnauld.   Hanover, 14 July 1686

. . . I agree that the connection of events, although it is certain, is not necessary, and that it is open to me to go or not to go on this journey; for although it is included in my notion that I shall go, it is also included that I shall go freely. And of all that in me which can be conceived *sub ratione generalitatis seu essentiae seu notionis specificae sive incompletae* [1] there is nothing from which it can be inferred that I shall go necessarily; whereas from the fact that I am a man it can be concluded that I am capable of thinking. Consequently, if I do not go on this journey, it will not violate any eternal or necessary truth. Nevertheless, since it is certain that I shall go, there is bound to be some connection between me, who am the subject, and the accomplishment of the journey, which is the predicate; *semper enim notio praedicati inest subjecto in propositione vera.* [2] Thus if I did not go there would be a falsity which would destroy my individual or complete notion, or that which God conceives of me, or did conceive even before he decided to create me. For this notion involves *sub ratione possibilitatis* [3] existences, or truths of fact, or decisions of God, on which facts depend. . . .

. . . You approve, sir, the interconnections of God's decisions; you recognize as certain my principal proposition, in the sense which I gave to it in my reply. You are simply in doubt whether I made the interconnection independent of the free decisions of God; and this quite rightly troubles you. But I have made it clear that according to

[1] 'in general terms, or in terms of its essence or of its specific or incomplete notion'.

[2] 'for in a true proposition the notion of the predicate is always included in the subject'.

[3] Cf. p. 64, note.

my view it depends on these decisions, and that it is not necessary though it is intrinsic. You insisted on the difficulty that would be involved in saying that if I do not go on this journey as I am bound to do, I shall not be I; and I explained how it may be said or may not. Finally I gave a decisive reason, which in my opinion takes the place of demonstration; namely, that in every affirmative true proposition, necessary or contingent, universal or singular, the notion of the predicate is contained in some way in that of the subject, *praedicatum inest subjecto*.[1] Or else I do not know what truth is.

Now I ask no more connection here than that which exists *a parte rei*[2] between the terms of a true proposition; and it is in this sense only that I say that the individual substance includes all its events and all its denominations, even those which are commonly called extrinsic (that is, they belong to it only by virtue of the general interconnection of things and because it expresses the whole universe in its own way), *there must always be some foundation of the connection of the terms of a proposition, which foundation must lie in their notions*. This is my chief principle, on which I hold that all philosophers ought to be agreed. And one of its corollaries is the common axiom that nothing happens without a reason, which can always be given to explain why the thing turned out thus rather than otherwise, though this reason often inclines without necessitating, a perfect indifference being a chimerical or incomplete supposition. It will be seen that from the aforesaid principle I draw surprising consequences; but this is only because people are not accustomed to thinking out sufficiently the clearest apprehensions. . . .

You may perhaps be surprised that I deny the action of one bodily substance on another, when it seems to be so evident.

[1] 'the predicate is included in the subject'.
[2] Cf. p. 71, note 2.

But besides the fact that others have denied it before me, we must bear in mind that it is rather a play of the imagination than a distinct conception. If a body is a substance, and not a mere phenomenon like the rainbow, nor an entity united by accident or by aggregation like a heap of stones, it cannot consist of extension; and it must necessarily be conceived as something which is called substantial form, and which corresponds in some way to a soul. I became convinced of this in the end, as it were in spite of myself, after having held a very different opinion in earlier days. Still, approve as I may of the Schoolmen in this general and, if I may so put it, metaphysical explanation of theirs of the principles of bodies, I still subscribe fully to the corpuscular theory in the explanation of particular phenomena; in this sphere it is of no value to speak of forms or qualities. Nature must always be explained mathematically and mechanically, provided it is remembered that the very principles or laws of mechanics or of force do not depend on mathematical extension alone, but on certain metaphysical reasons. . . .

To Arnauld. Hanover, 14 July 1686

. . . Also I do not much approve of the behaviour of those who are always appealing to their ideas, when they are at the end of their proofs, and who misuse the principle that every clear and distinct conception is valid.[1] I hold that we must always look for some mark in a distinct apprehension; and as we often think without ideas, by using ciphers (in place of the ideas in question) whose signification we falsely suppose ourselves to know, and make up for ourselves impossible chimeras. I hold that the mark of a genuine idea is that its possibility can be proved, either *a priori* by conceiving its cause or reason, or *a posteriori* when experience teaches us

---

[1] *lit.* 'good'. It will be seen that later in the same paragraph Leibniz speaks of 'a *genuine* idea', and also of 'a *true* idea'.

that it in fact exists in nature. For this reason definitions, in my view, are real when it is known that the thing defined is possible; otherwise they are nominal only, and should not be trusted, since if by chance the thing defined implied a contradiction, two contradictory consequences might be inferred from one and the same definition. Hence you were absolutely right to inform Fr. Malebranche and others that a distinction must be made between true and false ideas, and that too much rein must not be given to a man's imagination under pretext of its being a clear and distinct intellection.

Draft of a letter to Arnauld. 28 November/8 December 1686

. . . The action is attributed to that substance, whose expression is more distinct, and which is called the cause. For instance, when a body is floating in water, an infinity of movements of the particles of the water are necessary so that the place which the body leaves may always be filled by the shortest way. Hence we say that the body is the cause of these movements; because by its means we can explain distinctly what happens. But if we examine what is physical and real in the motion, we can as well suppose that the body is at rest, and that everything else moves in conformity with this hypothesis, since the whole motion is in itself nothing but a relative thing, namely a change of situation, such that we cannot know to what to attribute it in mathematical precision. Actually we attribute it to a body, by whose means everything is explained distinctly. . . .

Thus in strict metaphysical precision, we have no more reason to say that the ship causes the water to produce this large number of circles which serve to fill up the place of the ship, than to say that the water is caused to produce all these circles and that it causes the ship to move accordingly. But short of saying that God has expressly willed to produce this large number of movements in this co-ordinated manner, we cannot give the reason for them; and as it is not reasonable to have recourse to God in matter of detail, we fall back on the ship, although as a matter of fact in the last analysis the agreement of all the phenomena of the different substances comes simply from the fact that they are all the products of one and the same cause, namely God, who arranges that each individual substance expresses the decision which God has taken in regard to the whole universe.

I do not know whether the body, when the soul or substantial form is put aside, can be called a substance. It might well be a machine, an aggregate of several substances, so that, if I am asked what I should say *de forma cadaveris* [1] or about a square of marble, my reply is that they are perhaps unities *per aggregationem* [2] like a heap of stones, and are not substances. The same might be said of the sun, of the earth, of machines; and with the exception of man there is no body of which I can be assured that it is a substance rather than an aggregate of several substances, or perhaps a phenomenon. Nevertheless it seems to me certain that, if there are any corporeal substances, man is not the only one; and it appears probable that the brutes have souls, though they are without consciousness.

Finally, although I agree that the consideration of forms or souls is useless in particular physics, it is for all that of importance in metaphysics. In the same way geometers do not trouble themselves *de compositione continui*, [3] and physicists do not concern themselves whether one ball impels another, or whether it is God.

It would be unworthy of a philosopher to admit such souls

[1] 'about the form of the physical, human body', as distinguished of course f om the whole living being.

[2] 'by aggregation'.

[3] 'about the composition of a continuum'; i.e. how that which is continuous can have parts and yet be continuous, etc.

or forms unless there were a reason for it; but without them the fact that bodies are substances is not intelligible.

To Arnauld. Göttingen, 30 April 1687

. . . You suppose that I will not say that a body can move itself; and so, since the soul is not the real cause of the movement of the arm, nor is the body, the cause will therefore be God. But I am of a different opinion. I hold that all that is real in the state which is called motion proceeds as much from the corporeal substance as thought and will proceed from the mind. Everything happens in each substance in consequence of the first state which God gave to it in creating it, and, extraordinary intervention apart, His ordinary intervention consists simply in the conservation of the same substance, in conformity with its precedent state and with the changes which it carries within it. Nevertheless, it is quite right to say that one body impels another; that is to say that the fact is that one body never begins to have a given tendency except when another body which is touching it has a proportionate loss, in accordance with the constant laws which we observe in phenomena. And in fact, motions being real phenomena rather than entities, a movement as phenomenon is in my mind the immediate consequence or effect of another phenomenon, and similarly in the minds of others. But the state of a substance is not the immediate consequence of the state of another particular substance. . . .

If my opinion that substance requires a true unity were founded on a definition that I had myself made up contrary to common usage, then *the dispute would be simply one of words.* But in the first place philosophers have understood this term in much the same manner, *distinguendo unum per se et unum per accidens, formamque substantialem et accidentalem, mixta imperfecta et perfecta, naturalia et artificialia.*[1] In the second place, I approach the matter from a higher ground also, and, waiving the analysis of terms, *I hold that where there are only entities by aggregation, there will not be any real entities.* For every entity by aggregation presupposes entities endowed with a true unity, for it only takes its reality from the reality of those of which it is composed, so that it will not have any at all, if each entity of which it is composed is itself an entity by aggregation; or else it is necessary to look further for a different foundation of its reality, which, if it is at every stage necessary to go further in looking for it, can never be found. I agree, sir, that in all corporeal nature there are nothing but machines (which are often animated); but I do not agree that *there are nothing but aggregates of substances*; and if there are aggregates there must also be some true substances of which the aggregates are made up. We must then come down to either the mathematical points, out of which some authors compound extension, or to the atoms of Epicurus and M. Cordemoy (which are things that you and I alike reject), or else we must acknowledge that no reality can be found in bodies; or finally we must recognize some substances as having a genuine unity. I have already said in another letter that a combination of the Grand Duke's diamond and the Great Mogul's diamond may be called a pair of diamonds, but that is only an entity of reason: when they are put side by side, that will be an entity of imagination or of perception, that is to say a phenomenon; for their contact, their common movement, and their co-ordination to carry out one and the same design, make no difference as regards substantial unity. It is true that there is sometimes more, sometimes less foundation for our supposition, when we suppose that several things are combining to make one

[1] 'by distinguishing between that which is a unity of itself and that which is a unity adventitiously, between substantial and accidental form, and between imperfect and perfect, natural and artificial compounds'.

single thing, according as the things have more or less connection; but this is only a way of abbreviating our thoughts and of picturing phenomena.

It appears, too, that what constitutes the essence of an entity by aggregation is nothing but a manner of existence of the things of which it is composed; for example, what constitutes the essence of an army is simply a manner of existence of the men who compose it. This manner of existence, then, presupposes a substance, whose essence is not the manner of existence of a substance. Every machine, too, presupposes some substance in the pieces of which it is made; and there can be no plurality without true unities. To put it shortly, I maintain as axiomatic this identical proposition, whose differentiation can only be marked by the accentuation—namely, *that that which is not truly* an *entity cannot either be truly an* entity. It has always been held that unity and entity are reciprocal things. An entity is one thing, entities are quite another thing: but the plural presupposes the singular, and where there is no entity still less are there several entities. What could be more clearly stated? I therefore thought that I might be allowed to distinguish entities by aggregation from substances, since such entities have their unity in our mind only; which unity is based upon the relations or modes of genuine substances. If a machine is a substance, a circle of men holding one another's hands will be a substance too; so will an army, and so will every plurality of substances.

I do not mean that there is nothing substantial, or nothing but appearance, in the things which have no genuine unity; for I agree that they have always as much reality or substantiality as there is genuine unity in that of which they are composed.

You object, sir, that it may perhaps be of the essence of

body not to have a true unity. But in that case it will be
of the essence of body to be a phenomenon, deprived of all
reality, like an ordered dream; for phenomena themselves,
like a rainbow or a heap of stones, would be wholly imaginary,
if they were not composed of entities with a genuine unity.

You say that you do not see what leads me to admit that
there are such substantial terms, or rather corporeal substances, endowed with a genuine unity. It is because I do
not conceive of any reality at all as without genuine unity.
According to my view the notion of singular substance
involves consequences which are incompatible with its being
an entity by aggregation. I conceive of there being properties
in substance which cannot be explained by extension, shape,
and motion, besides the fact that there is no exact and fixed
shape in bodies because of the actual subdivision of the continuum *ad infinitum*. Moreover, motion inasmuch as it is
only a modification of extension and a change of neighbour-
hood, involves an imaginary element, so that it is not possible
to determine to which of the subjects that change it belongs,
unless we have recourse to the force in corporeal substance
which is the cause of the motion. I admit that there is no
need to mention these substances and qualities in order to
explain particular phenomena, but neither is there any need
to mention the intervention of God, the composition of the
continuum, the plenum, and countless other things. We
can explain mechanically, I fully admit, the particularities
of nature; but my point is that after having accepted or
assured the principles of mechanics themselves, we cannot
establish them *a priori* except by metaphysical arguments;
and even the difficulties *de compositione continui* [1] will never
be resolved so long as extension is regarded as constituting
the substance of bodies, and we go on embarrassing ourselves
by our own chimeras.

[1] Cf. p. 76, note 3.

I think, too, that to allow genuine unity or substance to man almost alone is to be as limited in metaphysics as those people were in physics who confined the world within a ball. And as genuine substances are so many expressions of the whole universe taken in a certain sense, and so many reproductions of Divine works, it is in agreement with the greatness and beauty of these works of God, since these substances do not hinder one another from accomplishing as much in this universe as each of them can and as much as superior reasons allow. . . .

I agree that there are degrees of accidental unity; that an ordered society has more unity than a confused mob, and that an organized body or a machine has more unity than a society—that is to say there is more point in conceiving them as one single thing, because there is more relation between the constituent parts. But in the end all these unities only receive their existence from thoughts and appearances, like colours and all other phenomena, which for all that are called real. The tangibility of a heap of stones or of a block of marble does not any the more prove its substantial reality than the visibility of a rainbow proves the substantial reality of the rainbow; and as there is nothing so solid that it has not some degree of fluidity, perhaps this block of marble is only a heap made of an infinity of living bodies, or is like a lake full of fish, although these living creatures cannot ordinarily be distinguished by the eye except in the case of bodies that are half rotted. We may say then of these composites and of similar things what Democritus so well said of them, namely, *esse opinione, lege, νόμῳ*.[1] Plato held the same view about everything which is purely material. Our mind notices or conceives a number of genuine substances which have certain modes; these modes involve relations to other substances, and so the mind takes occasion to

[1] 'they depend for their existence on opinion or custom'.

join them together in thought and to give an inclusive name to all the things together. This is a convenience for reasoning; but we must not allow ourselves to be misled into making of them so many substances or genuinely real entities. This only befits those people who go no further than appearances, or else those who make realities of all the abstractions of the mind, and who conceive of number, time, place, motion, figure, and sensible qualities as so many separate entities. Whereas I hold that philosophy cannot be better established, and reduced to some degree of precision, than by learning to recognize the only substances or complete entities, endowed as they are with a genuine unity in their different states following one another, all the rest being nothing but phenomena, abstractions, or relations.

No kind of arrangement will ever be found which can make a genuine substance out of a number of entities by aggregation. For example, if the parts which fit together into one and the same design are more competent to produce a genuine unity than are parts which are in contact, then all the officials of the Dutch East India Company will make a real substance far better than a heap of stones. But what else is a common design but a resemblance, or rather an ordered arrangement of actions and passions, which our mind notices in different things? If on the other hand we prefer the unity based on contact, we are faced by other difficulties. Hard bodies have perhaps nothing uniting their parts except the pressure of surrounding bodies and of themselves, and in their substance are no more united than a heap of sand, *arena sine calce*.[1] Or, consider a number of rings interlaced to make a chain: why should they compose a genuine substance thus any more than if they had openings in them through which they could be separated? It may be that one of the parts of the chain does not touch another and even

---

[1] 'sand without lime', i.e. without anything to bind it into mortar.

does not enclose it, and yet they are so interlaced that unless they are taken in a certain manner they cannot be separated, as in the figure here given. Are we to say in that case that the substance of the com-pound of these things is as it were in suspense and depends on the future address of whoever may wish to dis-entangle them? These are all fictions of the mind; and so long as we do not distinguish what is genuinely a com-plete entity, or substance, we shall never have any fixed point at which we can stop; and such fixed point is the one and only means of establishing solid and real principles.

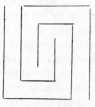

In conclusion, nothing should be taken as certain without foundations; it is therefore for those who manufacture entities and substances without a genuine unity to prove that there is more reality than I have just said; and I am waiting for the notion of a substance, or of an entity, which successfully comprehends all these things; after which parts and perhaps even dreams will be able one day to lay claim to reality, unless very precise limits are set to this *droit de bourgeoisie* [1] which is to be accorded to entities formed by aggregation.

I have written at some length on these matters, so that you may be able to form some opinion not only of my views, but also of the reasons which have driven me to adopt them. . . .

---

[1] Leibniz seems to mean a kind of inferior citizenship. A *bourgeois* was originally a member of a small township who had certain rights akin to those of a citizen in a city.

To Arnauld.   9 October 1687

. . . You reply that you have no clear idea of what I mean by the word *express*. If I mean by it a thought, you say, you do not agree that the soul has any more thought and knowledge of the movement of the lymph in its lymphatic ducts than of the movements of the satellites of Saturn; if I mean something else, you do not know what I mean, and consequently (supposing that I cannot explain myself distinctly) this term will be of no use to make clear how the soul can give itself the sensation of pain, since for that it would be necessary (so you say) for it to know beforehand that I am being stung, instead of learning of the sting by feeling the pain. In reply to your objection, I will first explain the term which you find obscure, and then apply it to the difficulty you raise. One thing *expresses* another (in my language) when there is a constant and ordered relation between what can be asserted of the one and what can be asserted of the other. In this sense a projection in perspective expresses its ground plan.[1] Expression is common to all forms, and is a genus of which natural perception, animal sensation, and intellectual knowledge are species. In natural perception and in sensation it is sufficient that what is divisible and material, and is to be found dispersed in a number of entities, should be expressed or represented in a single indivisible entity, or in a substance possessing a genuine unity. There can be absolutely no doubt of the possibility of a good representation of several things in one single thing; for our soul presents us with an example. This representation is accompanied by consciousness in a rational soul, and it is then that it is called thought.

Now such expression is to be found on all sides, because every substance sympathizes with every other and receives

[1] *son géométral.*   Cf. p. 60, note.

some proportionate change, answering to the least change which occurs in the universe; though this change is more or less noticeable in proportion as the other bodies or their activities have more or less relation to ours. On this point I think M. Descartes himself would have agreed; for he would certainly grant that because of the continuity and divisibility of all matter the effect of the least movement is extended over all the neighbouring bodies, and consequently from body to body *ad infinitum*, though diminishing proportionately. Thus our body must be affected to some extent by the changes in all the others.

Now to all the movements of our body there correspond certain perceptions or thoughts of our soul, more or less confused; so the soul in turn will have some thought of all the movements of the universe, and according to my opinion every other soul or substance will have some perception or expression of them. It is true that we do not perceive distinctly all the movements of our body, as for example the movement of the lymph; but (to make use of an example which I have employed previously) it is like this. It must be the case that I have some perception of the movement of each wave on the shore if I am to be able to apperceive that which results from the movements of all the waves put together, namely the mighty roar which we hear by the sea. Similarly we feel some confused result of all the movements which take place in us, but, being accustomed to this internal movement, we do not apperceive it distinctly and reflectively except when there is a considerable change for the worse, as at the beginning of an illness. And it would be an excellent thing if physicians devoted themselves to distinguishing more exactly these kinds of confused sensations which we have of our bodies. Now since we do not apperceive the other bodies except by the relation which they bear to ours, I was quite right in saying that the soul expresses better what belongs to our body, and that we only know of the satellites of Saturn or of Jupiter in consequence of a movement occurring within our eyes. . . .

With regard to minds, that is to say substances which think, and are capable of knowing God and of discovering eternal truths, I hold that God governs them by laws different from those by which He governs the rest of substances. All forms of substances express the whole universe; but it may be said that brute substances express the world rather than God, while minds express God rather than the world. Moreover God governs brute substances by the material laws of force, or of the communication of motion, whereas He governs minds by the spiritual laws of justice, of which the other substances are incapable. It is for this reason that brute substances may be called material, because the economy which God observes in regard to them is that of a Workman or a Mechanician; whereas in regard to minds, God fulfils the function of Prince or Legislator, which is infinitely more exalted. And since God is nothing in regard to these material substances but that which He is in regard to everything, namely the general Author of all entities, He takes on, in regard to minds, a different character, such that He must be conceived as invested with will and moral qualities; since He is Himself a mind, and as it were One among us, even to the point of entering with us into a social community of which He is the chief. It is this society or general Commonwealth of Minds under this sovereign Monarch which is the noblest part of the universe, composed of so many little gods under this great God. For created minds differ from God only as less from greater, as finite from infinite. And we may be truly assured that the whole universe was created only to contribute to the adornment and to the happiness of this City of God. This is why everything is so disposed that the laws of force, or purely material laws, conspire in all the universe to execute the laws of justice or of love, and that nothing can hurt the souls that are in the hand of God, and that all things must work together for the greatest good of those who love Him. This is why, since minds must keep their personality and their moral qualities, to the end that the City of God may not lose any person, it must be that in particular they should keep some manner of reminiscence or consciousness, or the power of knowing what they are; on this depends all their morality, punishments, and chastenings. Consequently it is necessary that every mind should be immune from those revolutions of the universe which would render it entirely unrecognizable to itself, and would make of it, morally speaking, a different person. Whereas for brute substances it is sufficient that each should simply remain the same individual in the strict metaphysical sense, even though it is subjected to all imaginable changes, since in any case it is without consciousness or reflection. . . .

LETTER TO BAYLE [1]

ON THE CARTESIAN THEORY OF THE QUANTITY OF MOTION. 1687

WHEN I gave myself the valuable pleasure of reading your *Nouvelles de la République des Lettres*, I found there my objection to the famous Cartesian principle regarding the Quantity of Motion, together with the Reply of a Cartesian scholar from Paris, by name M. l'Abbé C.[2] I now send you my answer so that all the parts of the business may be collected together, if you consider that suitable. It is true that this is merely intended to clear up the matter, by following out rather than by justifying the objection I there raised; for M. l'Abbé has in fact offered no opposition to it, but grants me more than I want. However, I am very much afraid that the other Cartesians may repudiate what he says.

According to him, the Cartesian rule is limited in application, and is indeed a very small matter; he maintains that it is only a particular *Principle regarding the five Common Machines and concerned with isochronic powers, or movements recorded in equal times.* I had shown that in a certain case (which was sufficiently ordinary), and in an infinite number of other similar ones, two bodies have the same force although they have not the same quantity of motion. He grants this, and I ask no more. But he adds that this is not surprising, because in the case referred to the two bodies acquired their forces in unequal times: as if the principle ought to be limited to forces acquired in equal times. This is to grant me my case, and indeed I do not ask so much. But as against the

[1] Pierre Bayle (1647–1706), author of the famous *Historical and Critical Dictionary*. Cf. pp. 118–40.
[2] probably Jean de Catellan, Bishop of Vallence.

88

Cartesians I should be wrong to try to take advantage of the fact that they are so feebly defended. For I do not believe that M. l'Abbé C. would ever find one of them, at least among those who pass for geometricians, to approve of his restriction of the principle. You, sir, will be able to decide, and I have no doubt but that some clever Cartesians among your friends will admit it, if you think fit to consult them; which I should make bold to ask you to do, if I knew what your convenience allowed. The Cartesians claim in general that there is always maintained the same sum total of force, which they always estimate by the quantity of motion. And according to them, if some bodies transfer their force, or a part of their force, to others, there will be in all these bodies together the same quantity of motion as before, or the sum total of the products of the masses multiplied by their velocities will be the same. For example, if there is a body weighing 4 pounds, with a velocity of 1 degree, and we suppose that its whole force must now be transferred to a body weighing 1 pound, is it not true that the Cartesians assert that in this case the body must receive a velocity of 4 degrees for the same quantity of motion to be preserved? For mass 4 multiplied by velocity 1 produces the same result as mass 1 multiplied by velocity 4. According to my view, on the other hand, the body in question must only receive a velocity of 2 degrees (as I will prove below); so the difference between us is manifest enough. And in estimating in this way the force which the bodies have acquired, neither these gentlemen nor any others that I know of (with the exception of M. l'Abbé C.) have worried themselves about whether they were gained in a long or short, an equal or an unequal time. Time, indeed, has nothing to do with this calculation. When we see a body of a given magnitude travelling at a given velocity, can we not estimate its force without knowing in what length of time and with what detours and delays it may have acquired that velocity? It seems to me that in this case we can judge of the present state without knowing the past. When there are two bodies, perfectly equal and similar, whose velocities are the same but acquired in the one case by a sudden shock, and in the other by a descent of observable duration, are we for that reason to say that their forces are different? This would be like saying that that man is richer whose money has taken longer to acquire. But, what is more, it is not even necessary that the two bodies in my suggested instance should fall from their different heights in unequal times, as is supposed by M. l'Abbé C.; he did not see that the time taken over the descent may be changed at will, according as the line of descent is changed by being given a greater or less inclination, and that there are an infinite number of ways in which these two bodies may be made to descend from their different heights in equal times. For if we disregard the resistance of the air and similar hindrances we know that a body falling from the same height acquires the same velocity whether the descent be perpendicular and sudden, or sloping and not so fast. Consequently the distinction of times does not affect my objection. These things are so evident that I might perhaps return to M. l'Abbé C. the compliment of some of his expressions, but I think it is more fitting not to descend to these amusements. The fact is, I think, that my objection is so simple that its very simplicity operated to deceive him, since he could not believe that a comment which was so easy could have escaped the notice of so many able people. This is why, noticing the difference in the times, he leapt upon that, without giving himself leisure to reflect that it is only incidental. I have a sufficiently good opinion of his mind and of his sincerity to hope that he will now agree about this himself, and I think that what follows will help even more to make him see the truth of the matter. In order, too, to anticipate the doubts of those who may think it is a satisfactory answer to my objection to say that the insensible matter which presses heavy bodies downwards and causes their acceleration, has lost exactly the quantity of motion which it imparts to the bodies; I answer that I agree about this pressure which is the cause of weight, and that I hold that this Ether loses as much force (though not as much motion) as it imparts to the heavy bodies; but that all this does nothing to resolve my objection, even if I granted (contrary to the truth) that the Ether lost as much motion as it imparted. For my objection is expressly so stated that it does not matter how the force was acquired; I left that out of account so as not to enter into any disputes on any hypothesis in that regard. I take the acquired force and the acquired velocity as they are, without bothering about whether they were imparted suddenly by a shock from another body or little by little by a continual acceleration from gravity or from a spring. It is sufficient for me that the body now has this given force or rather this given velocity. And under those circumstances I show that its force must not be estimated by the velocity or quantity of motion; and that the body can give its force to another body without giving it its quantity of motion, and that therefore when this transference occurs, it may, and indeed it must, happen that the quantity of motion is diminished or increased in the bodies, while the same force remains.

I shall now prove what I put forward above, namely, *that if we suppose the whole force of one body, which weighs 4 pounds and whose velocity* (when it travels in a horizontal plane, in whatever manner it acquires its velocity) *is 1 degree, is transferred to another body weighing 1 pound, then the latter body will receive a velocity, not of 4 degrees in accordance with the Cartesian principle, but of 2 degrees only*; because in this way the bodies or weights would be in reciprocal ratio to the heights to which they could ascend by virtue of the velocities they possess. Now these heights are as the squares of their velocities. And if the body weighing 4 pounds with its velocity in a horizontal plane of 1 degree, on meeting and becoming attached to the end of a pendulum or perpendicular line, climbs to a height of 1 foot, the body weighing 1 pound will have a velocity of 2 degrees, in order to be able, when similarly attached, to ascend to a height of 4 feet. For it requires the same force to raise 4 pounds 1 foot, as to raise 1 pound 4 feet. But if this body weighing 1 pound was bound to receive 4 degrees of velocity, as Descartes believed, it would be able to climb to a height of 16 feet. And consequently the same force which raised 4 pounds 1 foot, would be able, if transferred to 1 pound, to raise it 16 feet. But this is impossible; for the effect is four times as great, which means that three times the force which was originally present has been acquired and derived from nothing. This is why I hold that in place of the Cartesian principle it is possible to set up another *Law of Nature* which I consider most universal and most inviolable, namely *that there is always a perfect equation between the full cause and the entire effect*. This principle does not assert merely that effects are proportional to causes, but more than this, that each complete effect is equivalent to its cause. And although this axiom is altogether metaphysical, it is none the less one of the most useful in physics, and provides a means of reducing forces to a geometrical calculus. But in order to show more clearly how it must be made use of, and why Descartes and others departed from it, let us consider his third rule of motion, as an example. Let us suppose that two bodies B and C, each weighing 1 pound, meet one another, B with a velocity of 100 degrees, and C with a velocity of 1 degree. Their total quantity of motion will be 101. But if C with its velocity can climb 1 inch, B with its velocity will be able to climb 10,000 inches. Thus the force of both together is capable of raising 1 pound 10,001 inches. Now according to the *third Cartesian rule*, after the shock they will travel together in company at a velocity of 50½, so that when multiplied by 2 (the number of pounds travelling together after the shock) there results the same quantity of motion, 101. But in that case these 2 pounds will only be capable of ascending together to a height of 2,550¼ inches (i.e. the square of 50½), which is the same as if they had the force to raise 1 pound 5,100½ inches, whereas before the shock there was force enough to raise 1 pound 10,001 inches. Thus nearly half the force will have been lost by virtue of this rule for no reason whatever, and without being used for anything. This is just as impossible as what we showed above in another case, where by virtue of the same Cartesian general principle three times the force could be acquired for no reason.

The famous author of the *Recherche de la Vérité*[1] has indeed seen some errors of M. Descartes in these matters; but as he presupposed the maxim which I reject, he held that of the seven Cartesian rules numbers 1, 2, 3, and 5 were true, whereas the only one which can be maintained is the first, which is self-evident. The same author of the *Recherche*, arguing on the supposition of bodies that are hard and without elasticity, maintains that they cannot spring back nor become separated after the shock, except when they meet one another with velocities in reciprocal relation to their magnitudes, and that in all other cases they will travel in company after the shock, preserving the original quantity of motion. But in this I find a serious difficulty. If body B, of magnitude 2 and velocity 1, and body C, of magnitude 1 and velocity 2, move directly against one another, he grants that they will spring back at their own velocities. But if we suppose the velocity or the magnitude of one of the bodies, say B, to be increased by ever so little, he maintains that both will travel together in the direction in which B previously travelled alone, and this at a velocity of approximately $\frac{4}{3}$, supposing that the change in B is so slight that in calculating the quantity of motion it is possible to

[1] Malebranche.

retain the original numbers without any error worth mentioning. But is it credible that simply because of the smallest conceivable change assumed in regard to the body B, there should arise so great a difference in the result that all springing back should cease, and that B, which had in the previous instance to turn back at a velocity of 1, should now not only not have to travel backwards, but should even travel forwards at a velocity of approximately $\frac{4}{3}$ —which is all the more strange in that before the shock it only travelled forward at a velocity of 1? Thus the other body, instead of making this one recoil, or advance less, as a result of the shock of impact, makes it advance more, and as it were attracts it to itself—which is beyond all probability. As it is the author of the *Recherche de la Vérité* to whom we are indebted for the correction of a number of Cartesian prejudices of some importance, elsewhere as well as on this matter, it seemed to me fitting that I should explain here what else remained to be said. As I am assured that he is as honourable as he is penetrating, I have no fear that he may take it ill of me, but rather await his approbation.

However, I think that M. Descartes, who in laying down his rules forgot to notice the cases where two unequal bodies move against one another with unequal velocities, would have been obliged in the case just mentioned to say the same as the author of the *Recherche*, so far as I can judge from his third rule, about which they are both agreed. But there will still occur the inequality of the effect and the cause, as it would be easy to show by calculation on the example of the third rule. This inequality is also to be found in what the author of the *Recherche* says in correction of M. Descartes's fourth, sixth, or seventh rules. In regard to the sixth rule, for example: let B be of weight 1 pound and velocity 4, and C of weight 1 pound and at rest. He maintains that they travel in company after the shock at a velocity of 2. Thus whereas previously there was a force capable of raising 1 pound 16 feet, there is now only a force capable of raising 2 pounds 4 feet, and half the force has been lost. According to M. Descartes, in this case B and C will travel in the same direction, and B's velocity will be 3, C's will be 1; thus in all there will be a force capable of raising 1 pound 10 feet, and more than a third of the force will have been lost.

What may have misled these worthy authors, and has caused most confusion in this matter, is that bodies whose velocities are reciprocally related to their extensions are observed to stop one another, both in a balance and outside. This is why their forces were believed to be equal, *all the more because no account was taken in bodies of anything except velocity and extension.* It is in this connection that it would have been of value to make use of the distinction between force and direction, or rather between the absolute force necessary to cause the existence of some effect (for example, to raise a certain weight to a certain height, or to compress a certain spring to a certain degree) and the force required to travel forward in a certain direction, or to maintain the direction. For although a body of magnitude 2 with velocity 1 and a body of magnitude 1 with velocity 2 stop one another or prevent one another from going forward, nevertheless if the first can raise a pound 2 feet, the second will be able to raise a pound 4 feet. This is paradoxical, but it cannot be doubted after what has just been said. It might be possible, however, to find some new interpretation of the principle of the quantity of motion, so that after such correction it might remain a universal principle; but it is not easy to see what it would be.

I will add a remark of some consequence for metaphysics. I have shown that force must not be estimated by compounding the velocity and the magnitude, but by its future effect. Yet it seems that force or power is something real at the present moment, and the future effect is not. Whence it follows that *it is necessary to admit in bodies something other than magnitude and velocity, unless we are willing to deny to bodies all power of action.* I hold, moreover, that we have not a sufficiently perfect conception even of matter and extension. The author of the *Recherche de la Vérité* has recognized the existence of such obscurity in regard to the soul and to thought, thereby differing from the Cartesians, but as regards matter and extension he appears to agree with them. . . .

EXPOSITION AND DEFENCE OF THE NEW SYSTEM

NEW SYSTEM OF THE NATURE AND COMMUNICATION OF SUBSTANCES, AS WELL AS OF THE UNION EXISTING BETWEEN THE SOUL AND THE BODY. 1695

IT is now some years since I conceived this system, and entered into communication about it with several learned men, and in particular with one of the greatest theologians and philosophers of our time,[1] who had heard of some of my opinions from a personage of the highest rank, and found them highly paradoxical. But when he had received my explanations, he retracted in the most generous and edifying way imaginable, expressed his approval of a part of my propositions, and withdrew his censure of the others with which he still did not agree. Since that time I have continued my meditations as opportunity offered, so as to give to the public well-considered opinions only: and I have tried also to satisfy the objections raised against my *Essays on Dynamics*, which have some connection with this. Some distinguished people, moreover, have desired to see my opinions more clearly expressed, and so I venture to offer these meditations, although they are in no way popular, nor such as to be to the taste of all kinds of minds. My chief aim is to give myself the benefit of the judgment of those who are enlightened in these matters, since it would be too difficult to seek out and call to my aid individually those who would be prepared to give me instruction—which I shall always be very happy to receive, provided the love of truth appears therein, and not merely a passion for preconceived opinions.

[1] Arnauld. Cf. pp. 52–87.

Although I am one of those who have done much work on mathematics, I have constantly meditated on philosophy from my youth up, for it has always seemed to me that in philosophy there was a way of establishing something solid by means of clear proofs. I had travelled far into the world of the Scholastics when mathematics and modern writers lured me out again, while still a young man. I was charmed with their beautiful way of explaining nature mechanically, and scorned, with justice, the method of those who only make use of forms or faculties, from which we learn nothing. But later, when I tried to get to the bottom of the actual principles of mechanics in order to give an explanation of the laws of nature which are known through experience, I became aware that the consideration of an *extended mass* is not of itself enough, and that use must also be made of the notion of *force*, which is fully intelligible, although it falls within the sphere of metaphysics. It seemed to me also that the opinion of those who transform or degrade the lower animals into mere machines, though it seems possible, is improbable, and even against the order of things.

At first, when I had freed myself from the yoke of Aristotle, I had believed in the void and atoms, for it is this which best satisfies the imagination. But returning to this view after much meditation, I perceived that it is impossible to find *the principles of a true unity* in matter alone, or in what is merely passive, since everything in it is but a collection or accumulation of parts *ad infinitum*. Now a multiplicity can be real only if it is made up of *true unities* which come from elsewhere and are altogether different from mathematical points, which are nothing but extremities of the extended and modifications out of which it is certain that nothing *continuous* could be compounded. Therefore, to find these *real unities*, I was constrained to have recourse to what might be called a *real and animated point* or to an atom of substance which must embrace some element of form or of activity in order to make a complete being. It was thus necessary to recall and in a manner to rehabilitate *substantial forms*, which are so much decried to-day, but in a way which makes them intelligible and separates the use which must be made of them from their previous abuse. I found then that their nature consists of force and that from this there follows something analogous to feeling and to appetite; and that therefore it was necessary to form a conception of them resembling our ordinary notion of *souls*. But just as the soul must not be used to explain the detail of the economy of the animal's body, so I judged in the same way that these forms ought not to be used to explain the particular problems of nature, although they are necessary to establish true general principles. Aristotle calls them *first entelechies*; I call them, more intelligibly perhaps, *primary forces*, which contain not only the *act*, or the fulfilment of possibility, but also an original *activity*.

I saw that these forms and these souls must be indivisible like our mind; and indeed I recollected that this had been the opinion held by St. Thomas concerning the souls of the lower animals. But this truth revived the great difficulties about the origin and duration of souls and forms. For since every *simple substance* which possesses a true unity can have its beginning and end by miracle alone, it follows that they could not begin except by creation, nor come to an end except by annihilation. Thus (with the exception of such souls as God still wills to create expressly) I was obliged to recognize that the constitutive forms of substance must have been created with the world and that they go on subsisting always. Moreover, some of the Scholastics, such as Albert the Great and John Bacho, had a notion of some part of the truth about their origin. Nor ought our view to appear extraordinary, since we are only attributing to forms duration, which was granted to their atoms by the followers of Gassendi.

Nevertheless I deemed that we ought not to mix without

distinction or to confuse with other forms or souls, *minds* or rational souls, which are of a superior order and have incomparably more perfection than those forms embedded in matter which, on my view, are to be found everywhere, since in comparison with these others, minds or rational souls are little gods, made in the image of God, and having in them some glimmering of Divine light. This is why God governs minds as a prince governs his subjects, or as a father cares for his children; whereas He disposes of other substances as an engineer handles his machines. Thus minds have special laws which set them above the revolutions of matter, by the very order God has introduced into them; and it may truly be said that all the rest is made for them alone, the very revolutions being arranged for the felicity of the virtuous and the punishment of the wicked.

But to return to ordinary forms or *brute souls*, the fact that duration must now be attributed to them instead of to atoms as previously, might give rise to the doubt whether they do not pass from one body to another; this would be *metempsychosis*, more or less as some philosophers have thought occurred in the transmission of movement and of character. But this fancy is very far removed from the nature of things. There is no such passing. It is here that the *transformations* of MM. Swammerdam, Malpighi, and Leeuwenhoek, who are among the best observers of our day, have come to my assistance and have made me admit more readily that the animal and every other organized substance does not begin when we think, but that its apparent generation is only a development, a kind of increase. I have noticed, too, that the author of the *Recherche de la Vérité*,[1] M. Regis, M. Hartsoeker, and other clever men have not been very far removed from this opinion.

But there still remained the more important question of what becomes of these souls or forms at the death of the

[1] Malebranche.

animal, or at the destruction of the individual unit of organized substance. This question is the more awkward, inasmuch as it seems unreasonable that souls should remain useless in a chaos of confused matter. This ultimately made me decide that there was only one sensible thing to believe; that is to maintain the conservation not only of the soul but also of the animal itself and of its organic machine; even though the destruction of its grosser parts has reduced it to such smallness that it evades our senses, just as it did before birth. Moreover, nobody can mark precisely the true time of death, which may for a long time pass for a mere suspension of observable actions, and fundamentally is never anything else but that in the case of simple animals; witness the *resuscitations* of flies which have been drowned and then buried under powdered chalk, and several similar instances, which make us realize that there might be other resuscitations, and in cases which were much further gone, if men were in a position to readjust the machine. And it looks as though it were something of this nature which was discussed by the great Democritus, thoroughgoing atomist though he was, although it was made fun by Pliny. It is therefore natural that since the animal has always been living and organized (as some people of fine penetration are beginning to recognize), it should also always continue to be so. And since there is thus no first birth or entirely new generation of the animal, it follows that it will suffer no final extinction or complete death, in the strict metaphysical sense; and that consequently instead of a *transmigration* of souls, there occurs only a *transformation* of one and the same animal, according as its organs are differently folded, and more or less developed.

But rational souls obey much more exalted laws, and are immune from anything which could make them lose the status of citizens of the society of minds, since God has so well provided that no changes of matter could make them lose the moral qualities of their personality. And it may be said with truth that everything tends to the perfection not only of the universe in general, but also of these created beings in particular, who are destined for so high a degree of happiness that the universe becomes concerned in it by virtue of the divine goodness which is communicated to each created being, in so far as sovereign wisdom can permit.

As regards the ordinary body of animals and other corporeal substances, which have hitherto been held to suffer complete extinction, and whose changes depend rather on mechanical rules than on moral laws, I was pleased to note that the ancient author of the book *Of Regimen*, which is attributed to Hippocrates, had some notion of the truth when he expressly says that animals neither are born nor die, and that the things which are thought to come into being and to perish merely appear and disappear. This was also the opinion of Parmenides and of Melissus in the pages of Aristotle. For these ancient thinkers are sounder than is supposed.

I am as willing as any man to give the moderns their due; but I think they have carried reform too far, among other things in confusing the natural with the artificial, through not having had sufficiently exalted ideas of the majesty of Nature. They conceive that the difference between her machines and ours is but the difference between the great and the small. This recently led a very clever man[1] to remark that when looking at Nature from near at hand she appears less admirable than we thought, being no more than a workman's shop. I believe that this does not give a sufficiently just idea, or one sufficiently worthy of her, and there is no system except mine which properly exhibits the immense distance which really lies between the least productions and mechanisms of Divine wisdom and the greatest achievements of the skill of a limited mind. This

[1] Fontenelle.

difference is one not merely of degree, but of kind also. It must be recognized that Nature's machines possess a truly infinite number of organs, and are so well protected and armed against all accidents, that it is not possible to destroy them. A natural machine still remains a machine in its least parts, and, what is more, it always remains the very same machine that it was, being merely transformed by the different foldings it receives, and being sometimes stretched, sometimes contracted and as it were concentrated, when we think that it is destroyed.

Furthermore, by means of the soul or form, there is a true unity which corresponds to what is called the *I* in us; a thing which could not occur in artificial machines, nor in the simple mass of matter, however organized it may be. This can only be regarded as like an army or a flock, or like a pond full of fish, or a watch made up of springs and wheels. Yet if there were no true *substantial unities*, there would be nothing real or substantial in the collection. It was this that compelled M. Cordemoy to abandon Descartes, and to adopt Democritus's theory of atoms, in order to find a true unity. But *atoms of matter* are contrary to reason, besides the fact that they also are composed of parts, since the invincible attachment of one part to another (granted that this could be reasonably conceived or supposed) would not destroy their diversity. It is only *atoms of substance*, that is to say unities which are real and absolutely without parts, which can be the sources of actions, and the absolute first principles of the composition of things, and as it were the ultimate elements into which substantial things can be analysed. They might be called *metaphysical points*; there is about them *something vital* and a kind of *perception*, and *mathematical points* are their *points of view* for expressing the universe. But when corporeal substances are contracted all their organs constitute to us but a *physical point*. Thus physical points are indivisible in appearance only: mathematical points are exact, but they are nothing but modalities. It is only metaphysical points, or points of substance (constituted by forms or souls), which are both exact and real; and without them there would be nothing real, since without true unities there would be no plurality.

Once I had established these things, I thought I had reached port; but when I set myself to reflect on the union of the soul with the body, I seemed to be cast back again into the open sea. For I could find no way of explaining how the body causes something to happen in the soul, or vice versa, nor how one created substance can communicate with another. M. Descartes left the field at this stage, as far as we can gather from his writings; but his disciples, realizing that the common opinion is inconceivable, maintained that we are aware of the qualities of bodies because God produces thoughts in the soul on the occasion of the movements of matter; and when our soul wishes to move the body in its turn, they deemed that it is God that moves it for the soul. And as the communication of motion seemed to them likewise inconceivable, they maintained that God gives motion to a body on the occasion of the motion of another body. This is what they call *the System of occasional causes*, which has become very fashionable owing to the fine reflections of the author of the *Recherche de la Vérité*.[1]

It must be admitted that they have gone a great way in regard to this problem by showing what cannot possibly take place; but their explanation of what does in fact occur does not remove the difficulty. It is quite true that in the strict metaphysical sense there is no real influence exerted by one created substance on another, and that all things, with all their realities, are continually produced by the power of God: but to solve these problems it is not enough to make use of the general cause, and to drag in what is called the *deus ex machina*. For when this is done without giving any

[1] Malebranche.

further explanation in terms of the order of secondary causes, this is properly speaking to fall back on miracle. In philosophy, we must attempt to give an account showing in what way things are brought about by the Divine wisdom, in conformity with the notion of the subject in question.

Being thus constrained to grant that it is impossible for the soul or for any other true substance to receive anything from without, except by Divine omnipotence, I was insensibly led to adopt a view which surprises me, but which seems inevitable, and which does in fact possess very great advantages and considerable beauties. This view is that we must say that God first created the soul, and every other real unity, in such a way that everything in it must spring from within itself, by a perfect *spontaneity* with regard to itself, and yet in a perfect *conformity* with things outside. And thus, since our internal sensations (those, that is to say, which are in the soul itself and not in the brain or in the subtle parts of the body) are but phenomena dependent upon external entities, or rather are really appearances, and, as it were, well ordered dreams, these internal perceptions within the soul itself must arise in it from its own original constitution, that is to say through the natural representative ability (capable of expressing entities outside itself in relation to its organs) with which it has been endowed since its creation, and which constitutes its individual character. It follows from this that, since each of these substances exactly represents the whole universe in its own way and from a certain point of view, and since the perceptions or expressions of external things reach the soul at a determined point by virtue of its own laws and, as it were, in a world apart, as if nothing else existed but only God and itself (if I may make use of a way of speaking employed by a certain writer with a most exalted mind and famous for his holiness), there will be a perfect agreement between all these substances, producing the same effect as would occur if these communicated with one another by means of a transmission of species or qualities, as the common run of philosophers maintain. Furthermore, the organized mass, within which is the point of view of the soul, is itself more nearly expressed by it, and finds itself in its turn ready to act of itself according to the laws of the corporeal machine whenever the soul desires, without either disturbing the laws of the other, the animal spirits and the blood having precisely at the given moment the motions necessary to make them respond to the passions and perceptions of the soul; and it is this mutual relation, regulated in advance in every substance in the universe, which produces what we call their *communication*, and which alone constitutes *the union of the soul and the body*. And this makes it possible to understand how the soul has its seat in the body by an immediate presence, which could not be closer than it is, since it is present in the way in which the unity is present in that resultant of unities which is a plurality.

This hypothesis is very possible. For why should not God be able in the first instance to give to substance a nature or internal force capable of producing for it in order (as if it were an *automaton, spiritual and formal, but free* in the case of a substance which has a share of reason) everything that is going to happen to it, that is to say all the appearances and expressions it is going to have, and that without the assistance of any created thing? This is rendered all the more probable by the fact that the nature of substance necessarily requires and essentially involves a progress or change, without which it would have no force to act. And since it is the very nature of the soul to be representative of the universe in a very exact way (although with varying distinctness), the sequence of representations which the soul produces for itself will naturally correspond to the sequence of changes in the universe itself: while on the other hand the body has also been adjusted to the soul, in regard to the experiences in which the latter is conceived as acting outside itself. This is all the more reasonable in that bodies are only made for those minds which are capable of entering into society with God, and of celebrating His glory. Thus once we recognize the possibility of this *hypothesis of agreements*, we recognize also that it is the most reasonable one, and that it gives a wonderful idea of the harmony of the universe and of the perfection of the works of God.

There is in it this great advantage also, that instead of saying that we are free only in appearance and in a manner adequate for practice, as several ingenious men have held, we must rather say that we are determined in appearance only; and that in strict metaphysical language we are perfectly independent as regards the influence of all other created things. This again shows up in a marvellously clear light the immortality of our soul, and the ever uniform conservation of our individual self, which is perfectly well regulated of its own nature, and is beyond the reach of all accidents from outside, whatever the appearances to the contrary. No system has ever so clearly exhibited our exalted position. Since each mind is as it were a world apart, sufficient unto itself, independent of all other created things, including the infinite, expressing the universe, it is as lasting, as subsistent, and as absolute as the very universe of created things itself. We must therefore conclude that it must always play its part in the way most suited to contribute to the perfection of that society of all minds which constitutes their moral union in the City of God. Here, too, is a new and wonderfully clear proof of the existence of God. For this perfect agreement of all these substances, which have no point of communication with one another, could only come from the one common cause.

Besides the fact that this hypothesis is recommended by all these advantages, it may be added that it is something more than a hypothesis, since it seems hardly possible to explain things in any other intelligible way, and since several serious difficulties which have hitherto exercised men's minds seem to disappear of themselves when once it is properly understood. Ordinary ways of speaking can still be easily retained. For it may fairly be said that when the particular disposition of a given substance is the explanation of a change taking place in an intelligible manner, so that we can infer that it is to this substance that the others have been adjusted in this regard from the beginning, in accordance with the order of the decrees of God, then that substance ought to be conceived as in that respect *acting* upon the others. Further, the action of one substance on another is not a giving forth, or transplanting of an entity, as is commonly supposed; and it can reasonably be understood only in the way I have just described. It is true that we can easily conceive of matter both as giving out and as taking in parts; and it is in this way that we rightly explain in terms of mechanics all the phenomena of physics; but as the material mass is not a substance, it can be seen that action in regard to substance itself can only be such as I have just described.

These considerations, metaphysical though they may appear, are yet wonderfully useful in physics, for establishing the laws of motion, as my *Dynamics* will be able to establish. For the truth is that in the shock of impact each body suffers only from its own reaction, caused by the motion which is already in it. And as for absolute motion, nothing can determine it mathematically, since everything terminates in relations. This means that there is always a perfect equivalence of hypotheses, as in astronomy; so that whatever number of bodies we take, we may at our own discretion assign rest, or any given degree of velocity, to any particular one of them we wish, without its being possible for us to be refuted by the phenomena of motion, whether in a straight line, circular, or composite. It is, however, reasonable to attribute to bodies true motions, in accordance with the supposition which explains phenomena in the most intelligible way; and this way of speaking is in conformity with the notion of activity which we have just established.

Explanation of the New System of the Communication of Substances, in reply to what is said about it in the 'Journal' of 12 September 1695 [1]

... I recollect, sir, that I thought I was complying with your desire in imparting to you my philosophical hypothesis some years ago, though at the same time I pointed out that I had not yet decided to acknowledge it. In return I asked your opinion of it; but I do not remember receiving any objections from you, otherwise with my usual docility I should certainly not have given you occasion to raise the same ones a second time. Yet they are still not too late, although they reach me after publication, for I am not one of those for whom the being committed to a view takes the place of sound reasoning, as you will find when you are able to say you have adduced some precise and pressing reason against my opinions—which, it appears, is not your aim. You wish rather to speak as an able Academic, and thereby to provide an opportunity of going more deeply into the matter.

1. It was my aim here to expound, not the principles of extension, but the principles of that which is in fact extended, or of bodily mass. These principles, according to me, are the real units, that is to say the substances that possess a true unity.

2. The unity of a clock, to which you refer, is on my view quite other than the unity of an animal; the latter may be a substance possessing a true unity, like that in us which is called the *I*; whereas a clock is nothing but an assemblage.

[1] A letter from Foucher to Leibniz was published in this copy of the *Journal*, giving a number of objections to the New System. For an earlier letter of Leibniz to Foucher, see pp. 45–51.

3. It is not in the disposition of the organs that I find the principle of consciousness in animals; I agree that this disposition concerns nothing but the bodily mass.

4. I mention these things to prevent misunderstandings and to show that what you say about them is not contrary to what I have propounded. It seems that you do not make me out to be wrong when I demand true unities, and when that makes me rehabilitate substantial forms. But when you appear to say that the souls of brutes must have some share of reason if they are allowed to have sensation, that is a conclusion the proof of which I do not see.

5. You recognize with commendable sincerity that my hypothesis of harmony or concomitance is a possible one. But none the less you are still somewhat averse to it, no doubt because you believed that it was purely arbitrary, and did not realize that it follows from my view of unities, and that my whole contention stands or falls together.

6. You therefore ask me, sir, what can be the purpose of all this artifice which I attribute to the Author of nature—as if it were possible for too much artifice to be attributed to Him, and as if this exact correspondence of unities with one another through their own laws, which each received at the beginning, were not a thing admirably beautiful in itself and worthy of its Author. You further ask what advantage I find in this theory.

7. I might refer to what I have already said about this. Still, I answer in the first place that when a thing cannot not be so, it is not necessary to ask what can be the purpose of it before admitting it. What is the purpose of the incommensurability of the side with the diagonal?

8. In the second place I answer that this correspondence serves the purpose of explaining the communication of substances and the union of the soul with the body by means of the laws of nature established in advance, without having recourse either to a transmission of species, which is incon-

ceivable, **or to** a fresh intervention of God, which does not appear admissible. For we must realize that as there are natural laws in matter, so there are also natural laws in souls or forms, and these laws mean what I have just stated.

9. I am further asked how it happens that God is not content to produce all the thoughts and *modifications* of the soul, without these *useless* bodies which the soul (it is said) can neither *move* nor *know*. The answer is easy. It is that it was God's will that there should be a greater rather than a lesser number of substances, and He found it good that these *modifications* should correspond to something outside.

10. There is no *useless* substance; they all have their contribution to make to God's design.

11. Also I do not admit that the soul *does not know* bodies, though this knowledge arises without their influencing one another.

12. I should have no objection even to saying that the soul *moves* the body; in the same way as a Copernican rightly speaks of the rising of the sun, a Platonist of the reality of matter, a Cartesian of the reality of sensible qualities, provided these statements are sanely understood, so I believe that it is very true to say that substances act upon one another, provided it is understood that the one is the cause of changes in the other in consequence of the laws of harmony.

13. The objection touching the *lethargy* of bodies (namely that the bodies might be inactive even when the soul believed them to be in motion) cannot stand because of this same unfailing correspondence, established by Divine wisdom.

14. I have no knowledge of these *vain, useless, and inactive masses*, to which reference is made. There is activity everywhere; indeed, I maintain this more than the received philosophy, because I hold that there is no body without motion, nor substance without force.

15. I do not understand the precise nature of the objection contained in the words: *In truth, sir, can we not see that these*

*views are formed with a set purpose, and that these systems,
coming after the event, have only been manufactured to vindicate
certain principles?* All hypotheses are formed *with a set
purpose*, and all systems come *after the event* to vindicate
phenomena or appearances. But I do not see which are
the principles in favour of which I am supposed to be prejudiced, and which I want to vindicate.

16. If this means that I am led to my hypothesis by *a
priori* reasons also, or by fixed principles, as is in fact the
case, this is rather a commendation of the hypothesis than
an objection to it. It commonly suffices for a hypothesis
to be proved *a posteriori*, because it satisfies the phenomena;
but when we have other reasons as well, and those *a priori*,
it is so much the better.

17. But perhaps what is meant is that when I had invented
a new view for myself, I was very glad to make use of it,
more to assume airs on account of its novelty than because
I recognized it to be useful. I do not know, sir, whether
you have so poor an opinion of me as to attribute such
thoughts to me. For you know that I love truth; and that
if I had such a feeling for novelties, I should be in a greater
hurry to produce them, especially those whose solidity is
recognized. But in order that those who know me less
well should not endow your words with a meaning which
we should not like, suffice it to say that in my view it is
impossible to explain *transeunt activity* in conformity with
the laws of nature in any other way, and that I believed that
the value of my hypothesis would be recognized in view of
the difficulty which the ablest philosophers of our time have
found in the communication of minds and bodies, and even of
bodily substances one with another. I do not know whether
you yourself have encountered any of these difficulties.

18. It is true that there are, on my view, forces in all
substances; but these forces are, strictly speaking, only in
the substance itself; and what follows from them in the

other substances is only by virtue of a *pre-established harmony*, if I may use the word, and not by any real influence, or by the transmission of some species or quality. As I have explained the nature of activity and passivity, the nature of force and of resistance can readily be inferred.

19. You say, sir, *that you know that there are still many more questions to be put before we can decide those which we have been discussing.* But perhaps you will find that I have already put them: I am not sure that your Academics have put into practice the valuable parts of their method more rigorously and effectively than I myself have done. I strongly approve of the attempt to prove truths from first principles; this is more useful than is commonly supposed, and I have often put this precept into practice. Thus I welcome what you say on this subject, and I hope your example will lead our philosophers to think about it as they should.

20. I will add a further reflection which seems to me to be of considerable assistance towards the better understanding of the reality and value of my system. You know that M. Descartes believed that the same quantity of motion is conserved in bodies. It has been demonstrated that he was mistaken in this; but I have shown that it is always true that the same motive force—instead of, as he thought, the same quantity of motion — is conserved. Even so, the changes which take place in the body as a consequence of the modifications of the soul caused him embarrassment, because they seemed to violate this law. He thought therefore that he had found a way out of the difficulty, which is certainly ingenious, by saying that we must distinguish between motion and direction of motion; and that the soul cannot increase or diminish the motive force, but that it changes the direction or determination of the course of the animal spirits, and it is in this way that voluntary motions take place. It is true that he made no attempt to explain

how the soul sets about changing the course of bodies—and in fact this seems as inconceivable as saying that it gives them motion, unless you have recourse, as I do, to pre-established harmony. But the truth is that there is *another law of nature*, which I have discovered and proved, and which M. Descartes did not know: namely, that *there is conserved* not only the same quantity of motive force, but also *the same quantity of direction from whatever side in the world it be taken*. That is to say: take any straight line you like, and take also any number of bodies, chosen as you please; you will find that, considering all these bodies together without leaving out any of those which act on any of those which you have taken, there will always be the same quantity of progression from the same side in all the lines parallel to the straight line you have chosen: provided care is taken that the sum total of progression is estimated by deducting that of the bodies which go in the opposite direction from that of those which go in the direction chosen. This law is as beautiful and as general as the other, and deserves as little to be violated: and this is so in my system, which conserves both force and direction, and, in a word, all the natural laws of bodies, notwithstanding the changes which occur in them as a result of those in the soul.

P.S.   Hanover, 3/13 January 1696.

I see clearly from your reflections that I need to throw some light on that idea of mine which a friend caused to be inserted in the *Journal de Paris*. You say, sir, that you do not see how I could prove what I propounded concerning the communication or harmony of two substances as different as the soul and the body. It is true that I thought I had supplied the means of doing so. And I hope that what follows will satisfy you.

Imagine two clocks or watches which are in perfect

agreement. Now this agreement may come about *in three ways*. *The first* consists of a natural influence. This is what M. Huygens tried with a result that surprised him. He suspended two pendulums from the same piece of wood; the continual strokes of the pendulums communicated similar vibrations to the particles of the wood; but since these different vibrations could not well persist independently and without interfering with one another, unless the pendulums were in agreement, it happened by some sort of miracle that even when their strokes had been purposely disturbed, they soon went back to swinging together, rather like two strings [1] which are in unison. *The second method* of achieving the constant agreement of two clocks, albeit imperfect ones, would be to have them continually supervised by a skilful craftsman who should be constantly setting them right. *The third method* is to construct the two clocks so skilfully and accurately at the outset that one could be certain of their subsequent agreement.

Now substitute the soul and the body for these two watches. Their agreement or sympathy will also arise in one of these three ways. *The way of influence* is that of ordinary philosophy; but as it is impossible to conceive of either material particles, or immaterial species or qualities, as capable of passing from one of these substances to the other, we are obliged to abandon this view. *The way of assistance* is that of the system of occasional causes. But I hold that this is bringing in the *deus ex machina* for a natural and ordinary thing, where reason requires it to intervene in the same way only as it contributes to all other things in nature. Thus there remains only my hypothesis, that it to say *the way of pre-established harmony*—pre-established, that is, by a Divine anticipatory artifice, which so formed each of these substances from the beginning, that in merely following its own laws, which it received with its being, it is yet in accord with the

[1] i.e. strings of a musical instrument.

other, just as if they mutually influenced one another, or as if, over and above His work of general co-ordination, God were for ever putting in His hand to set them right. After this I do not think there is anything for me to prove, unless I am desired to prove that God possesses the cleverness necessary for making use of this anticipatory artifice, of which we see samples among men, in proportion as they are clever people. And supposing that He can, it is clear that this is the finest way and the worthiest of Him. You had some suspicion that my explanation would be opposed to the rather different idea we have of mind and body. But now you see clearly, sir, that no one has better established their independence. For so long as it was necessary to explain their communication by a kind of miracle, it was always left open to some people to fear that the distinction between them might not be what it was supposed to be, because it was necessary to go to such lengths to uphold it. Now all these scruples disappear. My *Essays on Dynamics* are connected with this; in them I had to inquire more deeply into the notion of bodily substance, which on my view lies rather in the force of acting and resisting than in extension, which is but a repetition or diffusion of something anterior, that is to say, of this force. And as these thoughts of mine, which to some have appeared paradoxical, have caused me to exchange letters with various well-known men, I could produce a *Commercium Epistolicum* on the subject, into which would come my correspondence with M. Arnauld, of which I spoke in my previous letter. It will contain a curious mixture of thoughts about philosophy and mathematics, which will perhaps sometimes have the charm of novelty. I leave you to judge, sir, whether the explanations I have just given are suitable for sounding the opinions of enlightened people through the intermediary of your journal. But do not give my name, as it was not given in the *Journal de Paris* either.

Extract from a Letter of M. D L.[1] Regarding his
Philosophical Hypothesis in the Curious Problem,
Propounded to the Mathematicians by one of his
Friends, with an Explanation Regarding some Dis-
puted Points in Preceding 'Journals' between the
Author of the 'Principles of Physics'[2] and the
Author of the 'Objections'.[3] 1696

. . . Let me say [4] a word on the subject of the dispute between
two very clever people, the author of the *Principles of Physics*,
published recently, and the author of the *Objections* (included
in the *Journal* of 13th August and elsewhere), since my
hypothesis serves to end these controversies. I do not
understand how matter can be conceived as being extended,
and yet as being without parts either actual or mental. If
this be possible, I do not know what it is to be extended.
I even hold that matter is essentially an aggregate, and
consequently that it always has actual parts. Thus it is by
reason, and not only by the senses, that we judge that it is
divided, or rather that it is ultimately nothing but a plurality.
I hold that it is true that matter (and even each part of
matter) is divided into a greater number of parts than it is
possible to imagine. It is this that makes me often say that
each body, however small, is a world of created things infinite
in number. Thus I do not believe that there are atoms, that
is to say parts of matter which are perfectly hard, or invincibly solid; just as on the other hand I do not believe
either that there exists matter which is perfectly fluid. My

[1] M. D. L. is a pseudonym of Leibniz.
[2] Nicolas Hartsoeker (1656–1725), a Dutch physicist, mainly
concerned with the making of microscopes and telescopes. His
correspondence with Leibniz about his philosophy of nature
is extant.
[3] Foucher. Cf. p. 45, note.
[4] The first part of this letter repeats the illustration of the two
clocks, given above; the second part deals with the solution of a
purely mathematical problem; the third part is given here.

view is that each body is fluid in comparison with more solid ones, and solid in comparison with more fluid ones. I am surprised that it should still be said that there is always conserved an equal quantity of motion in the Cartesian sense; for I have proved the opposite, and already excellent mathematicians have accepted my view. However, I do not consider the hardness or consistency of bodies as a primary quality, but as a consequence of motion, and I hope that my *Dynamics* will show wherein this consists; just as the understanding of my hypothesis will also serve to remove several difficulties which still exercise philosophers. Indeed, I believe I can answer intelligibly all the doubts to which the late M. Bernier devoted a whole book, and those who are ready to ponder what I have previously published will perhaps already find therein the means of doing so.

EXPLANATION OF THE DIFFICULTIES WHICH M. BAYLE FOUND IN THE NEW SYSTEM OF THE UNION OF THE SOUL AND THE BODY

I take the liberty, sir, of sending you this explanation of the difficulties which M. Bayle found in the hypothesis which I suggested to explain the union of the soul and the body. Nothing could be more accommodating than the manner in which he has treated me in regard to it; and I consider myself honoured by the objections which he included in his excellent *Dictionary*, under the article 'Rorarius'. Moreover, so great and profound a mind as his cannot make objections without being instructive, and I will try to take advantage of the light he has thrown on these questions, both here and in several other places in his work. He does not reject what I said about the conservation of the soul and even of the animal,[1] but he does not yet appear to be satisfied by the way in which I claimed to explain the union and intercourse between the soul and the body, in the *Journal des Savans* of 27th June and 4th

[1] i.e. the whole animal, soul and bodily organism.

July 1695, and in the *Histoire des Ouvrages des Savans* of February 1696, pages 274 and 275.

These are his words, and they seem to show where it was that he found difficulty: *I am unable to understand* (he says) *that necessary connection between internal and spontaneous actions which would cause the soul of a dog to experience pain immediately after having experienced joy, even though it were alone in the universe.* I answer, that when I said that the soul would experience everything it now experiences, though there were only God and itself in the world, I did but employ a fiction, that is, I postulated what could not happen naturally in order to make it clear that the feelings of the soul are nothing but a consequence of what is already present in it. I do not know whether M. Bayle means to demonstrate the incomprehensibility of the necessary connection only in what he says below, or whether he also intends to indicate it at once by giving this example of the spontaneous transition from joy to pain. Perhaps he wishes to give us to understand that this transition is opposed to the axiom which teaches that a thing remains always in the state in which it once is, if nothing supervenes to cause it to change; and that therefore when an animal once feels joy, it will feel it always if it is alone, and there is nothing outside it to cause it to pass to pain. In any case, I remain in agreement with the axiom, and even claim that it is favourable to me, as indeed it is one of my fundamental principles. Is it not the case that from this axiom we conclude, not only that a body that is at rest will always remain at rest, but also that a body that is in motion will always retain this motion or change, that is to say the same velocity and the same direction, if nothing supervenes to prevent it? Thus it is not simply that in so far as depends upon itself a body remains in the state in which it is, but also when it is in a state of change it continues to change—and this in accordance with the very same law. Now according to me, it is the nature of created substance to change continually following a certain order, by which it is led *spontaneously* (if I may be allowed to use this word) through all the states which are to happen to it, so that He who sees everything sees in its present state all its states both past and to come. And this law of order, which constitutes the individuality of each particular substance, has an exact relation to what occurs in every other substance, and in the whole universe. Possibly I am not making too bold a claim, if I say that I can prove all this; but at the moment it is only a question of upholding it as a possible hypothesis, and one fitted to explain the phenomena. Now in this way the law governing the changing of the substance of the animal bears him from joy to pain, at the moment when there occurs in his body an interruption of continuity, because the law of the indivisible substance of this animal is to represent what occurs in his body in the manner in which we experience it, and even to represent in some fashion and in relation to this body everything that occurs in the world; for the unities of substance are nothing else but different concentrations of the universe, represented according to the different points of view which distinguish them.

M. Bayle continues: *I understand why a dog passes immediately from pleasure to pain when, after being famished and eating bread, he is struck with a stick.* I am not sure that this *is* sufficiently well understood. No one knows better than M. Bayle himself that just herein lies the great difficulty we find in explaining why what happens in the body causes a change in the soul; and that it is just this which has driven those who uphold occasional causes to have recourse to the care that must be taken by God to see that all changes which occur in a body shall be continually represented to its soul: whereas I believe that it is its own nature, given it by God, to represent to itself, by virtue of its own laws, what occurs in its organs. He continues:

But that his soul is so constructed that at the moment when he is struck he would feel pain even if he were not struck, but were to continue eating bread without let or hindrance, that is what I cannot understand. Neither do I recollect having said so; nor could it be said except by a metaphysical fiction, as when we suppose that God annihilates some body to create a void, both suppositions being equally contrary to the order of things. For since the nature of the soul was originally made in a manner fitted to represent to itself in succession the changes of matter, the supposed case could not arise in the natural order. God could have given to each substance its own phenomena independent of those of others, but in this way He would have made, as it were, as many unconnected worlds as there are substances; very much in the same way as we say that when a man dreams, he is in his own world apart, but that he enters the common world when he wakes. It is not that dreams themselves are unrelated to the organs and to the rest of the body, but that they are related in a less distinct manner. Let us continue with M. Bayle.

Further, the spontaneity of this soul (he says) *seems to me quite incompatible with feelings of pain, and in general, with all perceptions which are not pleasing to it.* This incompatibility would be certain if spontaneity and voluntariness were the same thing. Everything which is voluntary is spontaneous; but there are spontaneous actions which occur without choice, and which consequently are not voluntary. It does not rest with the soul to give itself always feelings which are pleasing to it; for the feelings which it is going to have are dependent on those which it has had. M. Bayle proceeds:

Moreover, the reason why this gifted man does not fancy the Cartesian system appears to me a false supposition, for it cannot be said that the system of occasional causes makes the action of God intervene by miracle (deus ex machina) *in the reciprocal dependence of the body and the soul: for as God does not intervene except in accordance with general laws, His action in this matter is not in any way out of the ordinary.* It is not for this reason alone that I do not fancy the Cartesian system; and some slight consideration of my own doctrine will show that I find in it positive reasons for adopting it. Even if the hypothesis of occasional causes had no recourse to miracle, it appears to me that mine would none the less possess other advantages. I have said that three systems can be imagined which might explain the communion between the soul and the body; that is, (1) the system of the influence of the one on the other, which is that of the Schools, taken in the common sense—this I agree with the Cartesians in believing to be impossible; (2) the system of a perpetual supervisor, who represents in the one what takes place in the other, very much as if a man were entrusted with the task of securing the agreement of two bad clocks, which would not of themselves be capable of agreeing—this is the system of occasional causes; and (3) the system of the natural agreement of two substances, such as would arise with two very accurate clocks—this system I hold to be as possible as the system of the supervisor, and more worthy of the Author of these substances, clocks, or automata. But now let us see whether the system of occasional causes does not in fact presuppose a perpetual miracle. M. Bayle says that it does not, because according to this system God would not act except through general laws. Granted, but on my view this is not enough to obviate the miracles; even were God to perform them continually, they would not cease to be miracles, if we take this word not in the popular sense of a rare and marvellous thing, but in the philosophical sense of that which is beyond the powers of created things. It is not enough to say that God made a general law; for besides the decree there must also be a natural means of carrying it out; that is to say, what occurs must be able to be explained by the nature with which things are endowed by God. The laws of nature are not so arbitrary or so indifferent as some people believe. If, for example, God decreed that all bodies should tend to move in circles, and that the radii of the circles should be proportionate to the size of the bodies, we should have either to say that there was a way of carrying this out by means of simpler laws, or else to admit that God brought it about miraculously, or at least by means of angels expressly entrusted with the task, something like the angels who in earlier times were supposed to be attached to the celestial spheres. The same would be true if someone maintained that God had endowed bodies with natural and primary gravities, by means of which each tended to move towards the centre of its own sphere, without being impelled by other bodies; in my opinion this system would require a perpetual miracle, or at least the assistance of angels.

Does the internal and active power which is communicated to the forms of bodies know the sequence of actions which it will produce? By no means; for we learn from experience that we do not know that we shall have such and such perceptions an hour hence. I reply that this power, or rather this soul or form itself, does not know them distinctly, but that it feels them confusedly. There are in every substance traces of everything that has happened to it and of everything that will happen to it. But the infinite multitude of these perceptions prevents us from distinguishing between them, in the same way as when I hear a loud and confused noise made by a crowd I am unable to distinguish one voice from another.

It would thus be necessary for these forms to be directed by some external principle in the production of their actions; is not this the deus ex machina *again just the same as in the system of occasional causes?* My foregoing answer shows that this conclusion does not follow. On the contrary, the present state of every substance is a natural consequence of its preceding state, but only an infinite intelligence can grasp this sequence—for it involves the whole universe—whether in souls or in any given portion of matter.

M. Bayle concludes with these words: *Finally, since he supposes, and rightly so, that all souls are simple and indivisible, it is impossible to understand how they can be compared to a pendulum, that it to say that by their original constitution they can vary their operations in utilizing the spontaneous activity received from their Creator. It is quite clear that a simple being will always act uniformly, if turned aside by no outside cause. If it were composed of several parts like a machine, its actions would show variety, because the particular activity of each part might at any moment change the course of the activity of the others; but in a single substance, where will you find the cause of a change of operation?* This objection I consider to be worthy of M. Bayle: it is one of those which most deserve to be elucidated. But I also believe that if I had not previously provided for it, my system would not deserve to be examined. I compared the soul to a pendulum only in regard to the regulated exactitude of its changes, which is but imperfect in the best of clocks, though perfect in the works of God; and it may be said that the soul is an immaterial automaton of the most exact kind. When it is said that a simple being always acts uniformly, a distinction has to be made: if *to act uniformly* is to follow perpetually the same law of order, or of continuance, as in a given set or sequence of numbers, I admit that of itself every simple being, and even every compound being, acts uniformly; but if by *uniformly* is meant similarly, then I do not agree. Let me explain the difference of meaning by an example: a movement in a parabola is uniform in the first sense, but not in the second, for the parts of the parabola are not similar to one another, as are those of a straight line. . . .[1]

[1] In the few lines here omitted Leibniz comments 'by the way' on Bayle's statement that a simple body left to itself describes a straight line. He points out that this is true if we consider only

We must also remember that the soul, simple though it is, has always a sensation which is composed of several perceptions at once; and this serves the purpose for my theory as much as if it were composed of parts, like a machine. For each preceding perception has some influence on those which follow, in conformity with a law of order which is to be found in perceptions as well as in motions. Moreover, the majority of philosophers, for several centuries, who have endowed with thoughts both souls and angels (whom they hold to be destitute of all body), not to mention the intelligences of Aristotle, admit the occurrence of spontaneous change in a simple being. I add that, since the perceptions which exist together in the same soul at the same time include a truly infinite multitude of small feelings, indistinguishable from one another, which the future will develop, we must not be surprised at the infinite variety of what must result from them in the course of time. All this is but a consequence of the representative nature of the soul, which is bound to express everything that is occurring and even everything that is going to occur in its own body, and in some manner in all other bodies, owing to the connection or correspondence between all the parts of the world. It would perhaps have been enough to say that since God has made corporeal automata, He could easily likewise have made immaterial ones to represent them; but I thought it would be well to develop this matter a little further.

For the rest, I have read with pleasure what M. Bayle says in the article 'Zeno'. Perhaps he will notice that what can be derived from it agrees better with my system than with any other; for whatever is real in extension and in motion

the centre of the body; but in the case of a rotating body, a point in it distant from the centre describes a circle when the centre is stationary, and a more complicated curve (of which Leibniz gives the co-ordinates) when the centre is moving in a straight line. But he does not press this mathematical point into service for his general argument here.

consists only in the foundation of the order and regulated sequence of phenomena and perceptions. The Academics and the Sceptics, no less than those who wished to reply to them, seem to have been in difficulties only because they sought a greater reality in the sensible things outside us than the reality of regulated phenomena. We conceive of *extension*, by conceiving an order in co-existences; but we ought not to conceive of it, nor ought we to conceive of space after the manner of a substance. It is like *time*, which presents to the mind nothing but an order among changes. And as to *motion*, what is real in it is the *force* or power, that is to say, that which in the present state carries with it a change for the future. The rest is but phenomena and relations.

The consideration of this system shows also that when we go deeply into things, we find more sound sense than we thought in the majority of philosophical sects. . . .

REMARKS UPON THE ARTICLE 'RORARIUS' IN M. BAYLE'S *DICTIONARY*

1. *My first comment* [1] *is that M. Leibniz exalts beyond anything that can be conceived the power and intelligence of Divine art.* I agree that he exalts it beyond anything that can be understood, but not beyond anything that can be conceived.

Imagine a ship having neither feeling nor knowledge, and with no being created or uncreated at the helm, to have the power to move itself of its own nature so skilfully that it always enjoys a favourable wind, avoids currents and shallows, and finds a haven just at the right moment. Suppose such a ship sailing thus for several years continuously, always turned in the very direction and situated in the very place required by the changes of atmosphere and the different situations of land and sea;

[1] Italics indicate quotations from Bayle's *Dictionary*. From this paper an extract only is given here.

you will agree that the infinitude of God is not greater than is necessary to endow a ship with such a faculty, *and you will even say that a ship's nature is not capable of receiving* this power *from God. Yet what M. Leibniz supposes regarding the machine of the human body is more wonderful and more surprising than all this.*

I will first reply to the question whether the supposition of such a ship is possible. And afterwards I will come to the comparison here made with the machine of the human body. In the first place I find it strange that M. Bayle should dare to decide the question in the negative, and to deny that this is possible to God, without adducing any reason, when he himself often agrees that anything which does not imply a contradiction or imperfection could be produced by the Divinity. I admit that M. Bayle would be right if God were being required to endow the ship with some faculty, perfection, or occult quality, by which it could of itself direct its own course, without any knowledge within itself and without any attraction or direction from without, like the Phaeacians' vessel in Homer's *Odyssey.* For such a supposition would be impossible, and would violate the principle of sufficient reason, since it would be impossible to give any explanation of such a perfection, and God would always have to be setting His hand to it by a perpetual miracle—unless some occasionalist thought it suitable to have recourse to his supposed general laws, since God might promulgate one in favour of this ship; nor could M. Bayle, who is anxious to divorce occasional causes from miracles, reasonably object to this. For myself, I reject these natural laws exemption from which is absolutely explicable by the nature of things. But while we reject this occult quality in the ship, we must admit that there is nothing to prevent there being a ship, born under a lucky star as it were, so that it always reaches port, without guidance by the winds and tides, through storms and shallows, simply by encountering favourable accidents. Certain it is that ships without men have sometimes reached their destined shore. Is there anything that makes it impossible for this to happen several times to the same ship, and consequently as many times as it puts to sea—which will only happen a certain number of times? Since the number of accidents is not infinite, not only God but even an exceedingly excellent finite spirit would be able to foresee all the accidents to which the ship would be exposed, and could find out by solving a geometrico-mechanical problem the structure of the ship and the places, times, and methods of its putting to sea which would make it adjust itself in the best way to this finite number of accidents. Do we not know that men are sufficiently skilful to make automata capable of turning at a specified place at street corners, and of adjusting themselves in this way to a certain number of accidents? And a Mind proportionally greater would provide against accidents in greater numbers. And if this excellent Mind did not find these accidents already given, but was free to make them arise or cease at His will, it would be incomparably easier still for Him to satisfy this demand, and to adjust in advance and by a pre-established harmony the ship to the accidents and the accidents to the ship. Thus it is the gravest mistake to doubt whether the infinity of God is great enough to be able to succeed in this.

2. *Let us apply to the person of Caesar the new system of the union of the soul and the body: according to this system we must say that the body of Julius Caesar exercised its motive power in such a way that from birth to death it followed a constant progression of changes which corresponded in the last degree of exactness to the perpetual changes of a particular soul which the body did not know, and which made no impression on it.*

Bodies do not know what takes place in the soul, and the soul makes no physical impression on the body. M. Bayle agrees with this; but God has supplied this lack not by Himself giving the body at intervals new impressions to make it obey the soul, but by making this automaton such in the first place that it will carry out what the soul commands punctually as to both time and place.

We must say that the rule according to which this faculty *of Caesar's body had to produce these actions was such that he would have gone to the Senate on such a day and at such an hour, that he would there have uttered such and such words, etc., even though it had pleased God to annihilate Caesar's soul the day after it was created.*

There is nothing strange in this when once we bear in mind that as great a craftsman as God can make an automaton which resembles a valet and is capable of performing his function, and of carrying out at a specified place whatever it was ordered to do over a long period of time. The body is an automaton of this kind in regard to the mind.

We must say that this motive power *punctually changed itself and modified itself in accordance with the volubility of the thoughts of that ambitious spirit, and that it assumed precisely such a particular state rather than any other, because the soul of Caesar passed from one particular thought to another.*

It seems that M. Bayle has let himself be deceived, for he has imagined that the ship or the man's body was endowed with some mysterious *faculty* or *power* capable of adjusting itself to the accidents or the thoughts without having any knowledge of them, and even without any intelligible reason. He is entirely justified in condemning such a faculty as impossible, but no one ever thought of such a thing. All that the automaton which played the valet would need would be a structure which would make it perform its functions by virtue of the rules of mechanics. It would not modify itself nor change itself to adjust itself to the thoughts of its master. It would follow its own course, and by that very means would exactly fall in with the will of him whom the craftsman who made it meant it to serve.

Can a blind force so conveniently modify itself as the result of an impression *conveyed 30 or 40 years previously, and never since renewed, and which has moreover been left to itself without ever having any knowledge of its lesson? Is this not much more incomprehensible than the navigation of which I spoke in the preceding paragraph?*

It becomes clearer and clearer that M. Bayle has not properly grasped my view, which is that the body modifies itself in the required way not by some kind of *impression* or power it has received, but by its own structure, which is adjusted to that end. The automaton which plays the valet will again serve to remove the whole difficulty. The structure with which it has been endowed suffices for all its functions, even if it is left to itself, even if its first impressions are not renewed, and even if it has no knowledge of the command or of the lesson given to it. And the difference between the body of Caesar and this automaton is but the difference between the greater and the less.[1]

4. *It is vain for upholders of the view that the brutes are nothing but automata to shelter themselves behind the power of God. It is vain to explain that God was able to construct machines, so artfully wrought that the voice of a man, the reflected light of an object, etc., strike them in precisely the right place so that they move in such and such a way. Every one, except a few of the Cartesians, rejects this supposition.*

It is rejected not as impossible but as unlikely.

And there is no Cartesian who would accept the view if it were extended to man, that is to say if it were maintained that

---

[1] Bayle points out (in § 3, which is omitted here) that the changes which occur in the soul, corresponding to all the actions and interactions between the organs of the body and between the body and other bodies, are *infinite* in number, and urges that this infinity makes the theory of a pre-established harmony between spontaneous unities quite incredible. Leibniz replies that the fact that the variety of changes is infinite does nothing to increase the difficulty; it only gives ground for 'wondering still further at the Divine artifice'.

God was able to make bodies which could perform mechanically all the things that we see other men do.

The Cartesian will not deny that it is possible for God to make such an automaton; but he will not allow that other men are in fact inanimate automata of this kind. He will think, and rightly, that they are like himself. According to my view, all alike are automata, the bodies of men as well as those of brutes, but all of them are animated, the bodies of brutes as well as those of men. Thus pure materialists, such as the followers of Democritus, no less than formalists, such as the Platonists and Peripatetics, are right in some things, and wrong in others. There is a great deal of justification for the view of the followers of Democritus that the bodies of men as well as those of brutes are automata and perform all their actions mechanically; but they were wrong in thinking that these machines were not accompanied by an immaterial substance or form, and that matter was capable of perception. The Platonists and the Peripatetics held that brutes and men have animated bodies, but they were wrong in thinking that souls change the rules of the motion of bodies; thus they denied the automatism of the body of both brute and man. The Cartesians were right to reject this influence, but they were mistaken in denying automatism to man and sensation to brutes. I hold that we must allow both to both men and brutes, that we must follow Democritus in making all the actions of mechanical bodies independent of souls, and that we must also go further than the Platonists in holding that all the actions of souls are immaterial and independent of the machine.

In denying this we do not claim to set limits to the power and knowledge of God. We simply mean that the nature of things requires that the powers *given to the created being should necessarily have certain limitations. It is absolutely necessary that the activity of created things should be proportioned to their essential state, that it should be exercised in accordance with the character which is fitted to the given machine ; for according to the axioms of the philosophers everything which is received is proportioned to the capacity of the subject.*

M. Bayle keeps on reverting to this supposed power given to the body to enable it to accommodate itself to the soul. I do not require any such thing; I do not go outside the limitations of created things, nor of the state of bodies or machines. There is nothing in the artifice of the Divine machine which surpasses the knowledge and the power of God. Since He knows everything which can be known, and can do everything which can be done, He knows the number (which is limited) of the volitions of man: and He has the ability to make a machine capable of carrying them out.

We may therefore reject as impossible M. Leibniz's hypothesis, since it involves greater difficulties than that of automatism.

This argument would be good if the theory of automata had been convicted of impossibility, but since the contrary is manifest and has been sufficiently proved by the Cartesians, it is only a question of greater and less, which involves no difficulty when it is a question of a power and a wisdom which are infinite. Although man reasons about matters which are abstract and which surpass the imagination, he none the less has in his imagination signs which correspond to them, such as letters and characters. There is no understanding so pure as not to be accompanied by some imagination. Thus there is always in the body something mechanical which corresponds exactly to the sequence of thoughts present in a man's mind, in so far as that which can be imagined enters into the matter, and consequently the automaton of his body has no more need of the influence of the soul, or of the supernatural assistance of God, than has that of the brute's body.

It maintains the existence of a continual harmony between two substances which do not act on one another.

Why not? since they originate from one and the same

Author who was willing and able to arrange that they should agree without acting on one another.

But if the valets were machines, and punctually performed this and that whenever their master commanded, such a thing could only be if the master really acted on them: he would utter words and would make signs which would really affect the organs of the valets.

But there are valets who are so well trained as not to need signs to be given to them. They anticipate them. Watches which strike, for instance, and alarm clocks are valets of this kind. Far from awaiting signs, they give them to us. The artificial valet, who imitates and counterfeits a real one, such as we have been speaking of above, does not even need to be wound or set by us, as do watches and alarm clocks. The Artificer would have prepared him for us. Such a valet is our body.

5. If we consider at this point the soul of Caesar, we shall find still more impossibilities. This soul was in the world without being exposed to the influence of any body or of any mind. The force it had received from God was the sole principle of the particular actions it produced at each moment; and if these actions were different one from another, this was not due to the fact that some were produced with the co-operation of certain sources of action, which did not contribute to the production of the others; for the soul of man is simple, indivisible, and immaterial. M. Leibniz agrees; and if he did not agree, but on the contrary was at one with the majority of the philosophers and even with some of the greatest metaphysicians of our age (Mr. Locke for example) in supposing that a thing composed of several material parts arranged in a certain way is capable of thinking, I should in that case regard his hypothesis as absolutely impossible,

(So M. Bayle does not yet regard it as impossible.)

and many other ways of refuting it would present themselves, which are here no concern of mine, since he does recognize the immateriality of the soul, and builds upon it.

To say that the force which the soul has received from God is the sole principle of its particular actions does not afford sufficient explanation of its actions. It is better to say that God has placed in every soul *a concentration of the world*, or the power of representing the universe from a point of view proper to that soul, and that it is this that is the principle of its actions, distinguishing them from one another and from the actions of another soul. For it follows that they will continually be undergoing changes representative of the changes in the universe, and that the other souls will undergo other changes, but corresponding ones.

Let us return to the soul of Caesar, and let us call it an immaterial automaton, to use M. Leibniz's own expression; and let us compare it with an Epicurean atom. I mean an atom which is surrounded by a void on all sides and which will never meet any other atom. The comparison is a very just one; for on the one hand this atom has a natural faculty of moving itself, and exerts it without being helped by anything whatever, and without being checked or deflected by anything at all; and the soul of Caesar is a mind which has the power of giving itself thoughts, and which exerts it without being influenced by any other mind, or by any body. Nothing assists it, nothing deflects it. If you consult common notions and common ideas of order you will find that this atom must never stop, and that having moved in the preceding moment, it must move in the present moment and in all subsequent moments, and that the manner of its motion must always be the same. This is a consequence of an axiom approved by M. Leibniz. From the fact that a thing remains always in the state in which it once is, if nothing supervenes to cause it to change, we conclude (*he says*) not only that a body which is at rest will always remain at rest; but also that a body which is in motion will always retain this motion or change, that is to say the same velocity and the same direction, if nothing supervenes to prevent it. *All the world knows clearly that this atom, whether it moves by*

*an innate faculty, as Democritus and Epicurus assure us, or
whether it moves by a faculty received from the Creator, always
proceeds uniformly and equally in the same line without its ever
happening to it to turn to right or to left or to turn back. Epicurus
was made fun of when he invented the motion of atomic 'swerve';
he postulated it gratuitously to get himself out of the labyrinth
of the fatal necessity of all things, and he could give us no reason
for this new part of his hypothesis. It offended against the
most obvious notions of our minds, for it is evident that if an
atom which has pursued a straight line for two days is to turn
aside from its route at the beginning of the third day it must
either encounter some obstacle, or conceive some desire of leaving
its path, or else contain some source of energy which becomes
active at that moment. The first of these reasons does not arise
in empty space, the second is impossible because an atom has
not the power of thought; the third is likewise impossible in a
body which is absolutely one.*

Before proceeding, it is well to point out a great difference
between matter and the soul. Matter is an incomplete
being: it lacks the original source of actions. And when it
receives an impression, that impression precisely, and what
is in it at the moment, is all that the matter contains. It is
for this reason that matter is not even capable of maintaining
of itself a circular motion, for this motion is not sufficiently
simple for it to be able to remember it, so to speak. It
remembers only what happens to it in the last moment, or
rather *in ultimo signo rationis*,[1] that is to say it remembers
the direction straight along the tangent, without having the
gift of remembering the instruction which would be given
to it to turn aside from that tangent, to make it remain all
the time on the circumference. This is why the body does
not maintain its circular motion, even though it has begun
such a motion, unless there is some reason compelling it to
do so. This is why an atom can only learn to go simply

[1] 'in the last stage in the order of reasoning'.

in a straight line, such is its stupidity and imperfection. The case is quite different with a soul or mind. As it is a true substance or complete being, which is the original source of its own actions, it remembers as it were (confusedly, of course) all its preceding states, and is affected by them. It not only holds its direction, as does the atom, but it holds also the law of the changes of direction, or the law of curves, which the atom is incapable of doing; and whereas in the atom there is but a single change, there is an infinite number of changes in the modifications of the soul, each of which holds its own law; for the Epicurean atom, although endowed with parts, is a thing internally united, whereas the soul, although it has no parts, contains within itself a great number, or rather an infinite number, of varieties, owing to the multitude of the representations of external things, or rather owing to the representation of the universe, which the Creator placed in it. If M. Bayle had considered this difference between the *conatus* of bodies and of souls, of which I had already some slight notion in my earliest youth, when I gave to the public my *Physical Hypothesis* (an idea which impressed the late M. Lantin of Dijon, as is proved by a letter he wrote me) he would not have brought up against me the comparison of an Epicurean atom with the human soul, as he does here.

6. *Let us make some use of all this. The soul of Caesar is a being to which the term unity is in the strictest sense applicable. The power of giving itself thoughts is a property of its nature, according to the system of M. Leibniz. It received it from God, both as regards its possession and as regards its exercise. If the first sensation which it gives itself is a sensation of pleasure,*

(I do not conceive that the soul *gives itself* first sensations. It received them from God with its being at the moment of creation, since it had some at the outset; and in its first sensations it received virtually all the rest.)

it is not easy to see why the second thought also should not be a sensation of pleasure; for when the total cause of an effect remains the same, the effect cannot change.

The total cause does not remain the same in this case. Present thoughts include a tendency to other thoughts. For the soul does not only have perception, but has appetite as well. But in tending towards new pleasures it sometimes encounters pains.

Now this soul at the second moment of its existence does not receive a new power of thinking, it merely retains the power which it had in the first moment, and is as independent of the impact of every other cause in the second moment as in the first; it must therefore reproduce in the second moment the same thought that it has produced just before.

Not at all; because it tends towards change in accordance with the laws of appetite, as body tends towards change in accordance with the laws of motion.

If you object that it must be in a state of change, and that it would not be so in the case that I have supposed, I answer that its changing will be similar to the changing of the atom. For an atom which moves continually along the same line acquires at each moment a situation which is new but similar to its preceding situation. In order, therefore, that the soul may persist in its state of change, it is enough that it should produce a new thought similar to the preceding one.

I have already explained above the great difference there is between the laws of change of a body, such as the atom, and those of the soul. And the very difference between the thought of the soul and the motion of the atom is evidence of this. Spontaneous motion consists in the tendency to move in a straight line; there is nothing which is so unified. But thought implies an actual material object, which is the human body; and this object is compound, and contains a very great number of modifications, whereby it is attached to the surrounding bodies, and by means of them in varying degree to all other bodies. And the tendencies of the soul towards new thoughts correspond to the tendency of the body towards new shapes and new motions. And as these new motions are capable of causing the object to pass from order to disorder, so their representations in the soul are capable of causing the soul to pass from pleasure to pain.

Let us not press this point too rigidly; let us grant a metamorphosis of thoughts. At the very least it would be necessary that the passage from one thought to another should include some ground of affinity. If I suppose that at a particular instant the soul of Caesar is looking at a tree which has flowers and leaves, I can conceive (if we assume that a created mind can give itself ideas, nothwithstanding those reasons which prevent our understanding it) that his soul might immediately wish to see a tree which has only leaves and then another which has only flowers; and that thus it will produce for itself in succession several images which will arise one from another. But we cannot represent as possible changes from white to black, *and from yes to no, nor the wild leaps from earth to sky which are common in the thought of man. We cannot believe that God was able to put into the soul of Julius Caesar the principle of what I am about to say. It no doubt happened to him on several occasions that when sucking he was pricked by a pin. It was therefore necessary (on the hypothesis we are here examining) for his soul to modify itself by a feeling of pain* immediately after the pleasant perceptions *of the sweetness of the milk, which it had experienced for two or three minutes in succession. By what source of energy was it forced to interrupt its pleasures, and to give itself suddenly a feeling of pain,* when nothing had warned it *to prepare for the change, and* when nothing new had taken place in the substance? *If you run through the life of this first Emperor you will find at every step material for a stronger objection than this one.*

Let us run through this statement. It is certainly true that the passage from one thought to another *must include some* link or *reason*, and this has been shown. If Caesar's soul had nothing but distinct thoughts, and gave them all to itself voluntarily, the passage from one thought to another might be like what M. Bayle suggests of the passage from one tree to another, for example. But besides the perceptions which the soul remembers, it has a heap of an infinite number of confused ones which it does not disentangle; and it is by these that it represents the bodies outside itself, and that it arrives at distinct thoughts dissimilar to the preceding ones because the bodies which it represents have passed suddenly to something which powerfully affects its own body. Thus the soul sometimes passes from white to black, or from yes to no, without knowing how, or at least in an involuntary manner. For what its confused thoughts and its sensations produce in it, is attributed to the bodies. It is not surprising, therefore, if a man who is eating jam and feels himself stung by an insect, passes immediately from pleasure to pain in spite of himself. For the insect was already affecting the man's body by getting near him before stinging, and the representation of this already affected his soul, albeit insensibly. Little by little, however, what is insensible becomes sensible, in the soul as in the body; this is how it happens that the soul modifies itself against its own inclination, for it is the slave of its feelings and of its confused thoughts which arise in accordance with the states of its own body and of other bodies in relation to its own. Here then are the sources of energy by which pleasures are sometimes interrupted and succeeded by pains, without the soul always having warning or being prepared, as for example when the stinging insect approaches us noiselessly, or else, if for instance it is a wasp, some distraction prevents our noticing its buzzing as it approaches. Thus it must not be said that nothing new has taken place in the substance of the soul, to make it arrive at the feeling of the sting; it is the confused presentiments, or, to put it more strictly, the insensible dispositions of the soul which represent the dispositions to the sting in the bodies.

7. *We might understand something of all this if we suppose that the soul of man is not a mind but rather a legion of minds, each of which has its functions which begin and end precisely as required by the changes occurring in the human body. As a consequence of this we should have to say that something analogous to a great array of wheels and springs or of portions of matter in agitation, arranged in accordance with the vicissitudes of our machine, awakened or put to sleep for such and such a time the activity of each of these minds; but in that case the soul of man would no longer be a substance, it would be an* ens per aggregationem, *an aggregate and a pile of substances, just like material things. What we are looking for here is one single thing which produces sometimes joy, sometimes pain, etc.; we are not looking for several things, of which one produces hope, another despair, and so on.*

M. Bayle is right to reject this view of the compound nature of the soul, for it would make it capable of destruction and dissipation since it would be an aggregate. But my theory does not require that the substance of the soul should be compound; it is enough if its thoughts are compound and embrace a large number of objects and modifications which are known distinctly or confusedly; and this experience teaches us to be actually the case. For although the soul is a simple and single substance, it never has perceptions which are simple and single. It always has, at one and the same time, a number of distinct thoughts which it can remember, and attached to these an infinity of confused thoughts, whose ingredient parts it cannot distinguish. Since this complex of thoughts only has to produce other compound thoughts, it has no need of any legion of minds. Each partial modification of the preceding state of the soul contributes to the subsequent total modification of the same soul, and gives it a new variation.

NEW ESSAYS ON THE HUMAN UNDERSTANDING

INTRODUCTION

SINCE the *Essay on the Human Understanding*, by a famous Englishman,[1] is one of the finest and most highly esteemed works of our time, I have resolved to make some remarks on it, because, having long meditated on the same subject and on the greater part of the matters therein considered, I thought this would be a good opportunity for publishing something under the title of *New Essays on the Human Understanding*, and for securing a favourable reception for my reflections by putting them in such good company. I further thought that I might profit by someone else's labour, not only to diminish my own (since in fact it is less trouble to follow the thread of a good author than to work at everything afresh), but also to add something to what he has given us, which is always an easier task than making a start; for I think I have removed certain difficulties which he had left entirely on one side. Thus his reputation is of advantage to me; and since I am moreover inclined to do justice to him, and am very far from wishing to lessen the high opinion commonly entertained of his work, I shall increase his

[1] John Locke (1632–1704). When his *Essay* was published in 1690 Leibniz sent him some short papers in criticism. Locke seems to have paid little attention to these. In 1700, Coste's translation of the *Essay* into French was published, and Leibniz set himself to write the *New Essays*, an elaborate work in which he examines and criticizes Locke's doctrines in a running commentary; he delayed publication, however, as a new edition of the French translation of the *Essay* was promised. Then in 1704 Locke died; and the *New Essays* were not published until 1765, nearly fifty years after the death of Leibniz.

reputation if my approval has any weight. It is true that I am often of another opinion from him, but, far from denying the merit of famous writers, we bear witness to it by showing wherein and wherefore we differ from them, since we deem it necessary to prevent their authority from prevailing against reason in certain important points; besides the fact that, in convincing such excellent men, we make the truth more acceptable, and it is to be supposed that it is chiefly for truth's sake that they are labouring.

In fact, although the author of the *Essay* says a thousand fine things of which I approve, our systems are very different. His bears more relation to Aristotle, mine to Plato; although we both of us depart in many things from the doctrine of these two ancient philosophers. He is more popular, while I am sometimes compelled to be a little more *acroamatic* and abstract, which is not an advantage to me, especially when writing in a living language. But I think that by making two characters speak, of whom one expounds the views derived from our author's *Essay*,[1] while the other gives my observations, I shall show the relation between us in a way that will be more to the reader's taste than dry remarks, the reading of which would have to be constantly interrupted by the necessity of referring to his book in order to understand mine. Nevertheless it will be well sometimes to compare our writings and to judge of his opinions by his own work only, although I have as a rule retained his expressions. It is true

[1] Philalethes gives Locke's views, and Theophilus those of Leibniz. The words of Philalethes are sometimes obviously a translation of Locke's own words, sometimes a paraphrase or summary of a particular passage in Locke, and sometimes a free re-statement of Locke's doctrine. Where his words are obviously meant to be a translation, instead of retranslating them I have printed Locke's own words in italics, as it may be of advantage to the reader to see at a glance what is the original Locke, and what is Leibniz's summary or re-statement. In some places of course it is difficult to tell whether to treat the French as translation or as paraphrase; but as a general rule it is clear enough.

that the necessity of having to follow the thread of another person's argument in making my remarks has meant that I have been unable to think of achieving the graces of which the dialogue form is capable: but I hope the matter will make up for this defect in the manner.

Our differences are on subjects of some importance. The question at issue is whether the soul itself is entirely void, like a tablet whereon nothing has yet been written (*tabula rasa*), as is the view of Aristotle and the author of the *Essay*, and everything marked on it comes solely from the senses and from experience, or whether the soul contains originally the principles of various notions and doctrines, which external objects simply recall from time to time, as is my view and that of Plato, and even of the Schoolmen, and of all those who attribute this meaning to the passage from St. Paul (Rom. ii 15), where he says that the law of God is writ in men's hearts. The Stoics call these principles *prolepses*, that is to say assumptions which are fundamental or taken as agreed in advance. The mathematicians call them *common notions* (κοιναὶ ἔννοιαι). Modern philosophers give them other fine names, and Julius Scaliger in particular called them *semina aeternitatis*[1] and again *zopyra*, meaning to say living fires, flashes of light, hidden within us, but caused to appear by the contact of the senses, like the sparks which the shock of the flint strikes from the steel. And it is not an unreasonable belief that these flashes are a sign of something divine and eternal, which makes its appearance above all in necessary truths. From this arises another question, whether all truths depend on experience, that is to say on induction and on instances, or whether there are some which have another basis also. For if certain events can be foreseen before we have made any trial of them, it is clear that we contribute in those cases something of our own. The senses, although they are necessary for all our actual

[1] 'seeds of eternity'.

knowledge, are not sufficient to give us the whole of it, since the senses never give anything but instances, that is to say particular or individual truths. Now all the instances which confirm a general truth, however numerous they may be, are not sufficient to establish the universal necessity of this same truth, for it does not follow that what happened before will happen in the same way again. For example, the Greeks and the Romans, and all the other peoples of the earth known to the ancients, always observed that before the passage of twenty-four hours day changes to night and night to day. But they would have been wrong if they had believed that the same rule holds good everywhere, for since that time the contrary has been experienced during a visit to Nova Zembla. And any one who believed that in our zone at least this is a necessary and eternal truth which will last for ever, would likewise be wrong, since we must hold that the earth and even the sun do not exist of necessity, and that there may perhaps come a time when that beautiful star and its whole system will exist no longer, at least in its present form. From which it appears that necessary truths, such as we find in pure mathematics, and particularly in arithmetic and geometry, must have principles whose proof does not depend on instances, nor consequently on the testimony of the senses, although without the senses it would never have occurred to us to think of them. This is a distinction that should be carefully noted; and it is one which Euclid understood so well that he often proves by reason what is evident enough through experience and sensible images. Logic also, together with metaphysics and morals, the one of which forms natural theology and the other natural jurisprudence, are full of such truths; and consequently proof of them can only arise from inner principles, which are called innate. It is true that we must not imagine that we can read in the soul these eternal laws of reason as in an open book, as the edict of the praetor can be read in his *album* without trouble or deep scrutiny. But it is enough that we can find them in ourselves by dint of attention, opportunities for which are afforded by the senses. The success of experiments serves also as a confirmation of reason, more or less as verifications serve in arithmetic to help us to avoid erroneous calculation when the reasoning is long. It is in this also that the knowledge of men differs from that of the brutes: the latter are purely empirical, and guide themselves solely by particular instances; for, as far as we can judge, they never go so far as to form necessary propositions; whereas men are capable of the demonstrative sciences. This also is why the faculty the brutes have of making *sequences* of ideas is something inferior to the reason which is in man. The sequences of the brutes are just like those of the simple empiricists who claim that what has happened sometimes will happen again in a case where what strikes them is similar, without being capable of determining whether the same reasons hold good. It is because of this that it is so easy for men to catch animals, and so easy for pure empiricists to make mistakes. And people whom age and experience has rendered skilful are not exempt from this when they rely too much on their past experience, as some have done in civil and military affairs; they do not pay sufficient attention to the fact that the world changes, and that men become more skilful by discovering countless new contrivances, whereas the stags and hares of to-day are no more cunning than those of yesterday. The sequences of the brutes are but a shadow of reasoning, that is to say, they are but connections of imagination, transitions from one image to another; for in a fresh experience which appears like the preceding one, there is the expectation that what was hitherto joined thereto will occur again, as though the things were connected in fact, because their images are connected in the memory. It is true that reason also teaches us to expect in the ordinary course of events to see occur in the future what conforms to a long experience of the past, but it is not therefore a necessary and infallible truth, and we may cease to be successful when we least expect it, when the reasons which have maintained it change. This is why the wisest people do not rely on it to the extent of not trying to discover, if it is possible, something of the reason of what happens, so as to judge when exceptions must be made. For reason alone is capable of setting up rules which are certain, and of supplying what is lacking to those which are not certain, by inserting the exceptions, and in short of finding connections which are certain in the force of necessary consequences. This often provides the means of foreseeing the event, without its being necessary to experience the sensible connections between images which is all that the brutes can do; so that to vindicate the existence within us of the principles of necessary truths is also to distinguish man from the brutes.

Perhaps our gifted author will not entirely dissociate himself from my opinion. For after having devoted the whole of his first book to the rejection of innate ideas, understood in a certain sense, he yet admits in the beginning of the second and in what follows that ideas whose origin is not in sensation arise from reflection. Now reflection is nothing but an attention to what is in us, and the senses do not give us what we already bring with us. This being so, can we deny that there is a great deal that is innate in our mind, since we are innate, so to speak, to ourselves, and since there is in ourselves being, unity, substance, duration, change, activity, perception, pleasure, and a thousand other objects of our intellectual ideas? And since these objects are immediate to our understanding and are always present (although they cannot always be apperceived on account of our distractions and our needs), why be surprised that we say that these ideas, and everything which depends on them, are innate in us? This is why I have taken as an illustration a block of veined marble, rather than a wholly uniform block or blank tablets, that is to say what is called *tabula rasa* in the language of the philosophers. For if the soul were like these blank tablets, truths would be in us in the same way as the figure of Hercules is in a block of marble, when the marble is completely indifferent whether it receives this or some other figure. But if there were veins in the stone which marked out the figure of Hercules rather than other figures, this stone would be more determined thereto, and Hercules would be as it were in some manner innate in it, although labour would be needed to uncover those veins, and to clear them by polishing, and by cutting away what prevents them from appearing. It is in this way that ideas and truths are innate in us, like natural inclinations and dispositions, natural habits or potentialities, and not like activities, although these abilities are always accompanied by some activities which correspond to them, though they are often imperceptible.

It seems that our gifted author claims that there is in us nothing *potential*, nor even anything which we do not always actually apperceive; but he cannot take this quite strictly, otherwise his opinion would be too paradoxical, since acquired habits also and the contents of our memory are not always apperceived, and do not even always come to our aid when needed, although we often easily recall them to mind on some trivial occasion which reminds us of them, in the same way as we only need the beginning of a song to make us remember the song. Moreover he limits his doctrine in other places by saying that there is nothing in us which we have not at least previously apperceived. But besides the fact that nobody can guarantee by reason alone how far our past apperceptions which may have been forgotten may have gone, especially in view of the Platonic doctrine of reminiscence, which, mythical though it is, is not incompatible, in part at least, with bare reason: besides this, I say, why should it be necessary that everything should be acquired by us by apperceptions of external things, and nothing be able to be unearthed in

ourselves? Is our soul of itself alone so empty that apart
from images borrowed from without it is nothing? This is
not, I am convinced, an opinion that our judicious author
could approve. And where are there to be found tablets
which have not in themselves a certain amount of variety?
We shall never see a perfectly level and uniform surface.
Why, therefore, should we not also be able to provide some
sort of thought from deep within ourselves, when we are
willing to delve there? Thus I am led to believe that fundamentally his opinion on this point does not differ from mine,
or rather from the common opinion, inasmuch as he recognizes
two sources of our knowledge, the senses and reflection.

I am not sure that it will be so easy to reconcile him with
us and with the Cartesians when he maintains that the mind
does not always think, and in particular that it is without
perception during dreamless sleep; and when he protests
that since bodies can exist without motion, souls also might
well exist without thought. But here I answer somewhat
differently from what is usual; for I maintain that, naturally,
a substance cannot exist without activity, and that there
never even exists a body without motion. Experience is
already in my favour on this point, and to be persuaded of it
it is only necessary to consult the illustrious Mr. Boyle's
book[1] against absolute rest. But I believe that reason also
supports it, and this is one of the proofs which I use for
refuting the theory of atoms.

Besides, there are a thousand signs which make us think
that there are at all times an infinite number of *perceptions*
in us, though without apperception and without reflection;
that is to say changes in the soul itself which we do not
apperceive because their impressions are either too small and
too numerous, or too unified, so that they have nothing
sufficiently distinctive in themselves, though in combination

[1] *Of Absolute Rest in Bodies.* Robert Boyle (1627-1691) was a
famous chemist and physicist.

with others they do not fail to have their effect and to make themselves felt, at least confusedly, in the mass. It is thus that habituation causes us not to notice the motion of a mill or waterfall, after we have lived near by for some time. It is not that the motion does not continue to affect our organs, and that something does not still take place in the soul to correspond to it, on account of the harmony of the soul and the body; it is that these impressions which are in the soul and in the body, when they are devoid of the attractions of novelty, are not strong enough to attract our attention and memory, when these are attached to more absorbing objects. For all attention demands some memory, and often when we are not admonished, so to speak, and warned to pay attention to certain of our present perceptions, we let them pass without reflection and even without observing them; but if someone draws attention to them immediately afterwards, and makes us notice, for example, some sound that has just been heard, we remember it, and we apperceive that we did have some sensation of it at the time. Thus there were perceptions which we did not immediately apperceive, apperception in this case only arising through our attention having been aroused after an interval, however small. In order the better to form an opinion of these minute perceptions which we cannot distinguish in the crowd, I generally make use of the example of the roar or noise which strikes us when we are on the shore. To hear this noise as we do, we must surely hear the parts of which the whole is made up, that is to say the noises of each wave, although each of these little noises only makes itself heard in the confused combination of all the others together, that is to say in the actual roar, and would not be noticed if the wave which makes it were the only one. For it is necessary that we should be slightly affected by the motion of this wave, and that we should have some perception of each of these noises, however small they may be; otherwise we should not have the perception of a hundred thousand waves, since a hundred thousand nothings cannot make a something. We never sleep so soundly but that we have some feeble and confused feeling, and we should never be awakened by the loudest noise in the world, if we had not some perception of its beginning, small as it is; just as we should never break a rope by the greatest exertion in the world, if it were not to some small extent strained and stretched by lesser efforts, although the slight extension they produce is not apparent.

These minute perceptions are therefore more efficacious in their consequences than we think. They it is that constitute that indefinable something, those tastes, those images of the qualities of the senses, clear in the mass but confused in the parts, those impressions which surrounding bodies make on us, which include the infinite, that link which connects every being with all the rest of the universe. It may even be said that as a result of these minute perceptions the present is big with the future and laden with the past, that everything is in league together (σύμπνοια πάντα, as Hippocrates said), and that in the smallest substance eyes as piercing as those of God could read the whole sequence of things in the universe:

Quae sint, quae fuerint, quae mox futura trahantur.[1]

These insensible perceptions are also the signs and constituents of personal identity: the individual is characterized by the traces or expressions of his previous states which these perceptions preserve by connecting them with his present state, and which can be known by a superior spirit, even though the individual himself may not be conscious of them, that is to say though he may no longer expressly recollect them. But they (these perceptions, I mean) also provide the means of rediscovering this recollection at need through periodic developments which may one day occur.

[1] 'The things that are, the things that have been, and those that are presently to come.'

This is why, because of them, death can only be a sleep, and cannot even go on being that, since, in animals, the perceptions only cease to be sufficiently distinguished and become reduced to a state of confusion which suspends apperception, but which cannot last for ever—not to speak here of man, who must in this have great privileges in order to retain his personality.

It is, moreover, these insensible perceptions which afford the explanation of that wonderful pre-established harmony of soul and body, and indeed of all monads or simple substances, which takes the place of the untenable theory of the influence of the one on the other, and which in the opinion of the author of the greatest of dictionaries [1] exalts the grandeur of the Divine perfections beyond what has ever been conceived. After this I should be adding but little if I said that it is these minute perceptions which *determine* us in many experiences without our giving them a thought, and which deceive the common herd by giving the appearance of an *indifference of equilibrium,* as if we were entirely indifferent whether, for example, we turned to the right or to the left. Nor is it necessary that I should point out here, as I have done in the book itself, that they cause that *uneasiness* which, on my showing, consists in something which differs from pain only as the small from the great, and which yet often creates our desire and even our pleasure, giving it a kind of savour. It is moreover, these insensible parts of our sensible perceptions which bring it about that there is a relation between those perceptions of colour, heat, and other sensible qualities and the motions in the bodies which correspond to them; whereas the Cartesians and our author, penetrating though he is, conceive of the perceptions which we have of these qualities as being arbitrary, that is to say, as if God had given them to the soul at His good pleasure without any

[1] i.e. Bayle. For the passage in Bayle's *Dictionary* referred to here, see p. 126.

regard to any essential relation between perceptions and their objects: an opinion which surprises me, and which seems to me hardly worthy of the wisdom of the Author of things, who does nothing without harmony and without reason.

In a word, the *insensible perception* is of as much use in pneumatics [1] as is the insensible corpuscle in physics; and it is equally unreasonable to reject the one or the other on the pretext that it is beyond the reach of our senses. Nothing takes place all at once, and it is one of my most important and best verified maxims that *nature makes no leaps*. This I called the *law of continuity* when I spoke of it in the first *News of the Republic of Letters*; and the use of this law in physics is very considerable: it means that the passage from the small to the great and back again always takes place through that which is intermediate, both in degrees and in parts, and that a motion never arises immediately from rest, nor is reduced to it except through a smaller motion, just as we never manage to traverse any given line or length without first traversing a shorter line—although till now those who have exhibited the laws of motion have not observed this law, believing as they did that a body can receive in a moment a motion contrary to its preceding one. All this brings us to the conclusion that *observable perceptions* come by degrees from those which are too small to be observed. To think otherwise is to have but little knowledge of the immensely subtle composition of things, which always and everywhere include an actual infinity.

I have also noticed that, by virtue of insensible variations, two individual things can never be perfectly alike, and that they must always differ more than *numero*. This at once puts out of court the blank tablets of the soul, a soul without thought, a substance without action, the void in space, atoms and even particles not actually divided in matter, absolute rest, complete uniformity in one part of time, place,

[1] An early name for the philosophy of mind or spirit.

or matter, the perfect globes of the second element which are the offspring of the original perfect cubes,[1] and a thousand other fictions of the philosophers—fictions arising from their incomplete notions, and not admitted by the nature of things, but merely allowed to pass because of our ignorance and of the slight attention we pay to the insensible; they can only be made tolerable by being limited to abstractions made by the mind, which protests that it is not denying any of the things which it considers irrelevant to the present inquiry but only setting them on one side. Otherwise, if we thought in good earnest that the things we do not apperceive are not there in the soul or in the body, we should fail in philosophy as in politics, by neglecting τὸ μικρόν,[2] insensible progressions; whereas an abstraction is not an error, provided we know that what we are ignoring is really there. This is the use made of abstractions by mathematicians when they speak of the perfect lines they ask us to consider, and of uniform motions and other regular effects, although *matter* (that is to say the mixture of the effects of the surrounding infinite) is always making some exception. We proceed in this way so as to distinguish the various considerations from one another, and to reduce the effects to their reasons as far as is possible to us, and to foresee some consequences; for the more careful we are to neglect no consideration which we can regulate, the more does practice correspond to theory. But it belongs to the Supreme Reason, which misses nothing, distinctly to understand the whole infinite, and to see all the reasons and all the consequences. All that we can do in regard to infinities is to know them confusedly, and at least to have distinct knowledge that they exist. Otherwise we should have a very poor recognition of the beauty and grandeur of the universe; we should also be unable to have a sound physics to explain the nature of bodies in general, and still less a sound pneumatics

[1] The reference is to the vortex theory of Descartes.
[2] *lit.* 'the small'; i.e. by neglecting very small items.

to include the knowledge of God, of souls, and of simple substances in general.

This knowledge of insensible perceptions serves also to explain why and how two souls, whether human or of some other identical species, never come perfectly alike from the Creator's hands, but each has always from the beginning its own relation to the point of view it will have in the universe. But this follows from what I pointed out previously about two individuals, namely that their *difference* is always more than a *numerical* one. There is also another important point on which I am obliged to differ not only from the opinions of our author, but also from those of the greater part of the moderns; that is, that like most of the ancients I hold that all superhuman beings, all souls, all simple created substances, are always joined to a body, and that there never are entirely separate souls. I have *a priori* reasons for this, but there will be found to be this advantage also in my doctrine that it solves all the philosophical difficulties about the state of souls, their perpetual conservation, their immortality, and their operation: the difference between one state of the soul and another is never and has never been anything other than that between the more and the less sensible, the more and the less perfect, or the other way round, and so the past or future state of the soul is as explicable as its present state. The smallest reflection suffices to show that this is reasonable, and that a leap from one state to another infinitely different state could not be natural. I am surprised that the schools should have causelessly given up natural explanations, and should have been ready deliberately to plunge into very great difficulties and thus to provide occasion for the apparent triumphs of free-thinkers; all of whose reasons collapse at once on this explanation of things, in which there is no more difficulty in conceiving the conservation of souls (or rather on my view of the whole animal) than there is in the change from the caterpillar into the butterfly, and in the conservation of thought during sleep—sleep to which Jesus Christ with divine propriety likened death. I have already said that no sleep can last for ever, and it will have least duration, or almost none at all, in the case of rational souls, which are always destined to retain the personality which has been given to them in the City of God, and which consequently have memory, so that they may be more susceptible of punishments and rewards. I add further that in general no derangement of its visible organs is capable of carrying things to the point of complete confusion in the animal or of destroying all its organs, and of depriving the soul of the whole of its organic body and of the ineffaceable remains of all its preceding traces. But the ease with which the ancient doctrine that angels have subtle bodies[1] has been abandoned (a doctrine that has been confounded with the corporeality of the angels themselves), the introduction of supposed intelligences without bodies among created things (a view that has been much strengthened by Aristotle's doctrine that such intelligences make the heavens revolve), and finally the mistaken opinion that has existed that the con- servation of the souls of the brutes cannot be maintained without falling into metempsychosis and transferring them from body to body, and the perplexity some have felt through not knowing what to do with them—all these things have, in my opinion, led to the neglect of the natural way of explaining the conservation of the soul. This has done much injury to natural religion, and has caused some people to believe that our immortality was but a miraculous grace of God. Our illustrious author also speaks of it with some doubt, as I shall subsequently point out. But it would be well if all those who are of this opinion had spoken of it as wisely and sincerely as he; for it is to be feared that some who

[1] i.e. made of some more rarefied stuff than ordinary matter. Locke uses the word in this connection (to represent the Latin *subtilis*) in the correspondence with the Bishop of Worcester.

speak of immortality through grace merely do so to preserve appearances, and at bottom are not very far from those Averroists and certain pernicious Quietists, who picture an absorption and reunion of the soul with the ocean of Divinity, a notion whose impossibility is perhaps shown up by my system alone.

It appears, moreover, that we differ also in regard to matter, in that the author thinks that the existence of a void is necessary to motion, because he believes that the small parts of matter are rigid.[1] I admit that if matter were composed of such parts, motion in a plenum would be impossible, just as if a room were filled with quantities of small pebbles without there being in it the least empty space. But I do not admit this supposition, for which, moreover, there does not appear to be any reason, although our gifted author goes so far as to hold that rigidity[1] or cohesion of parts is the essence of matter. Space should rather be conceived of as full of a matter originally fluid, susceptible of any division, and submitted indeed actually to divisions and subdivisions *ad infinitum*; with this difference, however, that it is divisible and divided unequally in different places on account of motions which are already helping to a greater or less degree to produce the divisions. This means that it has throughout a degree of rigidity as well as of fluidity, and that there does not exist any body which is absolutely hard or absolutely fluid; that is to say that it is impossible to find in any body any atom whose hardness is indefeasible, or any mass which is entirely indifferent to division. Besides, the order of nature, and particularly the law of continuity, make both equally impossible.

[1] Locke's own term is *solid*, and *solidity*. He says: *That which hinders the approach of two bodies, when they are moved one towards another, I call solidity . . . but if any one think it better to call it impenetrability, he has my consent* [*Essay*, Bk. II, ch. iv, § 1]. But I do not think that Leibniz's word here (*roide*) can properly be translated by *solid*. The word *hard* is rejected by Locke on the ground that a hard body is no more solid than a soft one.

I have also shown that *cohesion*, which could not of itself be the result of impulse or of motion, would cause a *traction*, strictly speaking. For if there were a body originally rigid, an Epicurean atom, for example, which contained a part projecting from it in the form of a hook (since we may imagine atoms of all kinds of shapes), this hook when impelled would draw with it the rest of the atom, that is to say the part which was not being impelled, and which did not fall in the line of impulse. Our gifted author, however, is himself opposed to these philosophic tractions, such as were formerly attributed to nature's abhorrence of a vacuum, and reduces them to *impulses*, maintaining in agreement with the moderns that one part of matter can only operate immediately on another by impelling it by contact; wherein I think they are right, because otherwise the operation is in no way intelligible.

I must not, however, conceal the fact that I have observed a kind of recantation on this point on the part of our excellent author, whose modesty and sincerity in this I cannot too highly praise, just as on other occasions I have admired his penetrating insight. It is in the reply to the second letter of the late Bishop of Worcester, printed in 1699, page 408, where, in order to justify the view he had upheld against this learned prelate, namely that matter was capable of thought, he says among other things: '*It is true, I say "that bodies operate by impulse, and nothing else"* (Essay, *Bk.* II, *ch.* viii, § 11). *And so I thought when I writ it, and can yet conceive no other way of their operation. But I am since convinced by the judicious Mr. Newton's incomparable book, that it is too bold a presumption to limit God's power, in this point, by my narrow conceptions. The gravitation of matter towards matter, by ways inconceivable to me, is not only a demonstration that God can, if he pleases, put into bodies powers and ways of operation, above what can be derived from our idea of body or can be explained by what we know of matter,*

*but also an unquestionable and everywhere visible instance,
that he has done so.   And therefore in the next edition of my
book I shall take care to have that passage rectified.'*[1] I find
that in the French translation of this book, which was no doubt
taken from the latest editions, this § 11 reads thus: 'It is
evident, *at least as far as we can conceive it*,[2] that bodies act
upon one another by impulse and not otherwise; for it is
impossible for us to understand that a body can act upon that
which it does not touch, which is as much as to imagine that
it can act where it is not.'[3]

I cannot but praise this modest piety on the part of our
famous author, who recognizes that God can do things beyond
what we can understand, and thus that there may be inconceivable mysteries in the articles of faith: but I should
not wish us to be obliged to have recourse to miracles in the
ordinary course of nature, and to allow the existence of
powers and operations which are absolutely inexplicable.
Otherwise we should be granting too much licence to bad
philosophers on the strength of what God can do. If we
admit these *centripetal faculties* or *immediate attractions* from
a distance without its being possible to make them intelligible, I see nothing to prevent our Scholastics from
saying that everything is done simply through their 'faculties'
and from upholding their 'intentional species', which go
from objects up to us, and find a way even of entering our
souls.   If this is true:

Omnia jam fient, fieri quae posse negabam.[4]

So that it seems to me that our author, judicious though he

---

[1] Italics indicate Locke's own exact words.

[2] These italics are Leibniz's.

[3] In the English edition § 11 runs as follows: *The next thing to be
considered is, how bodies produce ideas in us; and that is manifestly
by impulse, the only way which we can conceive bodies to operate in.*

[4] 'Everything will now happen which I declared to be impossible.'

is, is in this going rather too much from one extreme to the other. He makes difficulties about the operations of *souls*, when it is only a question of admitting what is not *sensible*, and here we have him granting to bodies what is not even *intelligible*, in allowing them powers and activities beyond everything which, in my opinion, a created mind can do and understand, since he grants them attraction, even at great distance and without limiting himself to any stated sphere of activity, and that in order to uphold a view which seems no less inexplicable, to wit, the possibility of thinking in matter in the natural order.

The question he is discussing with the celebrated prelate, who had attacked him, is *whether matter can think*, and as this is an important point, even for the present work, I cannot avoid going into the subject a little and taking some account of their dispute. I will set forth the substance of it as regards this subject, and will take the liberty of saying what I think about it. The late Bishop of Worcester, being apprehensive, though in my opinion without great cause, that our author's doctrine of ideas was liable to some abuses prejudicial to the Christian faith, undertook to examine certain parts of it in his vindication of the doctrine of the Trinity. He first gives this excellent author his due by recognizing that he holds the existence of the mind as certain as that of the body, although one of these substances is as little known as the other; he then asks (page 241 seq.) how reflection could possibly assure us of the existence of mind, if God can give matter the faculty of thinking (as our author believes, Bk. V, ch. iii), since in this case the way of ideas, which is required to discriminate between the properties of soul and of body, would become useless; whereas it was said in Book II of the *Essay on the Human Understanding* (ch. xxiii, §§ 15, 27, 28), that the operations of the soul provide us with the idea of mind, and the understanding together with the will makes this idea as intelligible to us as the nature of body is made intelligible to us by solidity and impulse. This is how our author replies in his first letter (page 65 seq.): '*I think it may be proved from my principles, and I think I have done it, that there is a spiritual substance in us . . . We experiment in ourselves thinking. The idea of this action, or mode of thinking, is inconsistent with the idea of self-subsistence, and therefore has a necessary connection with a support or subject of inhesion: the idea of that support is what we call substance* . . . for *the general idea of substance being the same everywhere, the modification of thinking, or the power of thinking, joined to it, makes it a spirit, without considering what other modifications it has, as whether it has the modification of solidity or not. As, on the other side, substance that has the modification of solidity, is matter, whether it has the modification of thinking or not. And therefore if your lordship means by a spiritual an immaterial substance, I grant I have not proved, nor upon my principles can it be proved, (your lordship meaning, as I think you do, demonstratively proved) that there is an immaterial substance in us that thinks. Though I presume, what I have said about the supposition of a system of matter thinking* (Bk. IV, ch. x, § 16) (*which there demonstrates that God is immaterial*) *will prove it in the highest degree probable, that the thinking substance in us is immaterial. . . . Yet, I have shown* [adds the author, page 68] *that all the great ends of religion and morality are secured barely by the immortality of the soul, without a necessary supposition that the soul is immaterial.*

In his reply to this letter the learned bishop, to show that our author was of another opinion when he wrote the second book of his *Essay*, cites from it on page 51 this passage (taken from the same book, chapter xxiii, § 15), where it is said that *by the simple ideas we have taken from our own minds we are able to frame the complex idea of an immaterial spirit. And thus by putting together the ideas of thinking, perceiving, liberty, and power of moving themselves, and other things, we have as clear a perception and notion of immaterial substances as we have of material.* He further cites other passages to show that the author opposed mind to body. He says (page 54) that the ends of religion and morality are best secured by proving that the soul is immortal by its very nature, that is to say immaterial. He further adduces (page 60) this passage, that *all our ideas of the several sorts of substances are nothing but collections of simple ideas*; and that thus our author believed that the idea of thinking and willing gave a different substance from that given by the idea of solidity and impulse; and (§ 17) regards these ideas as constituting body as opposed to mind.

The Bishop of Worcester might have added that from the fact that the *general idea* of substance is in body and in mind, it does not follow that their *differences* are *modifications* of one and the same thing, as our author has just said in the passage I quoted from his first letter. It is necessary to distinguish properly between modifications and attributes. The faculties of having perception and of acting, extension, and solidity, are attributes of perpetual and principal predicates; but thinking, impetus, shapes, and motions are modifications of these attributes. Further, we ought to distinguish between *physical* (or rather real) *genus*, and *logical* or ideal *genus*. Things which are of the same *physical* kind or which are *homogeneous*, are of the same matter so to speak, and can often be changed one into another by changing their modifications, like circles and squares. But two *heterogeneous* things may have a common logical genus, and then their *differences* are not simple accidental modifications of one self-same subject or of one self-same metaphysical or physical matter. Thus time and space are quite heterogeneous things, and we should be wrong to imagine some kind of common real subject which had only continuous quantity in general and whose modifications resulted in time or space. People may laugh at these philosophical distinctions between two genera, the one only logical, the other real, and between two matters, one physical—that of bodies—the other only metaphysical or general, as if someone said that two parts of space are of the same matter or that two hours are also of the same matter as one another. Yet these distinctions are not a mere matter of terms, but are in the things themselves; and they seem to be particularly relevant here, where their confusion has given rise to a false conclusion. These two genera have a common notion, and the notion of real genus is common to both matters, so that their genealogy would be as follows:

Genus	*Logical* merely, the variations consisting of simple *differences*.	
	Real, whose differences are modifications, that is to say matter.	*Metaphysical* merely, in which there is homogeneity.
		Physical, in which there is a solid homogeneous mass.

I have not seen our author's second letter to the bishop, and the answer the latter makes to it hardly touches the point about the thinking of matter. But *our author's reply* to this second answer comes back to it. 'God (he says, nearly in these words, page 397), superadds to the essence of matter what qualities He pleases; to some parts simple motion, to plants vegetation, and to animals sense. Those who agree with me so far exclaim against me when I go a step further and say, *God may give to matter thought, reason, and volition,* as if that would destroy the essence of matter. To make good this assertion they say that thought and reason are not included in the essence of matter: which proves nothing, for motion and life are just as little included in it. They also urge that we cannot conceive how matter can think: but our conception is not the measure of God's omnipotency.' After this he quotes the example of the attraction of matter, page 399 and particularly page 408, where he speaks of the gravitation of matter towards matter, attributed to Mr. Newton (in the words I have quoted above), admitting that we cannot conceive how the attraction takes place. This, in effect, is going back to qualities which are occult, or, what is more, inexplicable. He adds (page 401) that nothing is more likely to assist the sceptics than to deny what we do not understand, and (page 402) that we cannot conceive even how the soul thinks. He wants to maintain (page 403) that, since both substances, material and immaterial, can be conceived in their bare essence without any activity, it rests with God to give to the one or to the other the power of thinking. And he wants to take advantage of the admission of his opponent, who had granted sense in brutes, but would not grant them any immaterial substance. He claims that liberty and self-consciousness (page 408) and the power of making abstractions (page 409) can be given to matter, not as matter, but as enriched by a divine power. Finally he reports (page 434) the observation of a traveller as important and judicious as M. de La Loubère that the pagans of the East know of the immortality of the soul without being able to understand its immateriality.

With regard to all this I may say, before coming to the explanation of my opinion, that it is certain that matter is as little capable of mechanically producing sensation as of producing reason, as our author agrees; that I fully recognize that it is not allowable to deny what we do not understand, but I add that we have the right to deny (in the order of nature at least) what is absolutely unintelligible and inexplicable. I maintain also that substances, whether material or immaterial, cannot be conceived in their bare essence without any activity, activity being of the essence of substance in general; and finally that the conception of created beings is not the measure of God's power, but that their conceptivity, or power of conceiving, is the measure of the power of nature; for everything which conforms with the order of nature can be conceived or understood by some created being.

Those who understand my system will see that I cannot agree altogether with either of these excellent authors; their dispute, however, is very instructive. Let me explain myself distinctly: it must above all things be considered that the modifications which can attach to a subject naturally or without miracle, must come to it from the limitations or variations of a real genus, or of an original nature which is constant and absolute. This is how we distinguish in philosophy the modes of an absolute being from that being itself; for instance we know that size, shape, and motion are manifestly limitations and variations of corporeal nature. For it is clear how a limitation of extension gives figures, and that the change which therein takes place is nothing but motion. And every time we find some quality in a subject, we ought to think that if we understood the nature of this subject and of this quality, we should conceive how this quality could result from it. Thus, in the order of nature (miracles apart) God does not arbitrarily give to substances such and such qualities indifferently, and He never gives them any but those which are natural to them, that is to say qualities which can be derived from their nature as explicable modifications. Thus we see that matter does not naturally have the attraction mentioned above, and does not of itself go in a curve, because it is not possible to conceive how this takes place, that is to say, to explain it mechanically, whereas what is natural ought to be able to be rendered distinctly conceivable, if we were admitted into the secrets of things. This distinction between what is natural and explicable and what is inexplicable and miraculous removes all the difficulties: in rejecting it we should be upholding something worse than occult qualities, and in so doing we should be renouncing philosophy and reason, and throwing open sanctuaries for ignorance and idleness, by a stupid system which admits not only that there are qualities which we do not understand (of which there are only too many), but also that there are some which the greatest mind, even if God provided him with every possible advantage, could not understand—that is to say they would be either miraculous or without rhyme or reason. It would indeed be without rhyme or reason that God should perform miracles in the ordinary course; so that this do-nothing hypothesis would destroy equally our philosophy which searches for reasons, and the Divine reason which provides them.

We can now turn to the question of thinking. It is certain that our author recognizes in more than one place that thinking cannot be an intelligible modification of matter, or one which could be understood and explained; that is to say, a sentient or thinking being is not a mechanical thing like a watch or a windmill, so that we could conceive of sizes, shapes, and motions in such a mechanical conjunction that they could produce in a mass, in which there was nothing of the kind, something capable of thought and even of sensation, which thinking and sensing would likewise stop if the mechanism got out of order. Thus it is not natural to matter to have sensation and to think, and there are only two ways in which it could do so; one of which is for God to join to it a substance to which thought is natural, and the other for God to endow it with thought miraculously. In this, then, I am entirely of the opinion of the Cartesians, except that I extend it to brutes also, and hold that they have sensation, and souls which are, properly speaking, immaterial, and as incapable of perishing as the atoms of Democritus or Gassendi; whereas the Cartesians, being needlessly embarrassed about the souls of brutes, and not knowing what to do with them if they were preserved (since it did not occur to them that the animal might be preserved in a minute form), were compelled to deny them even sensation, contrary to all appearances, and to the judgment of mankind. But if it is argued that God, at least, could add the faculty of thinking to such a mechanism, I would answer that if this occurred, and if

God added this faculty to matter without at the same time endowing it with a substance of such a kind that this same faculty (as I conceive it) could be inherent in it, that is to say without adding an immaterial soul, then matter would have to be exalted miraculously so as to be able to receive a power of which it is not capable naturally: just as some Scholastics claim that God exalts fire to the point of giving it the power directly to burn spirits separated from matter—which would be a miracle pure and simple. It is enough that we cannot maintain that matter thinks unless we attribute to it an imperishable soul, or rather a miracle, and that thus the immortality of our souls follows from what is natural: since we could not maintain that they are extinguished except by a miracle, whether by exalting matter, or by annihilating the soul. For we know, of course, that the power of God could render our souls mortal, even though they may be immaterial or immortal by nature, since He can annihilate them.

Now this truth of the immateriality of the soul is undoubtedly of consequence. For it is of infinitely more use in religion and morals, especially in our day (when many people have scant respect for revelation by itself or for miracles), to show that souls are naturally immortal, and that it would be a miracle if they were not, than to maintain that our souls must naturally die, and that it is by virtue of a miraculous grace, based solely on the promise of God, that they do not die. We have, moreover, known for a long time that those who wished to destroy natural religion, and reduce everything to revealed religion, as if reason taught us nothing about it, have been held suspect, and not always without reason. But our author is not of their number. He upholds the proof of the existence of God and attributes to the immateriality of the soul *a probability of the highest degree*, which may consequently pass for a *moral certainty*, so that I imagine that having as much sincerity as penetration, he might quite well come to agree with the doctrine I have just expounded. This doctrine is fundamental in every reasonable philosophy, for otherwise I do not see how we can prevent ourselves from falling back into *fanatical philosophy*, such as the Mosaic philosophy of Fludd, which accounts for all phenomena by attributing them immediately and miraculously to God, or into a *barbarous philosophy* like that of certain philosophers and physicians of bygone days, who still savoured of the barbarism of their age, and who to-day are justly despised; these accounted for appearances by expressly fabricating suitable occult qualities or faculties, which were supposed to be like little demons or sprites able to do what was required of them out of hand—just as if there were watches able to tell the time by some 'horodeictic faculty' without the need of wheels, or mills able to crush grain by a 'fractive faculty' without the need of anything in the nature of millstones. As to the difficulty many people find in conceiving an immaterial substance, that soon ceases to be felt (in part at least) when there is no longer any question of substances separated from matter; such substances do not, I hold, ever naturally exist among created things.

BOOK I. OF INNATE NOTIONS

CHAPTER I

Whether there are any Innate Principles in the Human Mind

§ 21.[1] PHILALETHES.[2] If the mind assents so promptly to certain truths, may this not come from the consideration of the nature of things, which does not suffer it to think

---

[1] The number of the section refers to the section in the corresponding chapter and book of Locke's *Essay*; i.e. in this case to *Essay*, Bk. I, ch. i, § 21. It will be seen that Leibniz does not always follow the order of Locke's sections, but sometimes takes the points in an order that suits his own argument. A large part of the present chapter is omitted here.

[2] Cf. p. 142, note.

otherwise, rather than because these propositions have been printed naturally in the mind?

THEOPHILUS. Both these doctrines are true. The nature of things and the nature of the mind here agree. And since you oppose the consideration of the thing to the apperception of what is printed in the mind, your objection shows, sir, that those whose doctrines you are upholding understand by *innate truths*, only such as would be approved naturally, as if by *instinct*, and without apprehending them except confusedly. There are some of this nature, and I shall have occasion to speak of them. But what is called the *natural light* presupposes a distinct knowledge, and often enough the consideration of the nature of things is nothing else than the knowledge of the nature of our mind and of these innate ideas, for which there is no need to search outside. Thus I call innate those truths which have no need of such consideration for their verification . . .

§ 23. PH. . . . But what do you say, sir, to this challenge of one of my friends? *I would gladly have any one name,*[1] he says, *that proposition whose terms or ideas were either of them innate.*

TH. I should name the propositions of arithmetic and geometry, which are all of that nature; and as regards necessary truths, it is not possible to find any others.

§ 25. PH. Many people will find that very strange. Can it be said that the most difficult and profoundest sciences are innate?

TH. Actual knowledge of them is not innate, but rather what may be called virtual knowledge; just as the figure traced by the veins of the marble is in the marble, before they are uncovered by the workman.

PH. But is it possible that children, when they receive notions which come to them from outside, and give to them

---

[1] In the speeches of Philalethes italics indicate Locke's own exact words; in those of Theophilus the italics are Leibniz's.

their assent, should still have no knowledge of those which are supposed to be innate and to form part of their mind, on which, it is said, they are *imprinted in indelible characters* to serve as a foundation? *This would be to make nature take pains to no purpose; or at least, to write very ill, since its characters could not be read by those eyes which saw other things very well.*

TH. The apperception of what is in us depends upon the presence of attention and upon order. Now it is not only possible, it is also fitting, that children should pay more attention to the notions of sense, because attention is regulated by need. The event, however, makes it clear in the sequel that nature did not take pains to no purpose in printing in us innate knowledge, since without such knowledge there would be no means of arriving at actual knowledge of necessary truths in the demonstrative sciences, and at the reasons of facts; and so we should have nothing more than the brutes.

§ 5. PH. . . . But you will have rather more difficulty in answering what I am now going to propound to you, namely that if any one particular proposition can be said to be innate, then the same reasoning will enable it to be maintained that all propositions that are reasonable, and that the mind is ever capable of regarding as such, are already imprinted in the soul. . . . Even supposing that there are truths which can be imprinted in the understanding, without the understanding perceiving them, I do not see how *in respect of their original* they can differ from the truths which it is simply capable of knowing.

TH. The mind is not simply capable of knowing them, but also of finding them in itself. If it had only the simple capacity to receive knowledge, or the passive potency necessary for that, as much without determinations as that which the wax has to receive shapes and the *tabula rasa* to receive letters, then it would not be the source of necessary truths, as I have just proved that in fact it is. For it is incontestable that the senses are not sufficient to make us see their necessity, and so the mind has the dispositions (as much active as passive) to draw them itself out of its own depths; though the senses are necessary to give to it the occasion and the attention required for this, and to lead it rather to the one sort than to the other. Thus you see, sir, that these people, clever as they are in other respects, who are of a different opinion, seem not to have reflected sufficiently about the consequences of the difference between truths which are necessary or eternal and truths of experience, as I have already remarked and as our whole dispute makes clear. The original proof of necessary truths comes from the understanding alone, and all other truths come from experiences or from observations of the senses. Our mind is capable of knowing both the one sort and the other, but it is the source of the first; whatever number of particular experiences we may have of a universal truth, we cannot assure ourselves of it for always by induction, without apprehending its necessity by reason.

PH. But is it not true that if these words, *to be in the understanding*, have any positive meaning they mean to be perceived and apprehended by the understanding?

TH. To me they mean something quite different. It is sufficient if that which is in the understanding is capable of being found there, and if the original sources of proofs of the truths which are here in question are simply in the understanding: the senses may suggest, justify, and confirm these truths, but they cannot demonstrate their infallible and perpetual certainty.

§ 18. TH. . . . Thoughts are actions, and apprehensions or truths, in so far as they are in us, even though we are not thinking of them, are habits or dispositions; and we have clear knowledge of things of which we hardly think at all.

PH. It is very difficult to conceive how a truth can be in the mind, if the mind has never thought of that truth.

TH. To say that is like saying that it is difficult to conceive that there are veins in the marble before they are uncovered. It appears, too, that this objection comes very near to a *petitio principii*. All those who allow innate truths, without making them dependent on a Platonic reminiscence, allow some of which the mind has not yet thought. Besides, this reasoning proves too much. If truths are thoughts, it will deprive us, not only of truths of which we have never thought, but also of those of which we have thought but are not actually thinking now. If truths are not thoughts, but habits and aptitudes, natural or acquired, then there is nothing to prevent the existence in us of truths of which we have never thought, no, nor ever shall think.

BOOK II. OF IDEAS

CHAPTER I

In which the author treats of ideas in general, and examines by the way whether the soul of man thinks always

§ 1. PH. Having now examined whether ideas are innate, let us consider their nature and their differences. Is it not true that an *idea is the object of thinking*?

TH. I agree, provided that you add that it is an immediate internal object, and that this object is an expression of the nature or of the qualities of things. If an idea were the *form* of thinking, it would come into being and cease with the actual thoughts which correspond to it; but being the *object* of thought, it can exist anterior to and posterior to the thoughts. External sensible objects are only *mediate*, because they cannot act immediately on the soul. God alone is the *immediate external* object. It might be said that the soul itself is its own immediate *internal* object; but it is so only as containing ideas, or that which corresponds to things. For the soul is a little world, in which distinct ideas are a representation of God and confused ideas are a representation of the universe.

§ 2. Ph. Our friends, who supposed that at the beginning the soul is a blank tablet, void of all characters and without any ideas, ask themselves how it comes to receive ideas, and by what means it acquires such a vast store. To this they answer in one word: from experience.

Th. This *tabula rasa* of which they talk so much, is nothing in my opinion but a fiction which nature does not admit, and which is founded only in the incomplete notions of the philosophers, like the void, atoms, rest (whether absolute rest or the relative rest of two parts of a whole in relation to one another), or like primary matter conceived as quite formless. Things which are uniform and contain no variety are never anything but abstractions, like time, space, and the other entities of pure mathematics. There is no body whose parts are at rest, and there is no substance which has not something to distinguish it from every other substance. Human souls differ not only from other souls, but also among themselves, although the difference is not of the nature of those which are called specific. And in accordance with the proofs which I think I can supply, every substantial thing, be it soul or body, has its relation to every other substantial thing, which is peculiar to itself; and one must always differ from another by *intrinsic denominations*. It need hardly be said that those who talk so much of this *tabula rasa*, after emptying it of all ideas, could not say what remains, just as the Schoolmen have nothing left for their primary matter. I shall be told, perhaps, that this *tabula rasa* of the philosophers means that the soul has naturally and originally nothing but bare faculties. But faculties without any activity, in a word the pure potencies of the Schools, these too are nothing but fictions, of which nature knows nothing, and which are obtained by making abstractions. For where in the world will you find a faculty which shuts itself up in a mere potency and never exercises any activity? There is always a particular disposition to action, and to one action rather than another. And besides the disposition there is always a tendency to action; indeed there is always an infinite number of them in every subject at any given time; and these tendencies are never without some effect. Experience is necessary, I allow, for the soul to be determined to such and such particular thoughts, and for it to take notice of the ideas which are in us. But by what means can experience and the senses provide ideas? Has the soul windows? Does it resemble a tablet? Is it like wax? It is evident that all those who speak thus of the soul treat it at bottom as corporeal. I shall have brought against me the axiom, accepted among the philosophers, that *there is nothing in the soul save that which comes from the senses.* But we must except the soul itself and its affections. *Nihil est in intellectu, quod non fuerit in sensu; excipe, nisi ipse intellectus.*[1] Now the soul contains existence, substance, unity, identity, cause, perception, reasoning, and a quantity of other notions which the senses could not afford. This is in agreement with your friend the author of the *Essay,* who finds the source of a good part of our ideas in the reflection of the mind upon its own nature.

PH. I hope, then, that you will agree with this able author that all our ideas come from sensation or from reflection, that is to say, from the observations we make either of

---

[1] 'There is nothing in the intellect which was not previously in the senses; *provided we make the reservation,* except the intellect itself.'

external, sensible objects or of the internal operations of our soul.

TH. To avoid a dispute over which we have delayed too long, I must make it quite clear at the outset, sir, that when you say that ideas come to us from the one or the other of these causes I understand you to speak of the actual perception of them, for I think I have shown that they are in us before they are apperceived in so far as they contain anything distinct.[1]

CHAPTER IX

Of Perception

§ 1. PH. Let us now turn to the ideas of reflection in detail. *Perception, as it is the first faculty of the mind exercised about our ideas, so it is the first and simplest idea we have from reflection. Thinking signifies that sort of operation of the mind about our ideas, wherein the mind is active ; where it, with some degree of voluntary attention, considers anything. For in bare naked perception, the mind is, for the most part, only passive ; and what it perceives, it cannot avoid perceiving.*

TH. We might perhaps add that brutes have perception, and that it is not necessary that they should have thought, that is to say, should have reflection or anything that can be the object of reflection. Moreover, we ourselves have minute *perceptions* which we do not apperceive in our present state. It is true that we could quite well apperceive them or reflect on them, if we were not deterred by their multitude, which distracts our mind, and if they were not effaced or rather obscured by greater ones.

§ 4. PH. I admit that *whilst the mind is intently employed in the contemplation of some objects it takes no notice of im-*

---

[1] In the remainder of this chapter Leibniz discusses Locke's contention that *the mind thinks not always.*

pressions of sounding bodies made upon the organ of hearing. A sufficient impulse there may be on the organ ; but if not reaching the observation of the mind, there follows no perception.

TH. I should prefer to distinguish between *perception* and *apperceiving*. The perception of the light or of the colour, for example, which we do apperceive, is composed of a number of minute perceptions, which we do not apperceive; and a noise of which we have perception, but of which we do not take notice, becomes *apperceptible* by a slight addition or increase. For if what precedes made no impression on the soul, neither would this little addition make any, and the whole would make none either. I have already touched on this point in ch. i of this book, §§ 11, 12, and 15.

§ 8. PH. *We are further to consider concerning perception, that the ideas we receive by sensation are often in grown people altered by the judgment, without our taking notice of it.* The idea imprinted on the mind by a globe of uniform colour is that of *a flat circle variously shadowed and with several degrees of light and brightness coming to our eyes. But we have by use been accustomed to perceive what kind of appearance convex bodies are wont to make in us, what alterations are made in the reflections of light by the difference of the sensible figures of bodies ;* and so we put in the place of what appears to us the actual cause of the image, and confuse judgment with vision.

TH. Nothing is more true, and this it is which provides the painter with the means of deceiving us by the artifice of a perspective which we can well understand. When bodies have flat surfaces, we can represent them without making use of shadows, by employing outlines only, and by simply making pictures in the fashion of the Chinese, only more in proportion than theirs. This is the usual way of drawing medals, so that the draughtsman may keep closer to the precise features of the originals. But there is no way by drawing, of exactly distinguishing the inside of a circle from the inside of a spherical surface bounded by that circle, without the assistance of shadows, since the insides have in neither case any distinct points or distinguishing features, although there is all the same a great difference which must be shown. This is why M. Des Argues laid down precepts about the effect of tints and shadows. When a painting deceives us there is a double error in our judgments; for in the first place we substitute the cause for the effect, and think we are seeing immediately that which is the cause of the image, rather like a dog who barks at a mirror. For, strictly speaking, we only see the image, and are affected by nothing but rays of light. And since these rays of light need time (however short), it is possible that the object might have been destroyed during this interval and no longer exist by the time the ray reaches the eye; and what no longer exists cannot be the present object of vision. In the second place we are mistaken in substituting one cause for another, and thinking that what only comes from a flat painting is derived from a body; so that in this case there is in our judgments at the same time both a *metonymy* and a *metaphor*; for the very figures of rhetoric become *sophisms* when they impose upon us. This confusion of the effect with the cause, whether real or alleged, often enters into our judgments in other places as well. It is involved when we feel our bodies, or what touches them, and when we move our arms, by an immediate physical influence, which we think constitutes the communion of the soul and the body; whereas the truth is that we feel and change in this way only what is within us.

§ 8. Ph. I shall here insert a problem which was sent to the illustrious Mr. Locke by that very ingenious and studious promoter of real knowledge, the learned Mr. Molyneux. It was stated very much as follows: *Suppose a man born blind, and now adult, and taught by his touch to distinguish between a cube and a sphere of the same metal, and nighly of the same bigness, so as to tell, when he felt one and the other, which is the cube, which the sphere. Suppose, then, the cube and sphere placed on a table, and the blind man be made to see: quaere, whether by his sight, before he touched them, he could now distinguish and tell which is the globe, which the cube?* I beg you, sir, to tell me your opinion on this matter.

TH. I should need time to think about this question, which seems to me a remarkable one; but since you urge me to reply on the spot, I venture to say, between ourselves, that I believe that if the blind man knew that the two figures he was looking at were the cube and the globe, he would be able to distinguish them, and say without touching them: This is the globe, this the cube.

PH. I fear that you must be numbered with the crowd of those who have wrongly answered Mr. Molyneux. For in the letter which contained this question, he stated that he had propounded it to various men of acute mind, apropos of Mr. Locke's *Essay on the Human Understanding*, and had found hardly one who began by giving him what he considered the right answer, although they became convinced of their mistake on hearing his reasons. This acute and judicious author answers: *Not. For, though he* (the blind man) *has obtained the experience of how a globe, how a cube affects his touch, yet he has not obtained the experience, that what affects his touch so or so must affect his sight so or so ; or that a protuberant angle in the cube, that pressed his hand unequally, shall appear to his eye as it does in the cube.* The author of the *Essay* declares that he is altogether of the same opinion.

TH. Perhaps Mr. Molyneux and the author of the *Essay* are not as far removed from my opinion as at first appears, and perhaps the reasons for their view, which were apparently contained in the letter of Mr. Molyneux, who had successfully made use of them to convince people of their mistake, were purposely suppressed by Mr. Locke so as further to exercise the minds of his readers. If you will closely consider my answer, you will find that I have included in it a condition which may be taken to be implied in the question, that is, that it is only a question of distinguishing; and that the blind man knows that the two shaped bodies which he has to distinguish are there, and therefore that each of the appearances he sees is either that of the cube or that of the globe. In this case it seems to me certain that the blind man who has just ceased to be blind can distinguish them by the principles of reason, combined with what sensuous knowledge he has previously acquired by touch. I am not speaking of what he perhaps will do actually and on the spot; for he will be dazzled and confused by novelty, as well as little accustomed to drawing conclusions. The foundation of my opinion is, that in the globe there are no points distinguished from the side of the globe itself, all of it being uniform and without angles, whereas in the cube there are eight points distinguished from all the others. If there were not this method of distinguishing figures, a blind man could not learn the rudiments of geometry by means of touch. Yet we see that men born blind are capable of learning geometry, and even have always some rudiments of a natural geometry; moreover geometry is most often learnt simply by sight, without the use of touch, as it could be, and indeed would have to be, learnt in the case of a paralytic or any other person who was more or less incapable of touch. And these two geometries, the geometry of the blind man and that of the paralytic, must meet and agree and even come back to the same ideas, although they have no common images. This shows again how necessary it is to distinguish *images* from *exact ideas*, which consist of definitions. Indeed, it would be most interesting and even instructive thoroughly to examine the ideas of a man born blind, and to hear his descriptions of figures. For he can give such descriptions, and can even understand the doctrine of optics, in so far as it is dependent on ideas that are distinct and mathematical, although he cannot manage to conceive anything which is chiaroscuro, that is to say the image of light and colours. This is why a certain man, born blind, after listening to some lessons on optics, which he seemed to understand pretty well, when asked what he thought about light replied that he imagined it must be something pleasant like sugar. In the same way it would be very important to examine the ideas of a man born deaf and dumb about things without shapes, ideas which we ordinarily describe in words, and which he must acquire in a quite different way, although it may be equivalent to ours, as the writing of the Chinese has the same effect as our alphabet, although it is infinitely different from it, and might seem to have been invented by a deaf man. I have heard, through the courtesy of a great prince, of a man in Paris, born deaf and dumb, whose ears finally came to perform their proper office; this man has now learnt French (for it was from the French Court that he was summoned not long ago) and can tell many curious things about the conceptions he had in his former state, and about the change in his ideas, when his sense of hearing began to function. These people who are born deaf and dumb can go further than we think. There was one at Oldenburg in the time of the last count, who became a good painter, and showed himself very rational in other respects. A very learned man, Breton by nationality, told me that at Blainville, a place ten leagues from Nantes, belonging to the Duke of Rohan, there was about 1690 a poor man living in a hut, near to the castle outside the town, who was born deaf and dumb, and who took letters and other things to the town, finding the houses by means of signs made him by the people who used to employ him. At last the poor man became blind too, and still did not give up performing services, and carrying letters to the town on the strength of what he was told by touch. He had in his hut a plank which went from the door to the place where his feet were, and which made him aware by its movement when any one came in. People are most negligent not to acquire exact knowledge of the ways of thinking of such persons. If he is no longer alive, there is likely to be someone in the vicinity who could still give us some information about him, and make us understand how he was shown the things he was to do. But to return to what the man born blind, who is beginning to see, will think about the globe and the cube, when he sees them without touching them, I answer that he will distinguish them in the way I have said, if someone informs him that one or the other of the appearances or perceptions he has of them belongs to the cube or to the globe; but without this preliminary instruction, I admit that it would not at first occur to him to think that these sorts of paintings which he received of them in the depths of his eyes, and which might arise from a flat painting on the table, represented bodies, until touch had convinced him of it, or until, by dint of reasoning about rays according to the laws of optics, he understood by the lights and the shadows that there was something there which arrested these rays, and that it was this which remained present to his sense of touch. He would arrive at this view finally, when he saw the globe and cube rolling along, and changing shadows and appearances as the result of their motion, or even when, the two bodies remaining at rest, the light which illuminated them changed its place, or his eyes changed their position. For these are more or less our methods of distinguishing at a distance between a picture or a perspective representing a body, and an actual body itself.

§ 11. PH. Let us return to perception in general. *Perception puts the difference between animals and inferior beings*.

TH. I am inclined to think that there is some perception and appetition in plants also, on account of the important analogy which exists between plants and animals; and if there is a vegetable soul, as is the common view, it must have perception. But I none the less attribute to mechanism all that takes place in the bodies of plants and animals, except their original formation. Thus I agree that the motion of the plant which is commonly called sensitive arises from mechanism, and I do not approve of having recourse to the soul for explaining the detail of the phenomena of plants and of animals.

§ 14. PH. It is true that I myself cannot but think that even in such kinds of animals, as oysters and cockles, *there is some small dull perception: for would not quickness of sensation be an inconvenience to an animal that must lie still where chance has once placed it, and there receive the afflux of colder or warmer, clean or foul water, as it happens to come to it?*

TH. Very true; and I hold that nearly as much could be said of plants; but as to man, his perceptions are accompanied by the power of reflection, which passes into action when need arises. But when he is reduced to a state like that of one who is in a lethargy, and is almost without sensation, reflection and apperception cease, and there is no longer any thought of universal truths. Nevertheless, his faculties and dispositions, innate and acquired, and even the impressions he has received in this state of confusion, do not for that reason cease, and are not wiped out, even though they are forgotten; they will even take their turn in contributing one day to some notable result. For nothing in nature is useless; every confusion is bound to be cleared up; the very animals, reduced to a state of stupidity, must one day return to more exalted perceptions; and since simple substances endure for ever, we must not judge of eternity by a few years.

BOOK IV. OF KNOWLEDGE

CHAPTER II

Of the degrees of our knowledge

§ 1. PH. *Knowledge* is *intuitive* when *the mind perceives the agreement or disagreement of two ideas immediately by themselves, without the intervention of any other.* In this case *the mind is at no pains of proving or examining* the truth. As the eye sees the light, the mind sees that white is not black, that a circle is not a triangle, that three is two and one. *This kind of knowledge is the clearest and most certain that human frailty is capable of;* it acts in a manner that is irresistible, and it leaves no room in the mind for hesitation. It is to know that the idea in the mind is such as it is perceived to be. *He that demands a greater certainty than this, demands he knows not what.*

TH. The *primary* truths which are known by *intuition* are of two kinds, like *derivative* truths. They are either *truths of reason* or *truths of fact*. Truths of reason are necessary, those of fact are contingent. The primary truths of reason are those which I call by the general name of *identical*, because it appears that they do nothing but repeat the same thing, without teaching us anything. They are affirmative or negative. . . .[1]

Someone perhaps, after listening patiently to all that I have just said, will at last lose patience and say that I am amusing myself with frivolous enunciations, and that identical truths serve no purpose whatever. But such a judgment would be due to insufficient reflection on these matters. The consequences of logic, for example, are proved by principles which are identical; and geometry relies upon the principle of contradiction in those demonstrations which reduce *ad impossibile*. I will content myself here with showing the value of identical propositions in the demonstrations of the consequences of reasoning. I say then that the principle of contradiction alone is sufficient to demonstrate the second and third figures of the syllogism from the first. Take an example in the first figure, in *Barbara*:

All B is C

All A is B

∴ all A is C.

[1] Here follows about a page of instances of identical propositions, affirmative and negative, hypothetical, disjunctive, etc.

Let us suppose that the conclusion is false (or that it is true that some *A* is not *C*), then the one or the other of the premises will be false also. Suppose the second is true: then the first, which asserts that all *B* is *C*, must be false. Then its contrary will be true; that is to say, some *B* is not *C*. And this will be the conclusion of a new argument, drawn from the falsity of the conclusion and the truth of one of the premises of the preceding argument. Here is the new argument:

Some *A* is not *C*

(which is opposite to the previous conclusion, supposed to be false).

All *A* is *B*

(this is the previous premise, supposed to be true).

∴ some *B* is not *C*

(this is the present conclusion, which is true, the opposite of the previous premise, which was false).

This argument is in the mood *Disamis* of the third figure, which is thus demonstrated obviously and at a flash from the mood *Barbara* of the first figure, without involving anything but the principle of contradiction. And I observed in my youth, when I was criticizing these things, that all the moods of the second and third figures can be obtained from the first by this one method, if we suppose that the mood of the first is valid, and consequently that, the conclusion being false and its contrary being taken for true, and one of the premises being taken for true also, it follows that the contrary of the other premise must be true. It is true that in the Schools of logic they prefer to make use of conversions.[1] . . .

[1] The validity of conversions themselves, Leibniz says, must be demonstrated from the primary principle, that of contradiction; it is therefore better to demonstrate the second and third figures direct, as above, and not to use conversion.

Since the demonstration of conversions also shows the value of *identical affirmative* propositions, which some take to be utterly frivolous, it is all the more relevant to include it here. I will only mention conversions without contraposition, which are sufficient for my purpose here, and which are either simple or *per accidens*, as they are called. Simple conversions are of two kinds: the universal negative, like *No square is obtuse-angled, therefore no obtuse-angled figure is square ;* and the particular affirmative, such as *Some triangles are obtuse-angled, therefore some obtuse-angled figures are triangles.* But conversion *per accidens*, as it is called, concerns the universal affirmative, such as *All squares are rectangles, therefore some rectangles are squares.* By *rectangle* here is always understood a figure whose angles are right angles, and by *square* a regular quadrilateral. We have now to demonstrate these three kinds of conversions, which are:

(1) No A is B, $\therefore$ no B is A.
(2) Some A is B, $\therefore$ some B is A.
(3) All A is B, $\therefore$ some B is A.

Demonstration of the first conversion in *Cesare*, which is of the second figure:

No A is B
All B is B
$\therefore$ no B is A.

Demonstration of the second conversion in *Datisi*, which is of the third figure:

All A is A
Some A is B
$\therefore$ some B is A.

Demonstration of the third conversion in *Darapti*, which is of the third figure:

All A is A
All A is B
$\therefore$ some B is A.

This shows that identical propositions which are most pure and appear to be most useless have considerable value in the abstract and in general. And that should teach us not to despise any truth. As regards the proposition that *three is equal to two and one*, which you adduce, Sir, as an example of intuitive knowledge, my comment is that it is simply the definition of the term *three*; for the simplest definitions of numbers are formed in this manner—*two* is one and one, *three* is two and one, *four* is three and one, and so on. It is true that there is hidden within these definitions an enunciation, which I have already mentioned, namely that these ideas are possible; and that is known in this case *intuitively*, so that we may say that there is intuitive knowledge contained in definitions when their possibility first appears. And in this way all *adequate* definitions contain primary truths of reason, and consequently intuitive knowledge. Finally, we may say in general that all primary truths of reason are immediate with an *immediacy of ideas*.

As regards *primary truths of fact*, these are the immediate internal experiences of an *immediacy of sensation*. It is among these that is included the first truth of the Cartesians or of Saint Augustine: *I think, therefore I am*, that is to say, *I am a thing which thinks*. But it is to be noted that the same is true of primary truths of fact as of identicals, that is to say that they can be either general or particular, and are as clear in the one case as in the other (since it is as clear to say that *A is A* as to say that *a thing is what it is*.) For not only is it clear to me immediately that *I think*, but it is just as clear to me that I have *different thoughts*, that now *I think of A* and now *I think of B*, etc. Thus the Cartesian principle is sound, but it is not the only one of its kind. So we see that all *primary truths* of reason or of fact have this in common that they cannot be proved by something more certain.

§ 2. Ph. I am very much pleased, sir, that you have developed further my remarks, in which I did no more than touch upon *intuitive* knowledge. Now *demonstrative knowledge* is simply a linking together of intuitive apprehensions in all the connections of the mediate ideas. For often the mind cannot join, compare, or apply its ideas to one another immediately, and so it is obliged to make use of other mediating ideas (one or more, as it happens) in order to discover the agreement or disagreement it is looking for; and this is called *reasoning*. For instance, in demonstrating that the three angles of a triangle are equal to two right angles, it finds out some other angles which it sees to be equal both to the three angles of the triangle and to two right angles. § 3. These intervening ideas are called *proofs*; and a quickness of the mind to find them is what is called *sagacity*. § 4. Even when these ideas have been found, it is not without pains and attention, nor by a single transient view, that this knowledge can be acquired; there must be *a progression of ideas by steps and degrees*. § 5. Before the demonstration there is a doubt. § 6. It is less clear than intuitive knowledge; just as a face reflected by several mirrors one to another grows weaker and weaker at each successive reflection, and is not at first sight so knowable, especially to weak eyes. *Thus it is with knowledge made out by a long train of proof.* § 7. And though in each step which reason makes in demonstrating there is an intuitive knowledge, or knowledge at sight, yet because in this long succession of proofs the memory does not retain so exactly this chain of ideas, men often embrace falsehoods for demonstrations.

Th. Over and above sagacity, whether natural or acquired by exercise, there is an art of finding mediating ideas (the *medium*); and this art is *Analysis*. Now it is well to consider here that it is sometimes a question of finding out the truth or falsity of a given proposition, that is, simply to answer the question *whether ?*—that is to say, Is it or is it not? At other times it is a matter of answering a question which is much more difficult (*ceteris paribus*); for instance,

where it is asked *by what means ?* or *how ?*—and where there is
more to be supplied. It is these questions only, which leave
part of the proposition blank, which mathematicians call
problems: for instance when we are asked to find a mirror
which collects all the rays of the sun at a point; that is to say
we are asked its shape, or how it is made. As for the first
kind of questions, where it is simply a matter of true and
false, and where there is nothing to supply in the subject or
predicate, here there is less *invention*; still there is some, and
judgment alone is not sufficient. It is true that a man of
judgment, that is to say, one who is capable of attention and
restraint, and who has the necessary leisure and patience and
is open-minded enough, can understand the most difficult
demonstration if it is properly put to him. But the most
judicious man in the world will not always be able to find
the demonstration without assistance. Thus there is some
invention in that too; and in geometry there used to be more
in earlier times than there is now. For when the art of
Analysis was less cultivated, it required more sagacity to
arrive at it. . . . It also happens that induction provides us
with some truths about numbers and figures, for which the
general reason has not yet been discovered. For we are
far from having arrived at the perfection of Analysis in
geometry and in numbers. . . .

But it is much more difficult to find out important truths,
and even more so to find out means of doing what is wanted,
just when it is wanted, than it is to find out the demonstration
of what someone else has discovered. Often beautiful truths
are arrived at by *Synthesis*, by passing from the simple to the
compound; but when it is a matter of finding out exactly the
means for doing what is required, Synthesis is ordinarily not
sufficient; and often a man might as well try to drink up the
sea as to make all the required combinations, even though it
is often possible to gain some assistance from the *method of
exclusions*, which cuts out a considerable number of useless

combinations; and often the nature of the case does not admit of any other method. But there are not always available the means for properly following this method. So it is to Analysis that we must look for a thread in the labyrinth, whenever it is possible; for there are cases where the very nature of the question requires that we should proceed by trial and error throughout, short cuts not always being possible.

§ 8. PH. Now since demonstration always presupposes intuitive knowledge, it is this, I imagine, which gave occasion to the axiom that *all reasoning is from things previously known and previously granted (ex praecognitis et praeconcessis)*. But we shall have occasion to speak of the faults of this axiom, when we come to speak of the *maxims* which are mistakenly supposed to be the foundations of our reasonings.

TH. I shall be curious to learn what fault you can find with an axiom which appears so reasonable. If it was necessary to reduce everything to intuitive apprehensions, demonstrations would often be of unbearable prolixity. . . . But there is another hindrance, namely that it is not easy to demonstrate all the axioms, and entirely to reduce demonstrations to intuitive apprehensions. And if attempts had been made to do this, perhaps we should still be without the science of geometry. . . .

§ 14. PH. Besides *intuition* and *demonstration*, which are the two degrees of our knowledge, all the rest is *faith or opinion, but not knowledge, at least in all general truths*. There is, however, *another perception of the mind employed about the particular existence of finite beings without us* ; and this is called *sensitive knowledge*. . . .

Sensitive knowledge, or the knowledge which establishes the existence of particular beings without us, goes beyond bare probability; but it does not possess all the certainty of the two degrees of knowledge of which we have been speaking. *There can be nothing more certain than that the idea we receive*

*from an external object is in our minds. But whether we can
thence certainly infer the existence of anything without us which
corresponds to that idea, is that whereof some men think there
may be a question made ; because men may have such ideas in
their minds when no such thing exists, no such object affects
their senses. But yet here I think we are provided with an
evidence which puts us past doubting.* We are invincibly
conscious of a different perception when we look on the sun
by day and think on it by night; and the idea which is revived
by the aid of memory is very different from the one which
actually comes into our minds by our senses. *If any one says
a dream may do the same thing, I make him this answer:* (1)
*That it is no great matter whether I remove this scruple or no:
where all is but dream, reasoning and arguments are of no use,
truth and knowledge nothing.* (2) *That I believe he will allow
a very manifest difference between dreaming of being in the
fire and being actually in it.* And if he persists in appearing
sceptical, I will tell him that it is enough that we certainly
find *that pleasure or pain follows upon the application of
certain objects to us, whose existence we perceive, or dream that
we perceive, by our senses: this certainty is as great as our
happiness or misery ; beyond which we have no concernment to
know or to be.* So that I think we may reckon *three degrees of
knowledge ; viz., intuitive, demonstrative, and sensitive.*

Th. I believe you are right, and I even think that to these
kinds of *certainty* or *certain knowledge* you might add *knowledge of the probable*; thus there will be two sorts of *knowledge*
as there are two sorts of *proofs*, of which the one produces
certainty, while the other arrives at *probability* only. But let
us turn to the quarrel between the Sceptics and the Dog-
matists over the existence of things without us. We have
already touched upon it, but we must return to it here. I have
in the past had much argument about this both personally
and by letter with the late M. l'Abbé Foucher, Canon of
Dijon, a man both learned and subtle, but somewhat too

much engrossed in the Academics, whose sect he would gladly have revived, just as M. Gassendi brought back upon the scene the sect of Epicurus. His criticism of the *Recherche de la Vérité*, and other small treatises which he had printed subsequently, have brought their author some fame. He also published in the *Journal des Savans* some objections to my System of Pre-established Harmony, when I communicated it to the public, after meditating on it for some years; but death prevented him from answering my reply. He always preached that we ought to guard against prejudices and to insist on great exactitude; but not only did he not devote himself to practising what he preached, wherein he was excusable enough, but he also seemed to me not to heed whether others did so, foreseeing no doubt that no one ever would. Now I pointed out to him that the truth of sensible things only consisted in the connection of phenomena, for which there must be a reason, and which is the thing that distinguishes them from dreams; but that the truth of our existence and of the cause of phenomena is of another nature, because it establishes some substances. I urged that the Sceptics spoil what is good in their statements, by carrying them too far, even wishing to extend their doubts to immediate experiences, and even to geometrical truths (which, however, M. Foucher did not do), and to other truths of reason, which he did a little too much. But, to return to you, Sir, you are right in saying that there is a difference ordinarily between sensations and imaginings; but the Sceptics would say that a difference of more and less is not a difference of kind. Besides, though sensations are habitually more vivacious than imaginings, there are none the less cases where imaginative people are as much or perhaps more struck by their imaginings than others are by the truth of things; so that I hold that the true criterion regarding the objects of the senses is the connection between phenomena, that is to say the linking up of what occurs in different places and times, and in the experience of different men, who are themselves very important phenomena to one another in this regard. And the connection of phenomena, which guarantees *truths of fact* with regard to sensible things outside us, is verified by means of *truths of reason*; as appearances in optics have light thrown upon them by geometry. Still it must be admitted that none of this certitude is of the highest order, as you have rightly recognized. For it is not impossible, metaphysically speaking, for there to be a dream which is consecutive and enduring like the life of a man; but it is a thing as contrary to reason as it would be for a book to be composed by chance through the type being jumbled up together anyhow. Besides it is also true, that provided phenomena are linked up, it matters not whether they are called dreams or not, since experience shows that we are not mistaken in the measures we take with phenomena, when they are taken in accordance with the truths of reason.

§ 15 PH. For the rest, *knowledge is not always clear, where the ideas are so. A man that has as clear ideas of the angles of a triangle, and of equality to two right ones, as any mathematician in the world, may yet have but a very obscure perception of their agreement.*

TH. Usually, when ideas are fundamentally understood, their agreements and disagreements appear. Nevertheless, I admit that there are sometimes ideas so compounded that much care is needed to develop what is hidden in them; and considering this, some agreements and disagreements may still remain obscure. As to your example, my comment is that the fact that we have the angles of a triangle in the imagination does not mean that we therefore have clear ideas of them. Imagination is incapable of providing us with an image common to acute-angled and obtuse-angled triangles, and yet the idea of triangle is common to both. Thus this idea does not consist in the images, and it is not as easy as one might think fundamentally to understand the angles of a triangle.

CORRESPONDENCE WITH CLARKE [1]

(Extract from a letter written in November 1715)

IT appears that even natural religion is growing very much weaker. Many hold that souls are corporeal; others hold that God Himself is corporeal. Mr. Locke and his followers are at any rate doubtful whether souls are not material and naturally perishable. Mr. Newton says that space is the organ which God makes use of to perceive things by. But if He stands in need of any medium whereby to perceive them, they do not then depend entirely on Him, and were not produced by Him. Mr. Newton and his followers have also an extremely odd opinion of the work of God. According to them God has to wind up His watch from time to time.[3] Otherwise it would cease to go. He lacked sufficient foresight to make it a perpetual motion. This machine of God's is even, on their view, so imperfect that He is obliged from time to time to come to its assistance especially out of the

[1] Samuel Clarke (1675–1729), English philosopher and divine; the most celebrated disciple of Newton.
[2] This paper by Leibniz begins the correspondence. It is given here complete.
[3] Clarke thinks that the passage to which Leibniz is referring is the following, from Newton's *Optics*: ' Whilst the comets move in orbs very eccentrical, with all variety of directions towards every part of the heavens; 'tis not possible it should have been caused by blind fate, that the planets all move with one similar direction in concentrick orbs; excepting only some very small irregularities, which may have arisen from the mutual actions of the planets and comets upon one another; and which 'tis probable will in length of time increase more and more, till the present system of nature shall want to be anew put in order by its Author.' (The translation from Newton's Latin is Clarke's.)

ordinary course, and clean it, and even to mend it, as a clock-maker might his handiwork; and the less skilful the workman is, the more often is he obliged to rehandle and correct his work. According to my view, the same force and vigour goes on existing in the world always, and simply passes from one matter to another, according to the laws of nature and to the beautiful pre-established order. And I hold that, when God performs miracles, it is not to uphold the needs of nature, but for those of grace. To think otherwise would be to have a very low opinion of the wisdom and power of God.

LEIBNIZ'S SECOND PAPER [1]

It is rightly said in the Paper which was sent to the Princess of Wales, and which Her Royal Highness did me the honour of sending me, that next to vicious passions *the principles of the Materialists* contribute much to support impiety. But I do not think the author was justified in adding that *the Mathematical Principles of philosophy are opposed to those of the Materialists*. On the contrary, they are the same except that Materialists follow the example of Democritus, Epicurus, and Hobbes, and restrict themselves to mathematical principles alone and admit nothing but bodies; while the Christian Mathematicians admit immaterial substances also. Thus it is not Mathematical Principles (in the ordinary sense of the term) but *Metaphysical Principles* which must be opposed to those of the Materialists. Pythagoras, Plato, and to some extent Aristotle had some knowledge of these, but it is my claim to have established them demonstratively, although I was giving a popular exposition, in my *Theodicy*. The great foundation of mathematics is the *principle of contradiction* or of *identity*, that is to say, that a statement cannot be true and false at the same time and that thus *A is A, and*

[1] This *Second Paper* was written in answer to Clarke's reply to Leibniz's *First Paper*. It is given here complete.

cannot be not A. And this single principle is enough to prove the whole of arithmetic and the whole of geometry, that is to say all mathematical principles. But in order to proceed from mathematics to physics another principle is necessary, as I have observed in my *Theodicy*, that is, the *principle of a sufficient reason*, that nothing happens without there being a reason why it should be thus rather than otherwise. This is why Archimedes, wishing to proceed from mathematics to physics in his book *On Equilibrium*, was compelled to make use of a particular case of the great principle of sufficient reason; he takes it for granted that if there is a balance in which everything is the same on both sides, and if, further, two equal weights be hung on the two ends of the balance, the whole will remain at rest. This is because there is no reason why one side should go down rather than the other. Now by this principle alone, to wit, that there must be a sufficient reason why things are thus rather than otherwise, is proved Divinity, and all the rest of metaphysics and natural theology, and even in some manner those physical principles which are independent of mathematics, that is to say, the principles of dynamics or of force.

Our author goes on to say that according to the mathematical principles, that is to say according to the philosophy of Mr. Newton (for mathematical principles here prove nothing one way or the other), *matter is the least considerable part of the universe.* This is because he holds that besides matter there is empty space, and because according to him matter only occupies a very small part of space. But Democritus and Epicurus maintained the same thing, except that in this they differed from Mr. Newton on the point of quantity; according to them there was perhaps more matter in the world than according to Mr. Newton. Wherein I think their view is preferable; for the more matter there is, the more opportunity is there for God to exercise His wisdom and His power; and it is for this, among other reasons, that I hold that there is no void at all.

It is said expressly in the Appendix to Mr. Newton's *Optics* that *space is God's sensorium*.[1] Now the word *sensorium* has always meant the organ of sensation. Let him and his friends now give a quite different explanation of their meaning: I shall not object.

Our author supposes that the presence of the soul is enough to enable it to perceive what is going on in the brain. But this is exactly what Malebranche and the whole Cartesian School deny, and rightly deny. Something quite other than mere presence is needed for one thing to represent what takes place in another. For this some explicable communication is necessary, some kind of influence either of the things upon one another or of a common cause. Space, according to Mr. Newton, is intimately present to the body which it contains and which is commensurate with it. Does it therefore follow that space perceives what takes place in the body, and remembers it after the body has left it? Besides, since the soul is indivisible and its immediate presence in the body could therefore be conceived to be at a point only, how could it then perceive what took place outside this point? I claim to be the first to have shown how the soul perceives what takes place in the body.

The reason why God perceives everything is not His simple presence, but His operation also; it is because He preserves things by an activity which continually produces all that there is in them of goodness and perfection. But since souls have no immediate influence on bodies, nor bodies on souls, their mutual correspondence cannot be explained by presence.

The real reason which chiefly causes us to praise a

---

[1] Clarke had objected to Leibniz's statement in his *First Paper* that 'Mr. Newton says that space is the organ which God makes use of to perceive things by'. Cf. p. 192.

machine, is derived rather from the effect of the machine than from its cause. We seek information less regarding the power of the mechanician than regarding his invention. Thus the reason alleged for praising God's machine—that He made it entirely without borrowing any matter from outside—is not enough. It is a shift to which the author has been compelled to resort. The reason why God is to be preferred above another mechanician is not only because He makes the whole, whereas the artisan has to seek for his material. This superiority would arise from power only. But there is another reason for the excellence of God, which arises from wisdom. This reason is that His machine also lasts longer and goes more correctly than that of any other mechanician whatever. The buyer of the watch does not trouble himself whether the workman made the whole of it, or whether he had the pieces of it made by other workmen and merely adjusted them himself, provided that it goes properly. And if the workman had received from God the gift of creating as well the material for the wheels, the buyer would not be satisfied if he had not also received the gift of adjusting them properly. And in the same way the man who wants to be satisfied with God's handiwork will not become so merely for the reason alleged here.

Thus it is needful that God's invention should not be inferior to that of a workman; it must even go infinitely beyond it. The mere production of everything would indeed exemplify the power of God, but it would not sufficiently show His wisdom. Those who maintain the opposite fall exactly into the error of the Materialists and of Spinoza, from whom they protest they differ. They recognize power, but not sufficient wisdom in the principle of things.

I do not say that the corporeal world is a machine or watch which goes without God's *interposition*,[1] and I am insistent

---

[1] Clarke had made the (usual) objection to Leibniz: 'The notion of the world's being a great *machine*, going on *without the inter-*

enough that created things stand in need of His continual influence. But I do maintain that it is a watch which goes without needing His *correction*: otherwise we should have to admit that God keeps improving upon His own work. God has foreseen everything, He has provided a remedy for everything in advance. There is in His works an already preestablished harmony and beauty.

This view does not exclude the providence or the government of God: on the contrary it makes it perfect. A true providence in God requires a perfect *foresight*, but moreover it further requires not only that He should have *foreseen* everything but also that He should have provided for everything by means of suitable preordained remedies: otherwise He would lack either wisdom to *foresee* things or power to *provide for* them. He would be like the God of the Socinians, who lives from day to day, as M. Jurieu said. It is true that God, according to the Socinians, fails even to foresee defects, whereas, according to these gentlemen who force Him to correct Himself, He fails to provide for them. But this seems to me to be still a very great lack; He would have to lack either power or good will.

I do not think I can be justly rebuked for having said that God is *Intelligentia Supramundana*. Will those who disapprove of it say He is *Intelligentia Mundana*, that is to say the Soul of the World? I hope not. However, they would do well to take care not to slip into this unintentionally.

The comparison with a king in whose kingdom everything went on without his interference is not to the point, since God preserves things continually, and since they cannot subsist without Him: thus His Kingdom is not a nominal one. To say this would be like saying that a king who had his *position of God*, as a clock continues to go without the assistance of a clockmaker, is the notion of *Materialism* and *Fate*, and tends (under pretence of making God a *Supra-mundane Intelligence*) to exclude *Providence* and *God's government* in reality out of the world'.

subjects so well educated, and by his care in providing for their subsistence, preserved them so well in their fitness for their several stations and in their good affection towards him, that he had no occasion ever to be amending anything amongst them, was only a nominal king.

Finally, if God is obliged to correct natural things from time to time, this must occur either supernaturally or naturally. If it occurs supernaturally, recourse is had to miracles to explain natural things; which is in effect a *reductio ad absurdum* of a hypothesis. For by miracles, anything can easily be accounted for. But if it occurs naturally, God will not be *Intelligentia Supramundana*, He will be included in the nature of things, that is to say, He will be the Soul of the World.

LEIBNIZ'S THIRD PAPER [1]

1. According to the usual way of speaking, *mathematical principles* [2] are those which consist in pure mathematics, for instance numbers, figures, arithmetic, geometry. But *metaphysical principles* concern more general notions, as for example cause and effect.

2. I am granted this important *principle, that nothing happens without a sufficient reason why it should be thus rather than otherwise.* But it is granted me in words and refused me in fact; which shows that the full force of it has not been properly understood; and in this connection the author makes

[1] Written in answer to Clarke's reply to the *Second Paper*. It is given here complete.

[2] Clarke had argued that the *Mathematical Principles of Philosophy* (i.e. Newton's philosophical doctrines) are opposed to *Materialism* because they demonstrate that the existing state of things can only have arisen from an Intelligent and Free Cause. As regards the propriety of the name; he says: 'So far as metaphysical consequences follow demonstratively from mathematical principles, so far the mathematical principles may (if it be thought fit) be called metaphysical principles'.

use of an example which exactly falls in with one of my demonstrations against real absolute space, the *idol* of some modern Englishmen. I call it 'idol' not in a theological sense, but in the philosophical sense in which Chancellor Bacon used the word when he said, a long time ago, that there are *idola tribus, idola specus*.[1]

3. These gentlemen maintain, then, that space is a real absolute being; but this leads them into great difficulties. For it appears that this being must be eternal and infinite. This is why there have been some who believed that it was God Himself, or else His attribute, His immensity. But as it has parts, it is not a thing which can be appropriate to God.

4. As for me, I have more than once stated that I held *space* to be something purely relative, like *time*; space being an order of co-existences as time is an order of successions. For space denotes in terms of possibility an order of things which exist at the same time, in so far as they exist together, and is not concerned with their particular ways of existing: and when we see several things together we perceive this order of things among themselves.

5. I have several proofs for refuting the conception of those who take *space* to be a substance, or at least an absolute being of some kind. But here I only wish to make use of the one which the present occasion requires. I say then that if space were an absolute being, there would happen something for which it would be impossible that there should be a sufficient reason, and this is contrary to our axiom. This is how I prove it. Space is something absolutely uniform, and without the things situated in it one point of space absolutely does not differ in any respect from another point of space. Now from this it follows that if we suppose that space is something in itself, other than the order of bodies among themselves, it is impossible that there should be a

---

[1] 'idols of the tribe, idols of the cave.'

reason why God, preserving the same positions for bodies among themselves, should have arranged bodies in space thus and not otherwise, and why everything was not put the other way round (for instance) by changing east and west. But if space is nothing other than this order or relation, and is nothing whatever without bodies but the possibility of placing them in it, these two conditions, the one as things are, the other supposed the other way round, would not differ from one another: their difference exists only in our chimerical supposition of the reality of space in itself. But in truth the one would be just the same as the other, as they are absolutely indiscernible; and consequently there is no occasion to search after a reason for the preference of the one to the other.

6. The same is true of *time*. Suppose someone asks why God did not create everything a year sooner; and that the same person wants to infer from that that God did something for which He cannot possibly have had a reason why He did it thus rather than otherwise, we should reply that his inference would be true if time were something apart from temporal things, for it would be impossible that there should be reasons why things should have been applied to certain instants rather than to others, when their succession remained the same. But this itself proves that instants apart from things are nothing, and that they only consist in the successive order of things; and if this remains the same, the one of the two states (for instance that in which the creation was imagined to have occurred a year earlier) would be nowise different and could not be distinguished from the other which now exists.

7. It will be seen from everything I have said that my axiom has not been fully understood, and that the author, while appearing to grant it, has really denied it. *It is true,* he says, *that nothing exists without a sufficient reason why it is thus rather than otherwise,* but he adds that this sufficient

reason is often the *simple* or *mere will* of God, as when it is asked why matter was not differently arranged in space, the positions as between bodies being preserved. But this is simply maintaining that God wills something without there being a sufficient reason for His will, contrary to the axiom or general rule governing everything which happens. This is to relapse into the loose indifference which I have amply refuted, and which I have shown to be absolutely chimerical, even in created beings, and contrary to the wisdom of God, as if He could operate without acting reasonably.

8. I am met with the objection that not to admit this *simple and mere will* would be to remove from God the power of choice, and that this would be to fall into fatalism. But quite the reverse is true. I maintain that God has the power of choice, since I base it on the reason for the choice which is in conformity with His wisdom. And it is not this fatalism (which is nothing but the order of the highest wisdom or of providence) but a brute fatalism or necessity, in which there is neither wisdom nor choice, that we ought to avoid.

9. I had observed that if we diminish the quantity of matter, the quantity of objects on which God can exercise His goodness is diminished. The author answers that instead of matter there are other things in the void on which He does not fail to exercise it. Be it so; though I do not agree, for I hold that all created substance is accompanied by matter. But be it so. I answer that more matter was compatible with those same things, and consequently the said object will still be lessened. The example of a greater number of men or animals is not to the purpose, for they would occupy the room of other things.

10. It will be difficult to make me believe that, in its ordinary use, *sensorium* does not mean the organ of sensation. Here are the words of Rudolphus Goclenius, in his *Philosophical Dictionary*: *Sensiterium: barbarum Scholasticorum* (he says) *qui interdum sunt simiae Graecorum. Hi dicunt*

αἰσθητήριον, ex quo illi fecerunt Sensiterium pro Sensorio, id est, organo sensationis.[1]

11. The simple presence of a substance, even an animated one, is not enough for perception: a blind man does not see, nor even does an absent-minded one. It is necessary to explain how the soul perceives what is outside itself.

12. God is not present in things by situation but by essence; His presence is manifested by His immediate operation. The presence of the soul is of quite another nature. To say that it is diffused throughout the body is to make it extended and divisible; to say that the whole of it exists in each part of each body is to make it divisible from itself. To attach it to one point, to spread it over several points are only improper expressions, idola tribus.[2]

13. If active force were lost in the universe by the natural laws which God has established in it, so that He needed a new impression to restore this force, like a workman setting right the imperfection of his machine, the disorder would occur not only with regard to us, but with regard to God Himself. He could have prevented it and have taken better steps to avoid such an untoward occurrence. Actually, indeed, He has done so.

14. When I said that God has prepared actual remedies against these disorders in advance, I do not mean that God lets the disorders come and then the remedies for them; but that He has found means in advance to prevent disorders from happening.

15. Our author attempts without success to criticize my expression, that God is Intelligentia Supramundana. To say that He is above the world is not to deny that He is in the world.

[1] 'Sensiterium: a barbarism of the Scholastics, who sometimes ape the Greeks. The latter say αἰσθητήριον, from which the former have manufactured the word sensiterium in place of sensorium, i.e. the organ of sensation.'

[2] Cf note, p. 199.

16. I have never given occasion for doubt whether God's conservation is an actual preservation and continuation of beings, powers, orders, dispositions, and motions; and I think I have perhaps explained it better than many others. But, says our author, *this is all that I contended for: herein consists the whole dispute.* To this I answer: Your most humble servant. Our dispute consists in quite different things. The question is whether God does not act in the most regular and perfect manner; whether His machine is liable to disorders which He will be obliged to set right by extraordinary means; whether the will of God is capable of acting without reason; whether space is an absolute being; wherein consists the nature of miracles: and many similar questions which set a great gulf between us.

17. Theologians will not agree with the thesis advanced against me, that there is no difference in relation to God between the natural and the supernatural. The majority of philosophers will approve it even less. There is an infinite difference, but it certainly seems not to have been given proper consideration. The supernatural surpasses all the powers of created things. We must take an example. Here is one which I have often made use of with success. If God wished to cause a free body to circle in the ether round about a given fixed centre, without any other created thing acting on it, this, I say, could only occur by miracle, not being explicable by the nature of bodies. For a free body naturally departs from a curve along the tangent. It is in this sense that I maintain that the attraction of bodies, properly so called, is a miraculous thing, since it cannot be explained by their nature.

LEIBNIZ'S FOURTH PAPER [1]

1. In things which are absolutely indifferent there can be

[1] Written in answer to Clarke's reply to the *Third Paper*. As will be seen, some paragraphs have been omitted here.

no choice and consequently no election or will, since choice must have some reason or principle.

2. A simple will without any motive (*a mere will*) is a fiction which is not only contrary to the perfection of God, but also chimerical and contradictory, incompatible with the definition of will and sufficiently refuted in my *Theodicy*.

3. It is indifferent whether three bodies which are equal and alike in every respect be placed in any order whatsoever, and consequently they never would be placed in order by Him who does nothing without wisdom. But also, being the Author of things, He will not produce any such; and consequently there are none in nature.

4. There are no two individuals indiscernible from one another. A clever gentleman, a friend of mine, when conversing with me in the presence of Her Electoral Highness[1] in the garden at Herrenhausen, thought he would certainly find two leaves exactly alike. Her Electoral Highness challenged him to do so, and he spent a long time running about looking for them, but in vain. Two drops of water or milk looked at under the microscope will be found to be discernible. This is an argument against atoms, which, like the void, are opposed to the principles of a true metaphysic.

5. These great principles of a Sufficient Reason and of the Identity of Indiscernibles change the state of metaphysics, which by their means becomes real and demonstrative; whereas formerly it practically consisted of nothing but empty terms.

6. To suppose two things indiscernible is to suppose the same thing under two names. Thus the hypothesis that the universe should have originally had another position in time and place from that which it actually had, and yet all the parts of the universe should have had the same position with regard to one another as that which they have in fact received, is an impossible fiction.

[1] Sophia, Electress of Hanover, mother of George I of England.

7. The same reason which shows that space outside the world is imaginary proves that all empty space is something imaginary; for they differ only as the great from the small.

8. If space is a property or an attribute, it must be the property of some substance. Of what substance is the bounded empty space, which the supporters of this view suppose to exist between two bodies, the property or affection?

9. If infinite space is immensity, finite space will be the opposite of immensity, that is to say mensurability or bounded extension. Now extension must be the affection of something extended. But if this space is empty, it will be an attribute without a subject, an extension of no extended thing. This is why in making space a property the author is accepting my position, according to which it is an order of things and not something absolute.

10. If space is an absolute reality, far from being a property or accident opposed to substance, it will have more subsistence than substances; God will be unable to destroy it, or even to change it in any respect. It will be not only immense in the whole, but also immutable and eternal in each of its parts. There will be an infinity of eternal things besides God.

11. To say that infinite space is without parts, is to say that it is not made up of finite spaces, and that infinite space might continue to exist though all finite spaces were reduced to nothing. It would be as if we were to say, on the Cartesian supposition of a corporeal extended universe without limits, that this universe might continue to exist though all the bodies which make it up were reduced to nothing.

13. To say that God could move the universe forward in a straight line or otherwise without changing it in any other way is another chimerical supposition. For two indiscernible states are the same state, and consequently it is a change which changes nothing. Further, there is no rhyme nor

reason in it. Now God does nothing without a reason, and it is impossible that there should be one here. Besides, it would be *agendo nihil agere*,[1] as I have just said, because of the indiscernibility.

14. These are *idola tribus*,[2] the purest chimeras and superficial imaginings. It is all founded merely on the supposition that imaginary space is real.

15. It is a similar, that is to say an impossible, fiction to suppose that God had created the world several million years sooner. Those who incline towards such kinds of fiction will be unable to reply to those who argue in favour of the eternity of the world. For since God does nothing without a reason, and since there is no reason assignable why He did not create the world sooner, it will follow either that He created nothing at all, or that He produced the world before any assignable time, which is to say that the world is eternal. But when we show that the beginning, whatever it was, is always the same thing, the question why it was not otherwise ceases to arise.

16. If space and time were something absolute, that is to say if they were something other than certain orders of things, what I am saying would be a contradiction. But since this is not the case, the hypothesis is contradictory, that is to say it is an impossible fiction.

17. It is very like what happens in geometry where, by the very supposition that a figure is greater, we sometimes prove that in fact it is not greater. It is a contradiction; but the contradiction is in the hypothesis, which for this very reason is shown to be false.

18. The uniformity of space means that there is neither *internal nor external reason* for discerning its parts, and for choosing between them. For such external reason for discerning could only be founded in the internal one; other-

---

[1] 'acting without doing anything'.
[2] Cf. p. 199, note.

wise it would be discerning the indiscernible, or choosing without discerning. Will without reason would be the 'chance' of the Epicureans. A God who acted by such a will would be a God only in name. The source of these errors is want of care to avoid what is derogatory to the Divine perfections.

19. When two incompatible things are equally good, and when one has no advantage over the other either in itself or in its combination with others, God will produce neither.

20. God is never determined by external things, but always by what is in Himself, that is to say by His knowledge, before anything exists outside Him.

21. There is no possible reason which could limit the quantity of matter. Therefore there cannot in fact be any such limitation.

22. And suppose such an arbitrary limitation did exist, it would always be possible to add something without derogating from the perfection of those things which already exist: and consequently it would always be necessary to add something, in order to accord with the principle of the perfection of Divine operations.

23. Thus it cannot be said that the present quantity of matter is the most fitting for the present constitution of things. And even if this were the case, it would follow that this present constitution of things would not be the most fitting absolutely, if it prevents the employment of more matter; it would therefore be necessary to choose another constitution of things, capable of something more.

29. God perceives things in Himself. Space is the place of things, and not the place of the ideas of God: unless we consider space as something which causes the union of God and things, in imitation of the imagined union of the soul and the body; which would still make God the Soul of the World.

32. Those who imagine that souls can give a new force to bodies, and that God does the same in the world so as to correct the imperfections of His machine, make God too like the soul, by attributing too much to the soul and too little to God.

33. For it is only God that can give nature new forces, and He does it supernaturally only. If He needed to do it in the natural course of things He would have made a very imperfect work. He would be, in the world, like what the soul is commonly held to be in the body.

38. Those who imagine that active forces[1] diminish of themselves in the world, do not properly understand the principal laws of nature, and the beauty of the works of God.

41. The author says that space does not depend on the situation of bodies. I answer that it is true that it does not depend on such and such a particular situation of bodies; but it is the order which makes bodies capable of having situation, and through which they have a situation with regard to one another when existing together; just as time is this order in relation to their successive position. But if there were no created beings space and time would only exist in the ideas of God.[2]

---

[1] Clarke says that when he spoke of active forces diminishing, he meant by active force 'nothing but motion, and the impetus or relative impulsive force of bodies, arising from and being proportional to their motion'. He quotes from Newton's *Optics*: 'Since therefore all the various motions that are in the world are perpetually *decreasing*, 'tis absolutely necessary, in order to preserve and renew those motions, that we have recourse to some *active* principles'. (The translation from Newton's Latin is by Clarke.)

[2] Several sections containing a further discussion of the nature of *miracles* are omitted here.

P.S.

All those who believe in the void allow themselves to be guided more by imagination than by reason. When I was a young man, I also was inclined to believe in the void and in atoms; but reason brought me back. Imagination was utterly contented. On this theory a limit is set to our researches; reflection is fixed and as it were pinned down; we suppose ourselves to have found the first elements—a *non plus ultra*. We should like nature to go no further; we should like it to be finite, like our mind; but this is to ignore the greatness and majesty of the Author of things. Actually the least corpuscle is subdivided *ad infinitum* and contains a world of new created things, which the universe would lack if this corpuscle were an atom, that is a body all of a piece and not subdivided. All the same, to want to put a void in nature is to attribute to God a very imperfect production; it is to violate the great principle of the necessity of a *sufficient reason*, of which many people speak with their lips without at all recognizing its force, as I showed recently when I made it clear by means of this principle that space is only an order of things, like time, and in no sense an absolute being. Not to mention many other reasons against the void and atoms, here are those which I derive from the perfection of God and from *sufficient reason*. I assume that any perfection which God could put in things without derogating from the other perfections in them, has been put there. Now let us imagine a space entirely empty; God could put in it some matter without in any way derogating from anything else whatever; therefore He did put some matter therein; therefore there is no space entirely empty; therefore everything is full. The same argument proves that there is no corpuscle which is not subdivided. Here also is the reason taken from the necessity of a *sufficient reason*. It is not possible that there should be a

principle determining the proportion of matter, or what is
filled, to the void, or of the void to the plenum. It will
perhaps be said that one must be equal to the other; but as
matter has more perfection than empty space, reason demands
that geometrical proportion be observed, and that there
should be more plenum in proportion as it is worthy of
preference. But then there would be no void at all, for the
perfection of matter is to the perfection of the void as something is to nothing. The same argument applies to atoms.
What reason can be assigned for limiting nature in the process
of subdivision? Purely arbitrary fictions, and unworthy of
true philosophy. The reasons alleged in favour of the void
are but sophisms.

LEIBNIZ'S FIFTH PAPER [1]

8.[2] But the good, whether true or apparent, in a word the
motive, inclines without necessitating, that is to say without
imposing an absolute necessity. For when God (for instance)
chooses the best, that which He does not choose and which is
inferior in perfection is none the less possible. If what God
chooses were necessary, everything else would be impossible,
which would be contrary to our hypothesis, for God chooses
between possibles, that is to say between several things, not
one of which implies a contradiction.

9. To say that God can only choose the best, and to infer
from this that what He does not choose is impossible, is to
confuse terms: namely, power and will, metaphysical necessity and moral necessity, essences and existences. For what
is necessary is so by its essence, because the opposite implies
a contradiction; but the contingent which exists owes its
existence to the principle of what is best, the sufficient

[1] Written in answer to Clarke's reply to the *Fourth Paper*.
Here Leibniz takes up the points at much greater length. It
will be seen that much of this paper has been omitted here.
[2] §§ 1-7 contain further answers to the charge of *fatalism*. Cf.
p. 197.

reason for things. And this is why I say that motives incline without necessitating; and that there is a certainty and infallibility, but not an absolute necessity, in contingent things.

10. And I have sufficiently shown in my *Theodicy* that this moral necessity is good, and in conformity with Divine perfection, and in conformity with the *great principle of existences*, which is that of the need of a sufficient reason; whereas absolute metaphysical necessity depends on the other great principle of our reasonings, the principle of *essences*, that is to say that of identity or contradiction: for what is absolutely necessary is the only possible course, and its contrary implies a contradiction.

11. I have shown also that our will does not always precisely follow the practical understanding, because it may have or find reasons for suspending its resolution until a further discussion.

14. . . . . I now come to the objection made against my comparison between the weights of a balance and the motives of the will. The author objects that the balance is purely passive and weighed down by the weights, whereas agents which are intelligent and endowed with will are active. To this I reply, that the principle of the necessity of a sufficient reason is common both to active and to passive things. They need a sufficient reason for their activity as well as for their passivity. Not only does the balance not act when it is weighed down equally on both sides, but equal weights do not act either, when they are in equilibrium in such a way that one cannot go down without the other going up to the same extent.

15. It must also be considered that, strictly speaking, motives do not act on the mind like weights on a balance; it is rather the mind which acts by virtue of the motives, which are its dispositions to act. Thus to maintain, as it is here

maintained, that the mind sometimes prefers weak motives above stronger ones, and even sometimes what is indifferent above motives, is to separate the mind from its motives, as if they were outside of it, as the weight is distinct from the balance; and as if there were in the mind other dispositions to action besides motives, by virtue of which the mind rejected or accepted the motives. Whereas the truth is that motives comprise all the dispositions which the mind can have to act voluntarily, for they comprise not only reasons but also inclinations, which come from the passions or from other preceding impressions. Thus if the mind preferred a weak above a strong inclination it would be acting against itself and otherwise than it is disposed to act. This shows that notions which differ on this point from mine are superficial and turn out to have nothing in them, when they are properly considered.

16. To say also that *the mind may have good reasons for acting* when it has no motives, and *when things are absolutely indifferent*, as is explained here, is a manifest contradiction. For if there are good reasons for the course it adopts, the things are not indifferent to it.

17. And to say that a man will act when he has reasons for acting, *even though the ways of acting may be absolutely indifferent*, is again to speak most superficially, and in a very unjustifiable manner. For in this case there is no sufficient reason for acting when there is not a sufficient reason for acting *in a particular manner*, since every action is individual, and not general or abstracted from its circumstances, and it needs some way of being carried out. Thus when there is a sufficient reason for doing a particular action, there is a sufficient reason also for acting in a particular way, and consequently the ways of acting are not indifferent. On every occasion that a man has sufficient reasons for a given particular action, he has sufficient reasons also for doing everything which is requisite for that action.

21. It must be admitted that this great principle,[1] although it has been recognized, has not been sufficiently made use of. And this is to a great extent why *First Philosophy* [2] has been so little productive and demonstrative hitherto. I infer from this principle, among other consequences, that there are not in nature two real absolute beings which are indiscernible from one another; because if there were, God and nature would be acting without reason in treating one differently from the other; and thus that God does not produce two portions of matter which are perfectly equal and alike. The author replies to this conclusion without refuting the reason for it, and he replies by a very feeble objection. *That argument*, he says, *if it was good would prove that it would be impossible for God to create any matter at all. For the perfectly solid parts of matter, if we take them of equal figure and dimensions (which is always possible in supposition) would be exactly alike.* But it is an obvious *petitio principii* to suppose this perfect agreement which, on my view, cannot be admitted. This supposition of two indiscernibles, as of two portions of matter which perfectly agree with one another, seems possible in the abstract, but it is not compatible with the order of things, nor with Divine wisdom, by which nothing is admitted without a reason. The vulgar imagine such things because they are satisfied with incomplete notions. And this is one of the faults of the Atomists.

22. Besides, I do not allow that there are in matter parts which are perfectly solid, or which are all of a piece, without any variety or particular motion in their parts, as the pretended atoms are conceived to be. To suppose that there are such bodies is another popular and ill-founded opinion. According to my demonstrations, each portion of matter is actually subdivided into parts differently affected, and no one altogether resembles another.

[1] i.e. the principle of sufficient reason.
[2] i.e. metaphysics.

23. I had maintained that two indiscernibles can never be found among sensible things, and that, for example, we should never find two leaves in a garden, nor two drops of water, which were perfectly alike. The author admits this with regard to leaves and 'perhaps' with regard to drops of water. But it might be admitted without question, or without the 'perhaps', of the drops of water too.

24. I hold that these general observations which apply to sensible things apply also in proportion to insensible things. And that in this respect it may be said, as Harlequin says in the *Emperor of the Moon*, ' 'tis there as 'tis here'. And it is a great argument against indiscernibles that no instance of them can be found. But the author objects to this consequence on the ground that sensible bodies are compounded, whereas there are alleged to be insensible bodies which are simple. I answer again that I do not admit of any. According to me, there is nothing simple except true monads, which have no parts and no extension. Simple bodies and even perfectly similar ones are a consequence of the false doctrine of a void and of atoms, or else of lazy philosophy, which does not press far enough the analysis of things, and thinks it can arrive at the primary corporeal elements of nature, since they would satisfy our imagination.

25. When I deny that there are two drops of water perfectly alike, or two other bodies indiscernible from one another, I do not mean that it is absolutely impossible to suppose them, but that it is a thing contrary to Divine wisdom and consequently that it does not exist.

26. I admit that if two perfectly indiscernible things did exist, they would be two. But the supposition is false, and contrary to the great principle of reason. The vulgar philosophers were mistaken when they thought that there existed things which differed *solo numero*,[1] or only because they were *two*: and it is from this error that their perplexities

[1] 'numerically only'.

about what they called the *principle of individuation* arose. Metaphysics has ordinarily been treated as a mere doctrine of terms, like a philosophical dictionary, without ever coming to a discussion of things. *Superficial philosophy*, like that of the Atomists and Vacuists, fabricates for itself things which higher reasons render inadmissible. I hope that my proofs will change the face of philosophy, in spite of feeble contradictions such as I meet with here.

27. The parts of time and of place, taken in themselves, are ideal things: thus they are perfectly alike, like two abstract units. But this is not the case with two concrete unities, nor with two actual times, nor with two occupied, that is to say truly actual, spaces.

28. I do not say that two points of space are one and the same point, nor that two instants of time are one and the same instant, as seems to be imputed to me. But it may be imagined through lack of knowledge that there are two different instants when there is one only, as I observed in § 17 of my foregoing reply that often in geometry we suppose there to be two, so as to show up an opponent's error, and find but one. If someone supposed that one straight line cut another at two points he would ultimately find out that these two pretended points must coincide and can only make one. This also happens when a straight line, which in all other instances cuts a given curve, becomes a tangent.

29. I have proved that space is nothing other than an order of the existence of things, which is observed when they exist simultaneously. Thus the fiction of a finite material universe, the whole of which moves about in an infinite empty space, cannot be admitted. It is altogether unreasonable and impracticable. For besides the fact that there is no real space outside the material universe, such an action would be without purpose; it would be working without doing anything, *agendo nihil agere*. No change which could be observed by any one whatever would be occurring. Such

things are the imaginings of *philosophers with incomplete notions*, who make of space an absolute reality. Mere mathematicians who do but concern themselves with the play of the imagination are capable of fabricating to themselves such notions; but they are destroyed by higher reasons.

30. Absolutely speaking, it appears that God is able to make the material universe finite in extension; but the contrary seems better to conform with His wisdom.

31. I do not allow that everything finite is mobile. Indeed, according to the hypothesis of my opponents, a part of space, though finite, is not mobile. What is mobile must be able to change its position in relation to something else, and it must be possible for a new state discernible from the first state to arise: otherwise the change is a fiction. Thus a mobile finite thing must be part of some other finite thing, so that a change that can be observed can take place.

32. Descartes maintained that matter has no limits, and I do not think he has been sufficiently refuted. And even if this is granted him,[1] it does not follow that matter would be necessary, nor that it should have existed from all eternity, since the unlimited diffusion of matter would but be an effect of the choice of God, who held it to be better so.

33. Since space is itself a thing ideal, like time, space outside the world must certainly be imaginary, as the Schoolmen themselves recognized well enough. The same is true of empty space in the world, which I also hold to be imaginary for the reasons I have given.

34. The author brings forward as an objection against me the vacuum discovered by M. Guericke of Magdeburg: this was made by pumping the air out of a container. It is claimed that there genuinely is a perfect void, or space empty

---

[1] Clarke had said: 'To say that God could not have altered the *time* or *place* of the existence of matter, is making it to be *necessarily infinite* and *eternal*, and reducing all things to *Necessity* and *Fate*'.

of matter, in part at least, in the container. The Aristotelians and the Cartesians, who do not admit the existence of a true void, replied to this experiment of M. Guericke's as well as to the experiment made by M. Torricelli of Florence (who emptied the air out of a glass tube by means of mercury), by saying that there is no vacuum at all in the tube or in the container since the glass has subtle pores, through which rays of light, magnetic rays, and other very fine things can pass. And I am of their opinion. For I hold that the container may be compared to a box full of holes placed in water, in which there are fish or other gross bodies, which being removed, their room would not fail to be filled with water. There is this difference only, that water, though it is fluid and more amenable than these gross bodies, is yet as heavy and as massive as they are, or even more so; whereas the matter which enters the container in the room of the air is much finer. The new supporters of the void reply in this instance that it is not the grossness of matter, but simply its quantity, which produces resistance, and that consequently there is necessarily more void where there is less resistance. They add that subtlety has nothing to do with it, and that the parts of quicksilver are as subtle and as fine as those of water, and that yet quicksilver has more than ten times the resistance. To this I answer, that it is not so much the quantity of matter as the difficulties it makes in giving way which causes the resistance. For example, floating timber contains less weight of matter than water of equal volume, and yet it resists a boat more than the water does.

35. And as to quicksilver, it contains in truth about fourteen times as much weight of matter as an equal volume of water; but it does not follow that it contains fourteen times more matter absolutely. On the contrary, water contains as much, if we take together both its own matter which has weight and a foreign matter of no weight which passes through its pores. For both quicksilver and water are masses of heavy

matter pierced with holes, through which there passes a great deal of matter which has no weight and which does not resist sensibly. Such, it appears, is the matter which composes rays of light, and other insensible fluids; such above all is that fluid which itself causes the weight or gravity of gross bodies, by withdrawing itself from the centre where it forces them to go. For it is a strange fiction to regard all matter as having weight or gravity, and even to regard it as gravitating towards all other matter, as if every body had an equal attraction for every other body in proportion to mass and distance; and this, by means of attraction properly so called, and not derived from an occult impulsion of the bodies. Whereas in truth the gravitation of sensible bodies towards the centre of the earth must be produced by the movement of some fluid. And the same is true of other gravitations such as those of the planets towards the sun or towards one another. A body is never moved naturally except by another body which impels it by touching it; and after this it goes on until it is hindered by another body touching it. Any other operation on bodies is either miraculous or imaginary.

36. As I objected that space, taken as something real and absolute without bodies, would be a thing eternal, impassive, and independent of God, our author has tried to elude this difficulty by saying that space is a property of God. In my previous paper I opposed this by saying that the property of God is immensity; but that space, which is often commensurate with bodies, and the immensity of God are not the same thing.

37. I further objected that if space is a property, and if infinite space is the immensity of God, then finite space will be the extension or mensurability of something finite. Thus the space occupied by a body will be the extension of that body: an absurd thing, since a body can change space, but cannot leave its extension.

38. I also asked: If space is a property, of what thing will a limited empty space, such as is imagined in the container emptied of air, be the property? It does not seem reasonable to say that this round or square empty space is a property of God. Is it perhaps the property of some immaterial, extended, imaginary substance which (it seems) our author pictures to himself in the imaginary spaces?

39. If space is the property or affection of the substance which is in space, the same space would be the affection now of one body, now of another body, now of an immaterial substance, now perhaps of God, when it is empty of any other substance, material or immaterial. But it must be a very strange property or affection to pass like this from subject to subject. Subjects would thus put off their accidents like garments, so that other subjects could put them on. After that, how would one distinguish accidents and substances?

40. If limited spaces are the affections of limited substances which are in them, and if infinite space is the property of God, it must follow (strange though it may seem) that the property of God is composed of the affections of created things; for all the finite spaces, taken together, make up infinite space.

41. If it is denied that limited space is an affection of limited things, it will not be reasonable either for infinite space to be the affection or property of an infinite thing. I have touched on all these difficulties in my previous paper, but it does not look as though any attempt has been made to answer them.

42. I have yet other reasons against this strange fancy that space is a property of God. If it is, space enters into the essence of God. Now space has parts, so there would be parts in the essence of God. *Spectatum admissi.*[1]

43. Moreover, spaces are sometimes empty, sometimes full: thus there would be in the essence of God parts which

---

[1] *Spectatum admissi risum teneatis, amici?* 'If you saw such a thing, my friends, could you restrain your laughter?'

are sometimes empty, sometimes full, and consequently subject to a perpetual change. The bodies which fill space would fill a part of the essence of God, and would be commensurate with it; and, on the supposition of a vacuum, a part of the essence of God would be in the container. This *God with parts* will be very like the Stoic God, who was the whole universe, considered as a divine animal.

44. If infinite space is God's immensity, infinite time will be God's eternity. We must say, then, that what is in space is in God's immensity, and consequently in His essence; and that what is in time is in the essence of God also. Strange phrases, which plainly show that our author is misusing terms.

45. Here is another instance: God's immensity makes Him present in all spaces. But if God is in space, how can it be said that space is in God, or that it is His property? We have heard of the property being in the subject, but never of the subject being in its property. In the same way God exists in every time; how then is time in God, and how can it be a property of God? These are perpetual ἀλλογλωττίαι.[1]

46. It looks as though the immensity or extension of things were being confused with the space according to which that extension is taken. Infinite space is not the immensity of God, finite space is not the extension of bodies, just as time is not their duration. Things keep their extension, but they do not always keep their space. Each thing has its own extension, its own duration; but it does not have its own time, and it does not keep its own space.

47. This is how men come to form the notion of space. They consider that several things exist at the same time, and they find in them a certain order of co-existence, in accordance with which the relation of one thing to another is more or less simple. This is their situation or distance. When it happens that one of these co-existent things changes its relation to a number of others without their changing with

[1] 'misuses of words'.

regard to one another, and when another thing makes its appearance and acquires the same relation to the others as the first one had, we say that it has taken its *place*, and we call this change a *motion* in that body wherein is the immediate cause of the change. And when several or even all of these co-existent things change in accordance with certain known rules of direction and velocity, we can always determine the relation of situation which any given body acquires with regard to every other: and even the relation which any other would have, or which the given body would have to any other, if it had not changed, or if it had changed in a different way. If we suppose or pretend that among these co-existents there were a sufficient number which suffered no change in themselves, we should say that those which have the same relation to these fixed existents as others had before, occupy the same *place* as those others occupied. That which includes all these places is called *space*. This shows that in order to have the idea of place, and consequently of space, it is enough to consider these relations and the rules of their changes, without needing to picture any absolute reality beyond the things whose situation is being considered. To give a kind of definition: *Place* is that which is said to be the same for *A* and for *B*, when the relation of co-existence between *B* and *C, E, F, G*, etc., entirely agrees with the relation of co-existence which *A* previously had with those bodies, supposing there has been no cause of change in *C, E, F, G*, etc. It may also be said (without ἔκθεσις [1]) that *place* is that which is the same at different moments for certain entities when they, although different, have relations of co-existence with other entities (these latter being supposed to be fixed from the one of these moments to the other) which agree entirely. And *fixed entities* are those in which there has been no cause for a change of the order of co-existence with others, or (which is the same thing) in which there has

---

[1] i.e. without particular enunciation.

been no motion. Lastly, *space* is that which results from places taken together. And it is well here to consider the difference between the place and the relation of situation of the body which occupies the place. For the place of *A* and *B* is the same, whereas the relation of *A* to the fixed bodies is not precisely and individually the same as the relation that *B* (which is to take its place) will have to the same fixed bodies; these relations only agree. For two different subjects, such as *A* and *B*, cannot have exactly the same individual affection, since one and the same individual accident cannot occur in two subjects, nor pass from one subject to another. But the mind, not content with agreement, seeks an identity, a thing which is truly the same, and conceives it as outside these subjects; and this is what is here called *place* and *space*. This, however, can only be ideal, comprising a certain order wherein the mind conceives the application of the relations: just as the mind can imagine an order consisting of genealogical lines, whose length would consist only in the number of generations, in which each person would have his place. And if we added the fiction of metempsychosis, and made the same human souls come in again, the persons might change their places in these lines. He who had been father or grandfather might become son or grandson, etc. And yet those genealogical places, lines, and spaces, although they expressed real truths, would only be ideal things. I will give another example of the mind's habit of creating for itself, upon occasion of accidents existing in subjects, something which corresponds to those accidents outside the subjects. The ratio or proportion of two lines *L* and *M* can be conceived in three ways: as a ratio of the greater *L* to the smaller *M*, as a ratio of the smaller *M* to the greater *L*, and lastly as something abstracted from both of them, that is to say as the ratio between *L* and *M*, without considering which is the anterior and which the posterior, which the subject and which the object. It is in this way that proportions are considered in music. In the first way of considering them, *L* the greater is the subject; in the second, *M* the smaller is the subject of this accident which philosophers call relation. But which will be the subject in the third way of considering them? We cannot say that the two, *L* and *M* together, are the subject of such an accident, for in that case we should have an accident in two subjects, with one leg in one and the other leg in the other, which is contrary to the notion of accidents. Thus we are bound to say that the relation in this third way of considering it is indeed outside the subjects; but that being neither substance nor accident, it must be a purely ideal thing, the consideration of which is none the less useful. For the rest, I have acted rather like Euclid, who, when he could not make it absolutely understood what is meant by *ratio*, in the geometricians' sense, defined properly what is meant by *the same ratios*. In the same way, in order to explain what *place* is, I have tried to define *the same place*. Finally I remark that the traces which mobile things sometimes leave on the immobile things on which they exercise their motion, have afforded to men's imagination occasion to form this idea, as if there still remained some trace even when there is nothing immobile: but this is ideal merely, and only means that *if there were something immobile actually there, the trace might be pointed out on it*. And it is this analogy which causes us to imagine places, traces, and spaces, although these things only consist in the truth of relations, and nowise in any absolute reality.

49. We cannot say that a certain duration is eternal, but we can say that the things which last for ever are eternal, because they are always acquiring a new duration. Whatever of time and of duration does exist, since it is successive, continually perishes. And how could a thing exist eternally which properly speaking never exists? And how could a thing exist, no part of which ever exists? In the case of time

nothing exists but instants, and an instant is not even a part of time. Whoever gives proper consideration to these observations will easily understand that time can only be an ideal thing. And the analogy of time and space will indeed make us judge that the one is as ideal as the other. Still, if, when it is said that the duration of a thing is eternal, this only means that the thing endures eternally, I have nothing further to say.

52. In order to prove that space without bodies is an absolute reality, the author raised it as an objection to my view that a finite material universe might move about in space. I answered, that it does not seem reasonable that the material universe should be finite; and even if it were supposed to be so, it is unreasonable that it should have any movement except in so far as its parts change their situation among themselves: because a movement of this kind would produce no observable change and would be without purpose. It is a different thing when its parts change their situation among themselves, for then we recognize a movement in space; but it consists in the order of the relations, which are changed. The author now answers that the truth of the movement is independent of its being observed, and that a ship can go forward without a man who is in it perceiving the motion. I answer that motion is independent of being observed, but it is not independent of being observable. There is no motion when there is no observable change. Moreover, when there is no observable change, there is no change at all. The contrary view is based on the supposition of a real absolute space, which I demonstratively refuted by the principle of the necessity of a sufficient reason of things.

53. I find nothing in the eighth definition of the *Mathematical Principles of Nature*, nor in the *Scholium* of this definition, which proves, or can prove the reality of space in itself. But I grant that there is a difference between a

genuine absolute movement of a body and a simple relative change of its situation with respect to another body. For when the immediate cause of the change is in the body, it is genuinely in motion and then the situation of the rest with respect to it will be changed in consequence, although the cause of this change is not in them. It is true that, to speak exactly, there is no body which is perfectly and entirely at rest; it is an abstraction which we make when we consider the thing mathematically. Thus I have left unanswered nothing of all the arguments alleged in favour of the absolute reality of space. And I have proved the falsity of this reality by one of the most reasonable and well founded of fundamental principles, against which no exception nor example can be brought. For the rest, it may be seen from all that I have just said, that I cannot admit a movable universe, nor any place outside the material universe.

54. I know of no objection which I do not think I have adequately answered. And as to this objection that space and time are quantities, or rather things having quantity, and that situation and order are not such, I reply that order also has its quantity: there is that which precedes and that which follows, there is distance or interval. Relative things have their quantity as well as absolutes: for example, ratios or proportions in mathematics have their quantity and are measured by logarithms, and yet they are relations. Thus although time and space consist in relations, they have their quantity none the less.

57. This enables us to see how to interpret the truth that God created things at the time which was pleasing to Him, for the time depends on the things which He resolves to create. Once the things have been resolved upon with their relations, there remains no further choice of time or place; for these considered apart have nothing real in them, nothing to determine them, and indeed nothing that is discernible.

58. So it cannot be said, as is said here, that the wisdom of God may have *good reasons* for creating this world at a given particular time; for this particular time, taken apart from things, is an impossible fiction, and there can be no *good reasons* for a choice there where everything is indiscernible.

60. It should not then be said, as is said here, that God created things in a particular space, or at a particular time, *which was pleasing to Him*, for since all times and all spaces are in themselves perfectly uniform and indiscernible, one cannot *please* more than another.

63. But it nowise follows that matter is eternal and necessary, unless we suppose that space is eternal and necessary: an altogether ill-founded supposition.

67. The parts of space are determined and distinguished only by the things which are in them, and the diversity of the things in space determines God to act differently on different parts of space. But space, taken apart from things, has nothing in itself to determine it, and indeed it has nothing actual about it.

68. If God has decided to place a certain cube of matter, He thereby also becomes determined on the place of the cube: but this is with respect to other particles of matter, and not with respect to detached space which has nothing in it to distinguish it.

93. I do not admit that every action gives a new force to the thing acted upon. It often happens at the meeting of bodies that each keeps its force, as when two hard bodies of equal size meet directly. Then the direction alone is changed, without there being any change in the force, each body taking the direction of the other, and turning back with the same velocity it had before.

94. I am, however, careful not to say that it is supernatural to give a body a new force, for I recognize that one body often receives a new force from another body, which loses as much of its own. But I say merely that it is supernatural for the whole universe of bodies to receive a new force; and thus that one body should gain force without others losing the same amount. This is why I say also that it cannot be maintained that the soul gives force to the body; for then the whole universe of bodies would receive a new force.

99. I do not here undertake to establish my *Dynamics*, or my doctrine of forces. This would not be the proper place. But I can reply very well to the objection raised here. I had maintained that active forces are preserved in the world. The objection is that two soft non-elastic bodies meeting together lose their force. I answer that this is not so. It is true that the wholes lose it in relation to their total movement, but the parts receive it, being internally agitated by the force of the meeting or shock. Thus this loss occurs in appearance only. The forces are not destroyed, but dissipated among the small parts. There is here no loss of forces, but the same thing happens as takes place when big money is turned into small change. I agree, however, that the quantity of motion does not remain the same, and in this matter I approve what is said on page 341 of Mr. Newton's *Optics* which the author here quotes. But I have shown elsewhere that there is a difference between the quantity of motion and the quantity of force.

104. I do not say that space is an *order* or *situation* which makes things situable. That would be talking nonsense. It is only necessary to consider my own words and to join them with what I have said above (§ 47), to show how the mind comes to form the idea of space, without its being necessary for there to be a real and absolute being, corresponding to

that idea, outside of the mind and outside of relations. I do not say then that space is an order or situation, but an *order of situations*, or an order according to which situations are arranged; and that abstract space is this order of situations which are conceived as possible. Thus it is something ideal, but the author appears not to want to understand me. I have already replied (§ 54) to the objection that an order is not capable of quantity.

105. The author objects that time could not be an order of successive things, because the quantity of time can become greater or smaller, while the order of successions remains the same. I answer that this is not so; for if the time is greater there will be more similar successive states interposed, and if it is less there will be fewer, because there is no void nor condensation nor penetration (so to speak) in times any more than in places.

106. I maintain that if there were no created things, the immensity and eternity of God would none the less subsist, but without any dependence on times or places. If there were no created things there would be no time or place, and consequently no actual space. The immensity of God is independent of space, as the eternity of God is independent of time. They only signify with regard to these two orders of things that God would be present and co-existent with everything which existed. Thus I do not admit what is here advanced, that if God alone existed time and space would exist as at present. On the contrary, on my view, they would exist in ideas only, like mere possibilities. The immensity and eternity of God are something more eminent than the duration and extension of created beings, not only in relation to the greatness, but also to the nature of the thing. These Divine attributes are not dependent upon things outside God, as are actual places and times. These truths have been sufficiently recognized by theologians and philosophers.

124. The natural forces of bodies are all subject to *mechanical laws*; and the natural forces of minds are all subject to *moral laws*. The former follow the order of *efficient causes*; and the latter follow the order of *final causes*. The former operate without liberty, like a watch; the latter are exercised with liberty, although they agree exactly with that kind of watch which another, superior, free cause has set beforehand to fit in with them. I have already spoken of this in the present paper (§ 92).

PART III

MISCELLANEOUS EXTRACTS FROM LEIBNIZ'S PHILOSOPHICAL WRITINGS

From a letter to Landgraf Ernst von Hessen Rheinfels
November 1686

I TAKE the liberty, Sire, once more to entreat Your Serene
Highness to be good enough to have the enclosed papers
given to M. Arnauld, and since they treat of matters removed
from the outer senses and dependent on pure intellection,
matters which are not pleasing to, and are most often despised
by, those who are most alive and most excellent in the
affairs of the world, I will here say something in favour of
these meditations. It is not that I am so ridiculous as to
desire that Your Serene Highness should amuse himself
therewith (this would be as unreasonable as to want the general
of an army to apply himself to algebra, although this science
is very useful for anything which has any connection with
mathematics). My aim is rather that Your Serene Highness
may better be able to form a judgment of the purpose and
value of such reflections, which might seem but little worthy
to occupy, even for a moment, a man to whom all moments
must be precious. In truth, in the way in which these things
are ordinarily treated by the Scholastics, they are but disputes,
distinctions, a play upon words. Yet there are veins of gold
among these barren rocks. I take it to be a fact that thought
is the principal and perpetual function of our soul. We
shall always think, but we shall not always live here. This
is why whatever renders us more capable of reflecting on
more perfect objects and in a more perfect manner, also
makes us naturally perfect. But the present condition of
our life forces us to have a great number of confused thoughts
which do not make us more perfect. Such is the knowledge
of customs, genealogies, and languages, and indeed all
historical knowledge of facts both civil and natural. This is

233

useful to us for avoiding dangers and for handling the bodies and men around us, but it does not enlighten the mind. The knowledge of routes is useful to a traveller on his journey; but that knowledge which has more relation to the functions to which he is destined *in patria* [1] is more important to him. Now we are destined one day to live a spiritual life, where substances separated from matter will occupy us much more than bodies. But in order to distinguish better between knowledge that enlightens the mind and that which merely leads it blindfold, consider these examples taken from the arts. If a workman knows, by experience or from tradition, that if the diameter is 7 feet the circumference of the circle is a little less than 22 feet; or if a gunner knows by hearsay, or because he has frequently measured it, that bodies carry furthest when thrown at an angle of 45 degrees, theirs is a confused knowledge, the knowledge of an artisan who will make very good use of it to earn his living and in the service of others. But the knowledge which enlightens our mind, is that which is distinct, that is to say, which contains the causes or reasons, as when Archimedes gave the proof of the first law, and Galileo that of the second. In a word, the only knowledge which can make us perfect is the knowledge of reasons in themselves, or of eternal and necessary truths, especially those truths which are most comprehensive and which bear most relation to the Sovereign Being. This knowledge alone is good in itself; all the rest is mercenary, and we should only learn it through necessity, by reason of the needs of this life, and so that we may be the better able to make room afterwards for the perfection of the mind, when we have put in order all that which concerns our subsistence. Yet the disorderliness of mankind, and what is called the care *de pane lucrando*,[2] and often vanity also,

[1] 'in his fatherland', i.e. when he is at home in his own country, and not travelling.
[2] 'of earning daily bread'.

causes us to forget the master for the valet and the end for the means. This, as the poet says, is exactly *propter vitam vivendi perdere causas*.[1] It is very much like a miser preferring gold to health, whereas gold exists but to serve the conveniences of living. Now since what perfects our mind (if we leave on one side the illumination of grace) is the demonstrative knowledge of the greatest truths by their causes or reasons, it must be admitted that metaphysics or natural theology, which treats of immaterial substances, and particularly of God and the soul, is the most important of all. And it is impossible to make progress in this without knowing the genuine notion of substance, which I explained in such a way in my last letter to M. Arnauld that he himself, who is so exact, and who had been shocked by it at the outset, gave to it his acceptance.

Finally, these meditations provide us with conclusions which are surprising but of marvellous utility for delivering us from the greatest scruples regarding God's care for His creatures, His prescience and preordination, the union of soul and body, the origin of evil, and other things of this kind. I will not here say anything of the great value of these principles in the human sciences; but at least I can say that nothing is more instrumental in raising our mind to the knowledge and love of God, so far as nature helps us. I admit that all this is of no use without grace, and that God gives grace to some people who have never dreamt of these meditations. But God desires also that we should omit nothing on our side, and that we should use the perfections which He has given to human nature, as opportunity offers, each of us according to his vocation; as His sole purpose in making us was that we should know and love Him, we cannot work for it too much, nor make a better use of our time and energies, unless we are otherwise engaged for the public and for the welfare of others.

[1] 'for the sake of life to lose the causes of living'.

From the Discourse of Metaphysic. 1686

... Suppose, for example, that someone marks a number of points on a sheet of paper entirely at random, in the manner of those who practise the ridiculous art of geomancy. I say that it is possible to find a geometrical line whose motion is constant and uniform in accordance with a certain rule, such that this line shall pass through all the points, and in the same order in which they were marked by the pen. ... Nor is there any instance of a face whose contour does not form part of a geometrical line, and which cannot be traced at one stroke by a given regulated movement. But when a rule is very complicated, that which conforms to it passes for being irregular. ...

From the same work

The ancient philosophers had very little knowledge of these important truths. Jesus Christ alone has expressed them divinely well, and in a manner so clear and so familiar that the dullest minds have been able to understand them: that is why His Gospel has completely changed the face of human affairs. He has made known to us the Kingdom of Heaven or that perfect commonwealth of minds which deserves to be called the City of God, whose admirable laws He has revealed to us. He alone has made us see the extent of God's love for us, and with what accuracy He has provided for all that concerns us. He has shown us that He who cares for the sparrows will not neglect the rational creatures who are infinitely dearer to Him; that all the hairs of our head are numbered; that heaven and earth shall pass away rather than that the word of God, and all that belongs to the economy of our salvation, shall be changed; that God has more care for the least among intelligent souls than for the whole machine of the world; that we ought not to fear those who have power to destroy the body, but cannot hurt the soul, which God alone can make happy or miserable; and that the souls of the just are in His hand, safe from all the revolutions of the universe, since nothing can act upon them save God alone; that not one of our actions is forgotten, but everything is included in the final reckoning, even idle words and the least spoonful of water that has been put to a good use; finally that everything must work for the greatest good of the righteous; that the just will be like suns, and that neither our senses nor our minds have ever tasted anything approaching the happiness which God prepares for those who love Him.

From a paper without superscription—Precepts for advancing the sciences. (*Date unknown*)

The human race, considered in relation to the sciences which minister to our happiness, appears to me like a disorderly rabble marching in the darkness, having neither leader nor order, without password or other signals to regulate their march, or by which to know themselves. Instead of holding one another by the hand so as to guide one another and make sure of our way, we run about at random and to and fro, and even hurl ourselves one against another, far from helping and supporting each other. This means that we advance but little, or else that we know not where we are. We even plunge into morasses and shifting sands of doubts without end, wherein is nothing solid nor firm, or else we drag ourselves into the principles of very dangerous errors. *Talibus in tenebris vitae tantisque periclis,*[1] it is given to no mortal to light a torch capable of dispersing this obscurity. Sects and leaders of sects serve merely to seduce us like the false lights of marsh fires; and it is left to the sun of our souls to enlighten us utterly, but in another

[1] 'In such darkness of life and in so great dangers'.

life. Nevertheless, what we can do here is to march together and in order, to share our journeyings, to make known the roads and to repair them: and finally to travel slowly, but with a firm unwavering tread, by the side of that pure and living stream of clear and simple knowledge, which has its source among us, which can serve as a comfort on our painful march, and as a thread in the labyrinth of these vast overgrown territories, a thread which grows gradually larger and increases our knowledge, until at last it leads us, albeit by a roundabout way, to a delightful plain—I mean the most important practical truths which serve to content the mind and to preserve the health of the body, as far as this can be done by reason.

We see then that what would help us most would be to unite our labours, to share them advantageously and to regulate them in an orderly way. But at the present, men barely touch what is difficult and has not yet been attempted; but all run in crowds to what others have already done, where they cease not from copying and even from striving with one another. What one has built is first overthrown by another, who claims to found his reputation on the ruin of someone else's; but his own reign is no better established nor of longer duration. The fact is that they seek glory much more than truth, and seek rather to dazzle others than to enlighten themselves. To escape from this unhappy position, we must abandon the spirit of sect, and the affectation of novelty. We must imitate the geometers, who are not Euclideans nor Archimedeans. They are all for Euclid and all for Archimedes, because they are all for their common master, that is, divine truth. . . .

. . . We are responsible for our talent to God, and to the commonwealth. There are so many men of ability of whom much might be expected, if they would combine what is serious with what is pleasant. It is not always a question of writing great works; if each one contributed only a single discovery, we should gain a great deal in a short time. A single remark or demonstration of consequence is enough to gain a man immortality. . . .

. . . What century could be more suited to this task than ours, which will perhaps one day be known as the century of inventions and wonders? And the greatest wonder that will be noted in it will perhaps be that great prince,[1] who is the acknowledged glory of our time, and for whom succeeding ages will long in vain. I do not mention here his merits as a statesman and in war, which belong neither to this place nor to this pen. What he has done for the sciences would alone be enough to immortalize him. There is no need to describe him in more detail, he is too unique and too easily recognized on all hands. Why then seek in the uncertain idea of future things what exists amongst us in reality, and is even beyond what an ordinary mind is capable of conceiving? Perhaps among the great numbers of men of ability in his flourishing kingdom, and especially among those at his court, which is an assembly of remarkable persons, there is someone who has long since drawn up, at his command, a general plan for the advancement of the sciences, worthy of the sciences and of the king, and far beyond anything that I should be able to do.

From a draft of a letter to Malebranche. June 1679

. . . The value and even the mark of true science consists in my opinion in the useful inventions which can be derived from it. But I have not yet seen that any Cartesian has found anything useful by means of the philosophy of his master; whereas we owe at least the beginnings of pendulums and alleged experiments with a vacuum to the meditations of Galileo. It seems that the harvest of Descartes' philosophy is finished, or else that the promise of it was destroyed while it was still growing by the death of its author. For the majority of Cartesians are but commentators, and I could

[1] Louis XIV.

wish that some one of them was capable of adding as much to physics as you have contributed to metaphysics. What is more, even if all Descartes' physics were granted, this would not take us very far. For, after all, the first and second elements are difficult things to handle. Are we ever likely to succeed in discovering and executing a formula to compare with this?—*Recipe libram unam secundi elementi, unciam semis corporis ramosi, drachmam materiae subtilis, misce, fiat aurum.*[1] I think we should perhaps need a book as big as this terrestrial globe to explain the relation between any given sensible body and the first elements, even supposing these are genuine and are known. This can be seen from experiments with the microscope. For there are perhaps as many as 800,000 tiny animals visible in a drop of water, and each of these animals is still about as far from the first elements as we are, since it still has a body which bears a considerable relation to ordinary animals. There is even cause to fear that there may not be any elements, everything in organic bodies being actually divided up *ad infinitum*. For if these microscopical animals were again composed of heterogeneous animals or plants or bodies *ad infinitum*, it is obvious that there would be no elements.

Notwithstanding all these considerations I still have a high opinion of M. Descartes, and perhaps few people recognize as well as I do the greatness of his mind. In truth, of all the authors who preceded him and whose works we possess only Archimedes and Galileo can enter the lists with him. It is true that few of Archimedes's meditations remain to us; and although I hold that Galileo invariably makes some fine comment whenever he is obliged to treat of any matter, whatever it is, so that it would have been a good thing if he had had the opportunity to write more, nevertheless I

[1] 'Take one pound of the second element, an ounce and a half of a ramous body, a drachm of subtle matter: mix well. Result: gold.' The term 'ramous' was applied (following ancient physics) to the particles of viscous or rigid bodies.

admit that he certainly has not so vast a genius as M. Descartes. But to make up for this he devoted himself more to what was solid and useful; whereas M. Descartes, through his ambition to establish a school, allowed himself to say a number of things, which were extremely ingenious, but often uncertain and sterile. All the same, I should always advise a lover of truth to study his system thoroughly; for there is to be found in it a wonderful mental dexterity; and his physics, uncertain as it is, may serve as a model for the true one, which must at least be as clear and as well co-ordinated as his. For a romance may be fine enough to be worthy of imitation by a historian. In short, Galileo excels in the art of reducing mechanics to science; Descartes is admirable at explaining by beautiful guesses the reasons for the effects of nature; and it would have been a good thing if he had been able to apply himself more to medicine, which is altogether conjectural, and yet necessary. But Archimedes, if we can trust the histories, had a talent lacking in both the others: that is, he had a marvellous mind for the invention of machines that are useful for the purposes of living.

Fragment without superscription.[1]   (*Date unknown*)

The best *apologia* that could be made for M. Descartes would be to complete his hyperbolic spectacles, which are the only useful things he discovered—if it were practicable to do so; and I could wish that Fr. Malebranche and others, who assume the task of defending everything he said, were obliged to do it.

From a letter to Basnage.   16/26 July 1695

The death of the illustrious M. Huygens is an inestimable loss. Few know this as well as I do. He equalled, in my

[1] Taken from Bodeman's *Catalogue of the Leibniz MSS. in the Royal Public Library at Hanover* (1895).

opinion, the reputation of Galileo and Descartes, and, with the help of what they had done, he surpassed their discoveries. In a word, he was one of the chief ornaments of our time. I often exhorted him to give us his reflections, even if it were only in scraps and in an informal manner. I hope that his book on the system of the world and the internal constitution of the planets has been finished. But as he was accustomed to putting his reflections in writing in pretty good order, I have hopes that a great treasure may be found among his papers.

From the 'Theodicy' (Preliminary Discourse). 1710

87. . . . It is to be hoped that M. Bayle now finds himself surrounded by that illumination which we lack here below, since there is every ground to suppose that he was never lacking in good will.

From the same work

172. . . . This view that has been held regarding Mr. Hobbes, that he taught an absolute necessity of all things, has seriously injured his reputation, and would have done him harm, even had it been his only error.

173. Spinoza went further; he appears to have expressly taught that there is a blind necessity, having denied the Author of things understanding and will, and imagining that the good and perfection have relation only to us and not to Him. It is true that Spinoza's opinion on this point is not without obscurity, for he attributes thought to God after having deprived Him of understanding: *cogitationem, non intellectum concedit Deo*. There are even passages in which he relents a little on the question of necessity. However, as far as I can understand him, he does not recognize any goodness in God, properly speaking, and teaches that all things exist by the necessity of the Divine nature, without

any choice on the part of God.   We will not amuse ourselves here in refuting so bad, and indeed so inexplicable, an opinion.

From a letter to des Bosses.   15 March 1715

We rightly regard bodies as being things, for even phenomena are real.   But if any one seeks to regard bodies as being substances he will surely need some new principle of real unity.   The man in Ireland [1] who impugns the reality of bodies seems neither to give adequate reasons nor to explain sufficiently what is in his mind.   I suspect that he is one of those people who seek to become famous by their paradoxes.

From a letter to Thomas Burnett.   8/18 May 1697

. . . I find that it is not possible to regulate currency without regulating at the same time the price of merchandise and commerce, at any rate in part, since silver is itself a piece of merchandise.   And I find that it involves a logical circle if we seek to estimate the value of a piece of silver by money, and thus that what our lawyers are accustomed to call *bonitas extrinseca*,[2] when they say for example that an *écu* is worth so many *gros*,[3] is at bottom a chimera.   As Mr. Newton holds a position of responsibility in regard to matters of currency, I should place great reliance on his judgment on this point, as well as on every other question; as also on the opinion of Mr. Locke, since he has made a profound study of commerce. . . . I would not have it thought in the world that I am the kind of man to set Mr. Newton problems of mere curiosity.   If I wished to set him problems, I should choose more useful ones—though I recognize that M. Bernoulli's problems are good ones.   But more important things are

[1] Berkeley.

[2] i.e. extrinsic valuation, as opposed to intrinsic weight or fineness.

[3] An *écu* was a French standard silver coin; a *gros* was a Dutch copper coin of small value.

needed to occupy such a man as Mr. Newton. . . . I beg you to present my compliments to Mr. Newton and to assure him that I hold him ever in the highest esteem, and that I do not accept the excuses he gives for not yet having given to the public his meditations on colours and other matters. A man of his power should prefer the public good to all other considerations; and everything which comes from his pen is so generally esteemed that he has no ground for complaining of the ingratitude of his readers. I beg you to stir up Mr. Newton's friends to put pressure on him and to give him no quarter. . . .

From a letter to Hartsoeker. 10 March 1707

. . . You say, sir, that homogeneous rays change colour when they penetrate bodies of another colour. Yet you yourself adduce in your book an experiment which supports Mr. Newton's opinion as opposed to yours. For you follow him in stating that bodies which otherwise are blue appear red, when they are exposed to a homogeneous red light: and the same with the others. For the rest, it is possible that a white body absorbs or at least diverts elsewhere as many rays as a coloured body, if we suppose, for instance, that this white is composed of red and blue parts, or, to speak more exactly, of parts some of which are fitted to reflect red rays and others blue rays, and in this way the blue parts will cause the loss of many red rays, and vice versa. And if we conceive what is ordinarily white as composed of little mirrors, it is clear that a good part of the mirror is black and diverts the rays elsewhere. Thus from the fact that a yellow colour sometimes seems as vivid as a white colour, it does not follow that rays other than the yellow ones are sent to us to make the body appear yellow: this would be changing homogeneous rays which are not yellow into yellow. Mr. Newton mentions at the end of his work a number of points which he leaves for others to investigate. They are worthy of your attention, as you have applied yourself to this matter.

From a letter to Bourget. 5 August 1715

I cannot say anything about the details of the generation of animals. All that I think I can affirm is that the soul of every animal has pre-existed, and has been in an organic body which at last, by many changes, involutions and evolutions, has become the present animal. Your conjecture that every animal in the human seed will ultimately achieve rationality is ingenious and might be true, but I do not see that it is necessary. If there were a good number of them which remained mere animals, there would be no harm done. I would not dare to affirm that the animals which M. Leeuwenhoek has rendered visible in the seed are exactly those which I have in mind; but neither would I dare to affirm that they are not so; and I am waiting impatiently to see what M. Vallisnieri is going to give us in refutation of them. In the meantime I should not wish to speak as decisively as you do, Sir, when you say that M. Leeuwenhoek's opinion is one of the emptiest of fables. M. Huygens, who was one of the most penetrating men of his time, did not think so. The prodigious quantity of these animals (which constitutes your first objection) is in no way against it. A similar abundance may be found in the seeds of some plants. There are some, for example, whose grain consists of a very fine dust. Also, I do not see that there is any difficulty in the introduction into the egg of one of these animals to the exclusion of the other (your second objection). A great many appear to be introduced, because they are so small, but there appears to be only one place, a *punctum saliens* [1] so to speak, which can receive them with effect. And this also satisfies your third objection, which is that their extreme smallness is out of

[1] 'salient point'; in old medical usage, the heart as it first appears in an embryo.

proportion to the egg. The case is the same as when a fruit is very large, but its seminal part is very small and insensible. The fourth objection is that the egg and the foetus are the same animal; but this proposition is not proved; it might be that the egg was only a receptacle suited for giving growth and for assisting transformation. The fifth objection is that according to modern zoologists, and particularly according to M. Vallisnieri, the animals which are found in the sperms must be animals of their species which propagate and perpetuate themselves, exactly in the same way as occurs with the other animals which are known to us. With this I am in entire agreement: but in my opinion, even if these animals were the true seminal animals, they would none the less be a particular species of living things, of whom some individuals would be raised to a higher stage by a transformation.

However, I would not venture to assert that your view is false, namely that the animal to be transformed is already present in the egg when conception takes place. But the view that it enters it by the conception seems more likely. Do not then let us decide anything with too much assurance, and above all let us not treat ill a man like M. Leeuwenhoek, to whom the public owes thanks for the pains he has taken in his researches. It is, of course, most permissible to oppose his view, and I am very glad that it should be done, but it is not just to despise him. There is one difficulty which seems to me to be common to all the hypotheses, and on which I should like to have M. Vallisnieri's opinion; namely, why in the copulation of certain species of animals a single egg is generally fertilized, and why, in these species, twins are comparatively rare.

From the same letter

... Two hypotheses are possible: one that nature is always equally perfect, the other that it is always growing in perfection. If it is always equally perfect, but variable, it is more probable that there is no beginning. But if it is always growing in perfection (supposing that it is not possible to give it the whole of perfection all at the same time), the matter could still be explained in two ways, that is to say by the ordinates of the hyperbola *B*, or by the triangle *C*. On the hypothesis of the hyperbola, there would be no beginning, and the instants or states of the world would have

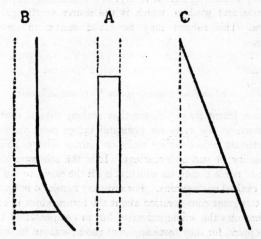

B   A   C

been growing in perfection from all eternity; but following the hypothesis of the triangle, there would have been a beginning. The hypothesis of equal perfection would be that of the rectangle *A*. I do not yet see the way to show demonstratively which we ought to choose by pure reason. However, although on the hypothesis of growth the state of the world could never be perfect absolutely, taken at any given instant, yet the actual sequence would none the less be the most perfect of all possible sequences, for the reason that God always chooses the best possible. . . .

Fragment without superscription.[1]   *(Date unknown)*

Goodness is in the will, wisdom is in the understanding. Wherein is power? Someone will say it is in body or matter. But body is not a substance unless it be taken to be a unity; and moreover there is power in God who is without matter. It is true, however, that power is in what corresponds analogically to matter, that is to say, in the common subject of goodness and wisdom, which is the source of changes or actions. This subject may be called matter in created things.

Fragment without superscription.[2]   *(Date unknown)*

I have learnt by experience that nothing defeats courage and removes the taste for beautiful things more than the importunate reflections we make on human misery, and on the vanity of our undertakings. It is the sole stumbling-block of noble minds, on which it is all the easier to fail the more exalted one's genius. For ordinary minds do not pause over this great consideration about the future which in some sort includes the whole universe: but in compensation they are happier, for they taste apparent goods, without its occurring to them to destroy the pleasure by too exact a reflection. And since a happy folly is better than a bitter prudence, I think we should do well to turn deaf ears to reason and give ourselves up to custom, or else to reason for our diversion only, if there be no means of reconciling wisdom with contentment. But, God be praised, we are not so unfortunate, and Nature would be a stepmother, if that which makes our perfection were the cause of our wretchedness.

[1] Taken from Bodeman's *Catalogue* (cf. p. 241, note).
[2] Ibid.

Comment on a book entitled: 'Reflections on Great Men who have died jesting'. [1] (*Date unknown*)

This little book is written with wit and learning, but there are signs in it of some moral laxity. I strongly approve that one should die joyfully, and consider that the Italian lawyer who gave orders that his funeral should be celebrated with rejoicings performed the action of a wise man, although it has been contested. But I should not wish an event which merits all our attention to be treated as of no account. This could be approved only by those who are ignorant of the dignity of man, and do not know that Providence put him at his post to render account of his movements; of which one of the most important is the manner of leaving it. Our author very rightly remarks that death is more to be desired than feared, but he adduces a bad reason for this when he says that man is not born to be happy. This is humorous, indeed. These gentlemen want to be unhappy by force, while charitable Nature has granted them almost everything necessary for their good. It is most untrue that there is ordinarily more unhappiness than happiness in life. The wretched thoughts and complaints against Nature of some persons are very unjust. It seems to me that the author rails in comfort against evils which he does not feel. Reason, which can make death pleasant to us, is not the misfortune of this life, but the greatest happiness of another. The author himself defends troubles on the ground that they make for vivacity. He is sure that a state which left nothing to be desired, would make us stupid. But I am not of his opinion when he holds that the verses which Ovid wrote in exile are better than those he wrote when in love. He does not seem to me to have rightly reported the words of M. Gassendi, when he was in danger of dying. M. Guy Patin, who was not

[1] Taken from Bodeman's *Catalogue* (cf. p. 241, note).

too much of a preacher, kept on telling him that he must think of death. M. Gassendi replied with this line from Virgil:

Omnia praecepi atque animo mecum ante peregi.[1]

M. de Meaux[2] and Madame de Maintenon have assured me that death came upon M. Pellisson by surprise, and that he did not by any means scorn the rites of the Church. I prefer to believe them rather than the author of this book, who attributes an unworthy avowal to a person who showed me friendship, and whom I, like most others, held in esteem.

From a letter without address or date[3]

I realized, sir, from the little talk I had the honour to have with you, that you meditate deeply on the nature of human freedom. And this it is which drives me to expound to you more clearly what I referred to in conversation, so that I may profit by your opinion of it. I hold that it is in the interests of piety and faith to reconcile the way in which our will acts not only with the dogmas of faith, but also with the great principles of reason, which hold sway everywhere else, and are the foundations of our knowledge. Otherwise we seem to be yielding the victory to impious men and atheists, or at the least to be confirming and strengthening them in their errors. This is why I never could fancy the opinion of those, who maintain that the principle of contradiction does not apply *in Divinis,* and that we do in fact find an exception to it in the case of the Trinity of the Divine Persons, as is admitted to some extent by those who introduce certain virtual distinctions. Now it is the same reason which

[1] 'I have imagined it all and have gone over it all beforehand in my mind.'

[2] Bossuet.

[3] Taken from Bodeman's *Catalogue* (cf. p. 241, note).

makes me doubt whether it is fitting to say that another principle, which is of hardly less general application than the principle of contradiction, does not apply with regard to freedom—the principle, namely, that nothing ever takes place without its being possible for one who knew everything to give some reason why it should have happened rather than not. All the more so, because it seems to me that this principle is of just the same use to us in matters of contingency, as is the principle of contradiction in matters of necessity. It is for this reason that the laws of motion depend on it, because they are not of geometrical necessity, since they originate from the will of God, regulated by wisdom. Now since the principle of contradiction is the principle of necessity, and the principle that a reason must be given is the principle of contingency, it seems to me that we must not except freedom from them. Archimedes takes it for granted that a balance will not tip more in one direction than in the other, when everything is equal on both sides, and in the same way all those who reason about morals and politics, with a view to discovering about human actions, tacitly make use of this same foundation, that there is always a reason or cause which inclines the will. We shall, moreover, never find a contrary instance, and no one but a Scholastic, buried in abstractions, thinks otherwise. To show that the will ought to be excepted it would be necessary to have a means of determining the limitation of this principle *a priori*. This we can never find; and any foundation which might be adduced for such a distinction will always go further than we wish. It therefore seems to me that we do not need to seek even this exception, and that free choice is not incompatible with the general principle I have just established. To explain myself more clearly: I say that Adam sinned without necessity, although He who knows everything could give a reason why he rather let himself sin than remain in innocence. Even Holy Writ, in the account it gives of the method adopted by the serpent to betray Eve, also seems to hint that there was some reason or inclination which prevailed over the will of Eve. It looks as though the soul is never in that state of complete indifference, in which nothing matters whether within or without. There is always a reason, that is to say a greater inclination, for what has in fact been chosen, which may come not only from arguments good or bad, but also from passions, habits, dispositions of the organs of the mind, external impressions, greater or less attention, etc. But this inclination does not master freedom, although it inclines it. There is a great deal of difference between a necessary cause and a certain concomitant. It is my view also that if we established the opposite, and claimed that the perpetual accompaniment of a stronger reason for choice destroys freedom, it would follow that inclination or the strongest reason would destroy freedom on every occasion that it accompanied it. From which it would follow further that we should almost never be free, since the cases when we are completely indifferent, or have a metaphysical freedom of choice, are at the least extremely rare, if they ever occur. Thus when we choose what is best, because it is best, it would be from necessity. Consequently the most perfect actions would be the least free and the least praiseworthy, since it is in freedom that we seek the reason for praise and blame, or rewards and punishments. The more perfect and the more inclined towards good a man was, the less free and praiseworthy he would be. Thus man would have to be reduced to a complete nudity, and despoiled of good qualities and graces, if he were to be allowed any merit. This is a vision favoured by some of our moderns, who seek the notion of freedom in indifference; which is as far removed from good sense as are their doctrines about probability and about knowledge of the badness of the action being necessary for sin. Whence has recently arisen that extraordinary distinction between philosophical and theological sin, which is

upheld by certain authors who maintain that an assassination
or an adultery is not a mortal sin, when the man who com-
mits it does not actually reflect that he is offending God;
because they imagine that otherwise the action is not sufficiently voluntary, that is to say, according to them, sufficiently indifferent, when the man does not give sufficient
thought to everything which might dissuade him from it.

Leibniz's Philosophical Dream.[1] *(Date unknown)*

I was happy to be among men, but not happy about human
nature. Often I thought with sorrow of the evils to which
we are subjected, of the short duration of our life, the vanity
of glory, the inconveniences which spring from pleasure, the
illnesses which crush our very spirit; finally the annihilation
of all our glories and all our perfections in the moment of
death, which seems to reduce to nothing the fruits of our
labours. These meditations made me melancholy. I had a
natural love of doing good and knowing the truth. Yet it
looked as though I were taking pains to no purpose, and as
though a fortunate crime were better than an oppressed
virtue, and the folly which satisfies preferable to the reason
which gives pain. But I resisted these objections, and the
better part triumphed in my mind through the consideration
of the Divinity, who must have ordered everything properly,
and who kept up my hopes by the expectation of a future
capable of making up for everything. The struggle in me
was renewed at the sight of any great disorder, either among
men, when I beheld injustice triumphant and innocence
afflicted, or in nature, when tempests or earthquakes made
havoc of towns and provinces, and caused the death of
thousands without distinction between the righteous and
the wicked, as if nature took no more account of us than we

[1] Taken from Bodeman's *Catalogue* (cf. p. 241, note). The
superscription is in the hand of a librarian.

take of the ants and worms we come across on our path. I was greatly moved by these spectacles, and could not prevent myself from pitying the condition of mortal men.

One day, wearied by these thoughts, I fell asleep, and found myself in a dark place, which was like a subterranean cave, very large and very deep, and swarming with men, who with strange haste pursued in this darkness wandering fires which they called honours, or tiny shining flies under the name of riches; many there were who searched on the ground to find shining pieces of rotten wood, which were called pleasures. These unlovely lights had each its followers; there were some who changed their course, and some who abandoned the pursuit altogether, through tiredness or through despair. Many of those who were running blindly about, and who often thought they had attained their goal, fell over precipices, whence naught was heard but their groans; some were stung by scorpions and other venomous creatures, which made them wretched and often mad with rage. But neither these examples, nor the arguments of some better informed persons, prevented the others from running the same risks, or from fighting in order to forestall others, or to prevent themselves from being forestalled. In the vault of this great cave, there were little chinks and barely perceptible cracks through which filtered some traces of the light of day, but it was so weak that much attention was required for it to be noticed. Often there were heard voices which said: 'Hold, mortals; whither go ye, wretched that ye are?' Others cried, 'Lift up your eyes to heaven'; but they did not stop, and only lifted their eyes to pursue these dangerous trifles. I was one of those who was extraordinarily struck by these voices. I kept on looking up, and at last I saw the little light which required so much attention. It seemed to me to grow in proportion as I looked fixedly at it. My eyes became as it were imbued with its rays, and when I used them immediately afterwards to see where I was and whither

I was going, I was able to discern what was around me, which was enough to save me from the dangers. A venerable old man, who had long been wandering in the grotto, and whose thoughts were not unlike mine, told me that this light was what in our world is called good sense and reason. I often changed my position to examine the different chinks in the vault through which this little light came, and when I was stationed in one place, where several lights could be perceived at the same time from their true point of view, I found an assemblage of rays which greatly enlightened me. This occupation was of great benefit to me, and made me more capable of acting in this obscurity. Finally, after having attempted several views, I was led by my good star to a place which was the sole and most advantageous spot in the grotto destined for those whom the Divinity wished to withdraw altogether from these dark regions. Barely had I begun to look up when I was surrounded by a great light gathered from all sides, and the whole grotto and its horrors were fully revealed to my eyes. But a moment afterwards a dazzling brightness took me by surprise. Presently it took shape, and I saw before me the appearance of a young man whose beauty charmed my senses. His mien had a majesty which inspired me with veneration mingled with awe, but the gentleness of his glances reassured me. But I began to feel a weakness overcoming me, and was about to faint, when I felt myself touched by a branch imbued with a marvellous liquid which I cannot compare with anything I have ever felt, which gave me the strength necessary to bear the presence of this celestial messenger. He called me by my name, and said in gracious tones: 'Give thanks to the Divine goodness which withdraws you from this mob'. At the same time he touched me a second time, and at that moment I felt myself raised up. I was no longer in the cave, I no longer saw a vault above me, and I found myself on a high mountain which revealed to me the face of the earth. I saw in the distance anything that I wished to look at only in a general way; but when I considered a particular place fixedly, immediately it grew, and in order to see it as if close at hand, I needed no other telescope than my attention. This gave me a wondrous pleasure, and emboldened me to say to my guide: 'Powerful spirit, for I cannot doubt but that you are one of the celestial angels, who pay court from near at hand to the Sovereign of the Universe, since you have been ready to enlighten my eyes, do as much for my mind'. He seemed to me to smile, and to take pleasure in hearing my wish. 'Your desires are granted,' he said, 'since you desire wisdom rather than the pleasures of the vain spectacles which the world offers to your gaze. But you will lose nothing of what is solid in these same spectacles. You will see them with eyes quite differently enlightened. Your understanding, being fortified from on high, will discover everywhere the brilliant enlightenments of the Divine Author of things; you will observe only wisdom and happiness where men customarily find nothing but vanity and bitterness. You will be satisfied by your Creator; you will be enchanted by the sight of His works. Your admiration will not be the result of ignorance, as is that of the common herd. It will be the fruit of the knowledge of the glories and wonders of God. Whereas among men secrets are despised when they are discovered, though they were previously regarded with astonishment; you will find that when you are admitted into the heart of nature, the further you go the greater will be your delights, because you will be only at the beginning of a chain which goes on to infinity. The pleasures which charm your senses, and that fabled Circe who changes men into beasts, will have no power over you, if you bind yourself to the beauties of souls which never perish and never cause displeasure. You will be of our company, and will go with us from world to world, from discovery to discovery, from perfection to perfection. You will pay court with us to the

Supreme Substance, which is beyond all worlds and which fills them without dividing Itself in doing so. You will be at one and the same time before His throne and among those who are distant from it. For God will establish His seat in your heart, and the heavens follow Him everywhere. Go then and lift up your mind above whatever is mortal, and whatever perishes, and bind yourself only to the eternal verities of the light of God. You will not always live here below this mortal life, so like that of the brutes; a time will come when you will be wholly freed from the chains of this body. Make good use, therefore, of the time which Providence grants you here, and know that your perfections to come will be proportioned to the care you take here below to attain them.'

From the 'Theodicy'. 1710

405. I had intended to stop at this point, having answered (so it seemed to me) all M. Bayle's objections on this subject, which I could find in his works. But recalling Laurentius Valla's dialogue *Of Free-will*, which was written against Boethius and which I have mentioned before, I thought it would be fitting to give a summary of it here, keeping the dialogue form, and then to go on from the point at which he stops, continuing the story which he begins. My aim is not so much to brighten up the subject-matter, but rather to explain myself at the end of my discourse in the clearest and most popular manner that is open to me. . . .

ANTONY. I know that you can give me wings, like a second Daedalus, to escape from the prison of ignorance, and to soar to the region of truth which is the dwelling-place of souls. I have derived no satisfaction from the books I have read, no, not even from the celebrated Boethius, who has won general approbation. I know not whether he himself has rightly understood what he says about God's understanding, and about eternity which transcends time I beg you to give me your opinion about the way of reconciling foreknowledge with freedom.

LAURENTIUS. I fear that I shall shock many people if I refute this great man. I will, however, subordinate this fear to my regard to the entreaties of a friend, on condition that you promise me——

ANT. What?

LAUR. That after you have dined with me you will not ask for supper also. By this I mean that you will be satisfied with the solution of the question you have put me, without asking me another.

ANT. I promise. Here is the heart of the difficulty. If God foresaw the treachery of Judas, it was necessary that Judas should betray; it was impossible that he should not betray. There is no obligation to perform the impossible. Therefore he did not sin, and did not deserve to be punished. This destroys justice and religion, together with the fear of God.

LAUR. God foresaw the sin, but He did not force the man to commit it. Sin is voluntary.

ANT. This volition was necessary, since it was foreseen.

LAUR. If my knowledge does not give existence to things past or present, neither can my foreknowledge give existence to future things.

ANT. This comparison is misleading. Neither the present nor the past could be changed; they are already necessary. But the future, in itself susceptible of change, becomes, through foreknowledge, fixed and necessary. Let us suppose that a pagan god boasts that he knows the future: I should ask him which of my feet I shall put foremost, and then I should do the opposite of what he predicted.

LAUR. This God knows what you will want to do.

ANT. How can He know, since I shall do the opposite of what He says, and I assume He will say what He thinks?

LAUR. Your supposition is a false one. God will not

answer you, or, if He did answer you, your veneration for Him would make you hasten to do what He said: His prediction would be to you a command. But we have changed our question. We are not concerned with what God will predict, but with what He foresees. Let us return to foreknowledge, and distinguish between the necessary and the certain. It is not impossible that that which is foreseen will not happen, but it is infallible that it will happen. It is possible for me to become a soldier or a priest, but I shall not become one.

ANT. That is where I have you. The philosophers' Rule demands that whatever is possible should be considered as existing. But if what you say is possible, that is to say an event different from what has been foreseen, did actually happen, then God would have been mistaken.

LAUR. Philosophers' Rules are not oracles for me. This one in particular is not accurate. Two contradictories are often both of them possible, but can they therefore both of them exist? But to enlighten you further, let us suppose that Sextus Tarquinius comes to Delphi to consult the oracle of Apollo and receives the answer:

Exul inopsque cades irata pulsus ab urbe.[1]

The young man complains: 'I have brought you a royal present, O Apollo; and yet you reveal to me so unhappy a fate'. Apollo answers: 'Your present is pleasing to me, and I perform what you ask of me; I tell you what will happen. I know the future but I do not make it. Go and complain to Jupiter and to the Fates'. It would be absurd of Sextus, would it not, if after this he went on complaining to Apollo?

ANT. He will say: 'I thank you, O holy Apollo, for not having paid me with silence, for having disclosed to me the truth. But how comes it that Jupiter is so cruel to me, and

[1] 'You will die poor and in exile, driven in anger from your fatherland.'

prepares so hard a fate for an innocent man, who is religious and who worships the gods?'

LAUR. 'You an innocent man?' answers Apollo. 'Know that you will be proud, that you will commit adulteries, and that you will be a traitor to your country.' Could Sextus answer: 'It is you who are the cause of this, O Apollo; you force me to do it by foreseeing it'?

ANT. I admit that he would have lost his reason if he answered thus.

LAUR. Neither then can the traitor Judas complain of God's foreknowledge. And this is the solution of your question.

ANT. The satisfaction you have afforded me has exceeded my hopes; you have done what Boethius was unable to do. I shall be grateful to you all my life.

LAUR. But let us pursue our story a little further. Sextus says: 'No, Apollo, I will not do what you say'.

ANT. 'What!' says the god, 'am I then to be a liar? I repeat again you will do everything that I have just said.'

LAUR. Perhaps Sextus will pray to the gods to change his fate, to give him a better heart.

ANT. He will receive the answer:

Desine fata deum flecti sperare precando.[1]

He will not be able to give the lie to divine foreknowledge. But what will Sextus say? Will he not burst into complaints against the gods? Will he not say: 'What? Am I not then free? Is it not in my power to follow virtue?'

LAUR. Apollo may say to him: 'Know, my poor Sextus, that the gods have made every man what he is. Jupiter has made the wolf ravening, the hare timid, the ass stupid, the lion brave. He has given you a soul which is wicked and incorrigible. You will act in accordance with your nature,

---

[1] 'Hope not that the fates of the gods may be turned aside by prayers.'

Jupiter will treat you as your actions deserve. By the Styx he has sworn it'.

ANT. I confess that it seems to me that Apollo, in excusing himself is accusing Jupiter more than Sextus. And Sextus would reply: 'Jupiter condemns in me his own crime—it is he alone who is guilty. He could have made me quite other than I am. But, made as I am, I am bound to act as he has willed. Why then does he punish me? Was I able to resist his will?'

LAUR. I confess that I also am brought to a standstill. I have called the gods Apollo and Jupiter on to the stage, to distinguish for you between the foreknowledge and the providence of God. I have shown that Apollo, or foreknowledge, is not injurious to freedom, but I cannot give you satisfaction concerning the decrees of the will of Jupiter, that is to say the commands of providence.

ANT. You have rescued me from one abyss, and you plunge me into a deeper one.

LAUR. Remember our contract. You have dined with me, and you are asking me for supper also.

ANT. Now I see your adroitness. You have caught me, it is not an honest contract.

LAUR. What more can I do? I have given you wine and meat of my own growing, such as my little estate can provide. Nectar and ambrosia you must ask of the gods—such divine food cannot be found among men. Listen to St. Paul, that chosen vessel who was caught up into the third heaven, who heard there unspeakable things. He will reply by invoking the parallel of the potter, the incomprehensibility of the ways of God, and our admiration for the depth of His wisdom. Yet it is well to note that we do not ask why God foresees the event, for that we understand; it is because it will happen. But we ask why He orders it so, why He hardens the heart of one, why He takes pity on another. We do not know what reasons He may have for it, but *the fact that He is very good and very wise is enough to make us judge them good.* And as He is just also, it follows that His decrees and His operations do not destroy our freedom. Some have sought for a reason. They have said that we are made of a corrupt and impure mass of mud. But Adam and the angels were made of silver and gold, and they sinned none the less. Sometimes, also, our hearts are hardened after regeneration. We must then seek another cause of evil, and I doubt if even the angels know it. For they continue happy and praising God. Boethius paid more attention to the answer of philosophy than to St. Paul's. This is the cause of his failure. Let us believe in Jesus Christ, who is the virtue and wisdom of God; He teaches us that God desires the salvation of all, that He desires not the death of a sinner. Let us trust in the Divine mercy, and let us not, through our vanity and our malice, become incapable of enjoying it.

This dialogue of Valla's is beautiful, although there are points to criticize in it here and there. But its chief defect is that it cuts the knot, and seems to condemn Providence under the name of Jupiter. Let us therefore proceed further with our little fable. Sextus, after leaving Apollo at Delphi, goes to seek Jupiter at Dodona. He offers sacrifices and then sets forth his grievances. 'Why have you condemned me, O great God, to be wicked and to be unfortunate? Change my lot and my heart, or recognize your fault.' Jupiter answers: 'If you are ready to renounce Rome, the fates shall spin you other destinies; you shall become wise, you shall be happy'. 'Why must I renounce the hope of a crown?' asks Sextus; 'can I not be a good king?' 'No, Sextus,' answers Jupiter, 'I know best what you need. If you go to Rome you are lost.' Sextus could not make up his mind to so great a sacrifice, left the temple, and gave himself up to his fate. Theodorus, the High Priest, who had witnessed the dialogue between the god and Sextus, addressed

Jupiter thus: 'Your wisdom is worthy of adoration, O great Master of the gods, you have convinced this man of his fault. Henceforth he must attribute his misfortunes to his evil will; he has not a word to say. But your faithful adorers are astonished: they would wish to admire your goodness as well as your greatness. It rested with you to give him another will'. 'Go to my daughter Pallas,' said Jupiter, 'she will teach you what I *had* to do.'

Theodorus journeyed to Athens. He was commanded to sleep in the temple of the goddess. As he dreamed, he found himself transported into an unknown country, where stood a palace of inconceivable brightness and vast size. The goddess Pallas appeared at the gate encircled with rays of blinding majesty.

> *Qualisque videri*
> *Coelicolis et quanta solet.*[1]

She touched the face of Theodorus with an olive branch, which she held in her hand. He immediately became able to bear the divine brilliance of the daughter of Jupiter and of all the things she was to show him. 'Jupiter, who loves you,' she said, 'has entrusted you to me to be instructed. Here you see the palace of the Fates, whose guardian I am. Here are representations, not only of what happens, but also of everything that is possible. Jupiter reviewed them all before the beginning of the existing world, arranged the possibilities into worlds, and chose the best of them all. Sometimes he comes to this place to give himself the pleasure of going through things, and of renewing his own choice, with which he cannot fail to be satisfied. I have only to speak and we shall see an entire world, which my father could have produced, and in it will be represented everything that can be required of it. And by this means it is possible to

---

[1] 'In the guise and grandeur in which she is wont to appear before the denizens of heaven.'

know too what would happen, if such and such a possibility
had to exist. And if the conditions are not clearly enough
determined, there will be as many such worlds as one can
desire, different from one another, which answer the same
question in different ways, and in as many ways as is possible.
You studied geometry when you were young, like all well-
educated Greeks. You know, then, that when the conditions of a point we are looking for do not sufficiently
determine it, and there are an infinite number of them, they
all fall in what the geometricians call a *locus*, and this *locus*
at least (which is often a line) is determined. In the same
way you can imagine an ordered series of worlds, all of which
(and they alone) contain the case you are concerned with,
and which vary its circumstances and consequences. But if
you suppose a case which differs from the actual world no
more than in one single definite thing and in the consequences
of that, then one certain determined world will afford the
answer. These worlds are all here; that is to say in idea.
I will show you some where you will find, not exactly the
same Sextus whom you have seen (that is impossible, since
he carries always with him what he is to be), but Sextuses
like him, who possess all that you already know of the true
Sextus, but not everything which is already in him without
being perceived, nor consequently all that is yet to happen
to him. You will find in one world a Sextus very happy and
exalted, in another a Sextus satisfied with a mediocre condition, Sextuses of all kinds and of an infinite number of
types.'

Thereupon the goddess led Theodorus into one of the
apartments. When he was inside it was no longer an
apartment, it was a world,

Solemque suum, sua sidera norat.[1]

By the command of Pallas, Dodona appeared with the

[1] 'A sun of its own it knew, and stars of its own.'

temple of Jupiter, and Sextus leaving it. He was heard to say that he would obey the god. He went to a town lying between two seas, like Corinth. There he bought a little garden, and while digging in it he found treasure. He became a rich man, loved and respected, and died in ripe old age, beloved by the whole city   Theodorus saw his whole life at a glance, like a performance on the stage. In this apartment lay a large book filled with writing. Theodorus could not refrain from asking what it meant. 'It is the history of the world we are now visiting,' answered the goddess, 'it is the book of its destinies. You have seen a number on the forehead of Sextus—look up in the book the place the number indicates.' Theodorus looked it up and found there the story of Sextus in more detail than the one he had seen in brief. 'Put your finger on whatever line you please,' said Pallas, 'and you shall see represented in actual fact in all its details what the line tells in outline.' He obeyed, and saw appear all the details of a part of the life of Sextus.

They passed into another apartment, and behold! another world, another Sextus, who, leaving the temple with the determination to obey the god Jupiter, went to Thrace. There he wedded the king's daughter, his only child, and succeeded him. He was adored by his subjects. They went to other rooms and beheld ever fresh scenes.

The apartments were arranged in a pyramid; the higher up they were the more beautiful they became, and the more beautiful the worlds they represented. At last they reached the topmost apartment, which completed the pyramid, and which was the most beautiful of all. For the pyramid had a beginning, but there was no end to it to be seen. It had an apex but no base; it grew and grew to infinity. This was because, as the goddess explained, out of an infinity of possible worlds, there is the best of all possible worlds, otherwise God would not have made up his mind to create one at all, but there is no world which has not less perfect ones below it, and that is why the base of the pyramid stretches down to infinity. When Theodorus entered this topmost apartment, he was caught up in an ecstasy. The goddess had to come to his aid and restore him by putting a drop of divine liquid on his tongue. He could not contain himself for joy. 'We are in the actual world,' said the goddess, 'and you are at the source of happiness. This is what Jupiter is preparing for you here, if you continue to serve him faithfully. Here is Sextus as he is and as he actually will be. He rushes from the temple in a rage, he scorns the advice of the gods. You can see him travelling to Rome, bringing destruction with him, violating the wife of his friend. Here he is exiled with his father, defeated, wretched. If Jupiter had here taken a Sextus who was happy at Corinth, or who was king of Thrace, it would no longer have been this world. Yet he could not fail to choose this world, which surpasses all others in perfection, and which forms the apex of the pyramid: otherwise Jupiter would have renounced his wisdom, and would have banished me, his daughter. You see that my father did not make Sextus wicked. He had been wicked from all eternity, and always of his own free will. Jupiter did nothing but grant him existence, which his wisdom could not refuse to the world which contains him. He made him pass from the region of possible to that of actual beings. The crime of Sextus serves great ends: it makes Rome free, from it is born a great empire, which will furnish great examples. But that is nothing compared with the totality of this world, whose beauty you will admire when, after a happy passing from this mortal condition into a better state, the gods shall have made you capable of knowing it.'

At this moment Theodorus awoke, gave thanks to the goddess, and praised the justice of Jupiter. Inspired by what he had seen and heard, he continued in his office of high priest with all the zeal of a true servant of his god, and with all the joy of which mortal man is capable. It appears to me that this continuation of the story throws light on the difficulty on which Valla did not wish to touch. If Apollo adequately represented the divine science of vision (which is concerned with existences), I hope that Pallas has represented well enough what is called the science of pure intelligence (which is concerned with everything that is possible), in which one must finally seek the source of things.

INDEX

INDEX OF PROPER NAMES

PHILOSOPHICAL INDEX

279

70
71
72

74
75
76
79
81
83

86
88